C000280575

# THE SCOTCH WHISKY DIRECTORY

# THE
# SCOTCH
# WHISKY
# DIRECTORY

## PHILLIP HILLS

MAINSTREAM
PUBLISHING

EDINBURGH AND LONDON

For flavour profiles of whiskies released since this book was
written, and other new information, please refer to the
Directory website, at www.scotchwhiskydirectory.com

First published in Great Britain in 2005 by
MAINSTREAM PUBLISHING COMPANY
(EDINBURGH) LTD
7 Albany Street
Edinburgh EH1 3UG

ISBN 1 84018 750 6

A catalogue record for this book is
available from the British Library

Typeset in Perpetua and Trade Gothic
Printed and bound in Great Britain by
The Bath Press Ltd

# ACKNOWLEDGEMENTS

The Directory is indebted to a great number of people, all of whom helped in one way or another and are listed below. Special thanks are due to the four tasters, each of whom tasted upwards of 300 whiskies. They are:

Jim McEwan of Bruichladdich Distillery Ltd
Richard Paterson of Whyte & Mackay
David Robertson of Macallan
David Stewart of William Grant & Sons Ltd

Thanks are also due to Frances Jack of the Scotch Whisky Research Institute, who provided a statistical analysis of the 20,000 bits of data which the tastings produced, to Richard Joynson of Loch Fyne Whiskies for supplying samples of whiskies which were hard to find, and to Maggie Braid for her support and encouragement throughout.

The following persons and firms provided assistance in various ways and they have our sincere thanks: Bill Lumsden of Glenmorangie; Gordon Steele of the Scotch Whisky Research Institute; Jamie Walker of the Adelphi Distillery Co.; Bill Bergius and Fiona Watson of Allied Distillers Ltd; Aaron Hillman of Angus Dundee Ltd; David McColm of ASDA; Alex Ross of Ben Nevis Distillery; Shirley Anne Hazelhurst of Berry Bros & Rudd; Gordon Wright of Bruichladdich Distillery Ltd; Robin Dodds of Burn Stewart Ltd; Alan Murray and Ewan Gunn of Cadenheads; Lisa McElhinney of Diageo; Vanessa Wright of Campbell Distillers Ltd; Alan Greig of Chivas Brothers Ltd; Christopher Donaldson of Cockburn & Campbell Ltd; Robin & Fred Laing of Douglas Laing & Co. Ltd; Jim Turle

& Ronnie Gemmell of the Edrington Group Ltd; Stephen Croft of Loch Lomond Distillers Ltd; Ian Urquhart of Gordon & MacPhail Ltd; Alistair and Donald Hart of Hart Brothers Ltd; David Cox and Freda Ross of Macallan; Jackie Cooper of Ian Macleod & Co. Ltd; Hamish Martin of Inverarity Vaults Ltd; Nial Mackinlay of Inver House Distillers Ltd; R. Miquel of Invergordon Distillers Ltd; Gordon Mitchell of Isle of Arran Distillers Ltd; Elaine Bennett of Whyte & Mackay; John Alden of John Dewar & Sons Ltd; James Catto & Co. Ltd; C.R. Parker of London & Scottish International Ltd; Richard Gordon of the Scotch Malt Whisky Society; Derek Gilchrist of Morrison Bowmore Distillers Ltd; Murray McDavid Ltd; Karen Wise of Oddbins; Skip Clary of Praban na Linne Ltd; Stuart Croucher of Safeways Stores plc; Andrew Symington of Signatory; Euan Mitchell of Springbank Distillery Co. Ltd; Denis Eames of the Tomatin Distillery Co. Ltd; Heather Graham and Libby Lafferty of William Grant & Sons Ltd; Bruce Lundie of William Lundie & Co. Ltd; Tim Steward of The Malt Masterclass Ltd and Dick Pountain.

Thanks are extended, too, to the management of all of the companies mentioned in Chapter 3, for the supply of whiskies for tasting and labels for illustration. It is a testament to the quality of the whiskies and the confidence which the proprietor companies have in their brands that they were prepared to submit them for tasting by persons as knowledgeable and critical as the Directory's tasting panel.

# CONTENTS

# INTRODUCTION

## What the Directory is For

The main purpose of the Directory is to provide information about Scotch whiskies. Not general information about whisky – for that the reader should consult the companion work, *Appreciating Whisky* – but about particular whiskies. That is, the whiskies which you will find in bars, in shops and in airports. The sheer number and variety of whisky brands is bewildering. The business of the Directory is to tell you enough about them to enable you to make an informed choice when you buy a whisky.

The Directory is a *consumer's* guide to Scotch whisky. Its aim is to assist people who are buying whisky with a view to drinking the stuff, by telling them what whiskies are available and by indicating what they may expect from each. People buy whisky for all sorts of purposes other than drinking it: for ostentation, for investment, from conformity to social norms, to name but a few. The Directory will be of little use to such folk. It is for people who buy whisky because they enjoy drinking it, or are buying it for someone else who will enjoy it.

We consume alcoholic liquors because the effects of intoxication are pleasing and because we like the taste. Nothing else really matters. There is no great secret in intoxication: the more you drink, the drunker you get – few whisky drinkers will need a directory to tell them that. The Directory is a guide to flavour. Its purpose is to tell you how the different whiskies taste and to do so in such a way that, beginning with whiskies you know and enjoy, you can go on to identify other whiskies whose flavours are likely to please you. You should also be able to use the Directory to develop your palate for whisky, by

9

progressing gradually from one set of flavours to another.

The Directory is a guide for the *rational* consumer. You may think that drink and rationality are uneasy bedfellows: that the more we drink, the less we reason. That's true up to a point but, even so, it does not therefore follow that we cannot rationally order our drinking. Even if your only object in drinking is oblivion, your action is not necessarily an irrational one: some people live lives of such misery that the drowning of sorrows is a perfectly logical thing to do. But this book is not for them. It is for people who take pleasure in their liquor. Its purpose is to enable them to enhance that pleasure.

Most people who buy a bottle of whisky, or order a glass of it, do so in the expectation that it will give them pleasure. They exercise choice. For that choice to be a rational one, it is necessary that the purchaser should know what it is that he or she is ordering. That's the difficult bit. How do we find out which whiskies suit our taste? There are four possible ways: by believing advertisements, by asking friends, by sampling and by consulting the Directory.

## Advertisements

Advertising is so much a part of our lives that we take it for granted, and most people don't give it much thought. We begin to question its value only when some major scandal shows us how great is the disparity between the claims of the advertisers and the effects of their products. For generations, smoking cigarettes was presented by the advertisers as sexy and macho. The reality, of course, was cancer, heart disease and emphysema – none of which enhance sexual attractiveness or are conducive to robust activity. It was not until 30 years *after* the effects of smoking were known that governments acted to restrain the mendacity of tobacco advertising – in the developed world, that is. In most developing countries, where literacy is low and poverty high, people are still persuaded to spend their little substance on stuff that will kill them.

Charged with systematic mendacity, most advertisers will retort that they only reflect the values of society, they don't create them. There is some truth in that, but not much. Mass-media advertising is so powerful that even the cynics cannot resist it completely and the naive – which probably means most of us – are dependent on it for the greater part of their values. At the time of writing, Americans are beginning to correlate epidemic obesity with the national pastime of eating hamburgers, and the larger fast-food chains are taking a lot of stick for pandering to the nation's desires – or, more precisely, for altering the nation's eating habits through the pervasiveness and ubiquity of their advertising.

We live in a culture which is pervaded by advertising. Advertising speaks in a language we understand, no matter how oblique its reference. Gone are the days when advertisers simply proclaimed the excellence of their product, when Guinness could boldly claim to be 'Good For You' (which was true) and Distillers Company assert that their Cambus grain whisky would give you 'Not A Headache In A Gallon' (which was not). Most advertising nowadays works by association: the product is shown in a context which the consumer regards as desirable and the desirability rubs off on the product. Our ability to interpret such messages is extremely sophisticated. Our response is not: if it were, there would be no epidemic of obesity.

Advertisers tailor their product's associations to suit both the product and the target consumers. So whisky adverts in Spain are about style and glamour, for in Spain Scotch is mainly drunk by younger people who respond to such messages. In Britain and America, where it is mainly an older person's drink, the associations are with tradition and authenticity. Whisky has done very well in recent years by climbing on the heritage bandwagon. 'Heritage' is a notion which embodies respect for tradition and history. It is able to do so by being extremely selective about what bits of tradition and history it includes. It is a subtle form of mendacity which works only because there is collusion between the misleader and the misled – and because most folk don't know much about history.

All whisky advertising is *brand* advertising. The brand is a sort of identity which is created for the whisky, with which consumers are encouraged to associate themselves. Most of the components of a brand are quite irrelevant to the flavour of the whisky, which is why it is possible consistently to sell poor stuff for lots of money. There is no point in complaining about this. It's how the world works and it's unlikely to change. However, the freedom that allows brand owners to mislead also allows us to say so. What is more, it allows us to say that not all advertisers are mendacious: there are a lot of people out there selling very fine whisky – and we are at liberty to shout on their behalf. The Directory is a shout. It is for people who assert their right to judge for themselves, in the light of standards that *they* set, and it is a shout for the people who make and sell good whisky and don't pretend it's anything else.

We should be clear what we are saying here: not that branding is a bad thing, but simply that if you choose your whisky solely because you like the images embodied by a brand's advertising you are surrendering your freedom. The Directory is on the side of liberty: it is for folk who prefer to swim against the stream of brand marketing; it is for those who wish to exercise their right to choose and to do so in the light of appropriate information.

## Friends

Now you may reasonably say that you don't need a directory and that you can find out for yourself which are good whiskies just by asking your friends and by going to the pub and trying the whiskies your friends recommend. The problem with friends is that one man's meat is another man's poison. Ditto for women. What pleases your friend is not necessarily what will best please you. And if one's own rationality is suspect in the face of media manipulation, how much more suspect must be that of one's friends, especially those friends whose advice is consequent on your buying the drinks?

Besides being suspect on grounds of self-interest, the advice of friends should be viewed with scepticism for more general reasons. What most people believe about anything is dictated by the fashions of society at large. If, 40 years ago, you had asked your friends which were the best whiskies, they would certainly have recommended only blended whiskies. This was not for want of malt whiskies, but simply because at that time most people thought that the only whiskies worth drinking were of the blended variety. This belief in its turn was the result of a century of relentless advertising of blended whiskies and disparagement of malts. In certain circles, the exact opposite is true today. There are lots of malt whisky buffs who scorn the idea of drinking blended whiskies, on the ground that all malt whiskies taste better than any blended whiskies. As the Directory will demonstrate, that is not the case: there are some very good and tasty blended whiskies, and there are some fairly undistinguished malts. If you mature a malt whisky in a worn-out cask, it will come out after five or ten years, having shed the disagreeable flavours of new whisky, but having acquired little in their place. By the same token, if you take some malt and grain whiskies, all of which are well-made and have been in decent wood, and mix them, you will get a very flavoursome blend.

## Sampling

One possibility is simply to work your way through all the whiskies, trying each a few times and in different circumstances. As an approach, this is pleasing in its simplicity and directness, but it has a downside: it's a long and expensive road and your liver may not survive it. Also, taste is a subtle and difficult matter (hence the ability of brand marketing to influence you) and, unless you are one in a million, you will need help to discriminate the flavours of each of hundreds of whiskies. Also, by the time you have got to the end of all the whiskies, you are likely to have forgotten what the first ones tasted like. If you are really keen, you will get round this by keeping a cellar book. The Directory has known people whom it respects who have done this, but can't help feeling that it's a bit nerdish and maybe there are better things to do with your life. It's only drink, after all.

## The Directory

It is the business of the Directory to do the legwork (if that's the right term) for you. The Directory provides a list of the principal branded Scotch whiskies and tells you what each of them tastes like. The whiskies have been tasted by four of the most expert tasters in the Scotch whisky industry and their findings have been collated with help from the statisticians of the Scotch Whisky Research Institute. The Directory's judgements on flavour can therefore claim to be the most objective of any yet published in respect of Scotch whisky.

That said, it is not the purpose of the Directory to tell you what is good whisky and what is not. The best whisky for you is the whisky which tastes best to you. Taste is irreducibly personal and you shouldn't allow anyone – not even the Directory – to tell you that what you like is no good. We can none of us have access to the subjective experience of anyone else, and the average wino has essentially the same equipment for sensory assessment as the connoisseur who lingers over an expensive malt – though the latter has, admittedly, more scope for the use of that equipment and his or her circumstances are probably more conducive to fine discrimination.

While maintaining our independence, we all ought to have a little humility when it comes to according objectivity to our taste sensations. And if we are to get the best out of our whisky, we should at least consider what is said by people who really are expert. The Directory therefore humbly submits the findings of four guys who undoubtedly know their stuff, in the hope that you, the reader, will be able to use their expertise to enhance your enjoyment.

## How the Directory is Arranged

### Part One: Information

Part One of the Directory tells you what you need to know in order to get the best out of the second part, which is the Whisky List. Most people will be inclined to go immediately to the Whisky List, to see what it says about their favourite whiskies. You are, however, recommended to read the first part, for if you do, you will find it a lot easier to use the second, since there are ways of using the latter which are less than obvious.

The Directory was conceived as a companion volume to *Appreciating Whisky*, a work by the same author which sets out in possibly unnecessary detail everything you need to know about Scotch whisky in order fully to appreciate it. The first part of the Directory covers some of the same ground, but in summary form. It is an improvement on its predecessor in the presentation of information about flavour, though. The flavour profiles, which are described in

Chapter 6, show you graphically how whisky tastes. They are fairly simple to use – but be sure to read Chapter 6, for they are more subtle than they seem.

Chapter 1 is a brief introduction to Scotch whisky. It assumes some knowledge of the subject and therefore does not deal with it at length. It touches mainly on those aspects which are relevant to the flavour of whisky. Chapter 2 expands on some of the remarks above: it is about branding and tells you some things you need to know about if you are to relate what you are told by advertisers to the reality you find in the bottle. Its aim in doing so is to assist you to achieve independence of judgement in matters to do with Scotch whisky.

Chapter 3 lists the principal Scotch whisky brands along with the companies which own them. The list for convenience is by company and it shows as far as possible the relationships between the companies. The brands belonging to each company which appear in the Directory are highlighted. Given the huge number of brands, and the fact that any given proprietor may bottle the same whisky under several brand names, it would be pointless and tedious to try to include every brand. If you wish to know about a brand which is not featured in the Directory, try others of its owner's brands – the chances are that one of them will be the same whisky. Unfortunately, it would be asking too much of brand owners to expect them to list the contents of each brand, or to tell us which brands have the same stuff in them.

From Chapter 4 onward, we treat of the things you need to know in order to evaluate a whisky: the origins of flavour and the principal flavours which you are likely to discover in a Scotch whisky. Chapter 5 tells you about the tasters and about the tasting. The results of the tastings were collated and are presented in Part Two as flavour profiles. Chapter 6 tells you how to read the profiles, as well as suggesting how you may use them to develop and extend your taste for whisky.

## Part Two: Evaluation

The Whisky List sets out all of the main Scotch whisky brands. The basic idea is pretty simple: if you wish to know about a given whisky, you look it up in the Directory. There you will find some basic particulars: the label, the type of whisky, the owner of the brand and a flavour profile which will show at a glance how the whisky tastes. The final chapter of Part One suggests ways in which you may extend your experience by means of the Directory.

Whiskies are listed in the Directory in alphabetical order by brand name. Where a brand has several expressions, the original bottling is listed first, followed by aged bottlings in date order and then by variants of other sorts.

There is little point in having a list to which people may refer if it is not complete. The reader wants to be able to look up whisky brands with a reasonable assurance of finding them in the Directory. That presents a problem at the outset, for the number of bottlings of genuine Scotch whisky around the world is very large indeed and to include them all would make the Directory unacceptably large and expensive. So the Directory has used a criterion of *significance* in choosing which whiskies to include and which to omit, as follows.

## Grain Whiskies

There are three main types of Scotch whisky: grains, malts and blends. Grain whisky is an alcoholic liquor made mainly from grains other than barley. In practice, this usually means maize, which is the cheapest source of starch available. A relatively small amount of malted barley is used to start the malting of the grain, to convert its starches to sugars. The sugars are fermented in the usual way with yeast and the resultant ale is distilled to get alcohol. The still used in grain whisky production is the patent-still. Its product does not have the complexity of malt whisky but, if well-made and matured in decent casks, grain whisky can be a very pleasant spirit indeed. By far the greatest part of grain whisky production is for use in blended whiskies. Very few single grain whiskies are bottled or at all widely available. All of those which are available are included in the Directory.

## Malt Whiskies

Malts are a different matter. There are over 100 malt whisky distilleries which either produce whisky, or have done so within living memory. If each malt had only a single expression, the number would not cause difficulty. But most malts are now available in lots of different bottlings and that 100 or so is multiplied many times. Since the flavour of a malt depends to a great extent on the cask in which it is matured, and the length and conditions of that maturation, and the variation in these factors is very great, it follows that the variety of possible single malt bottlings is too large for any directory to cope with.

Nor ought it to try. Most Scotch malt whisky is used for blending: even today, single malts make up little more than 5 per cent of total Scotch whisky sales by volume. The rest goes into blends. The blender wants consistency in his malts, so he ensures that the malt distilleries in his control produce a uniform product. He demands the same of any supplier. As a result, uniformity is the goal of all but a handful of distilleries. Not for them the fancy methods of a Macallan or an Aberlour. Most buy their malt from an industrial maltings, use the same yeast strains for brewing, source their stills from the same coppersmith, use techniques which are indistinguishable from those of their neighbours and get their casks from the same supplier. The result is that – *pace* malt buffs around the globe – there are many malts which differ little, one from the other. The Directory sees no point in including lots of malt whiskies which taste pretty similar and have no marks of distinction of any other sort. So where a malt whisky does not have a proprietary bottling and is not significantly different from many others, the Directory does not include it.

## *Proprietary Bottlings*

The Directory seeks to include all standard proprietary bottlings of malt whiskies. However, there have to be some exceptions. The last ten years have seen the emergence of a new and lucrative specialist malt whisky market. The response of the distillers to this has for the most part been unedifying. Malts have appeared as nature never intended; casks of all sorts and ages have been unearthed (sometimes literally) and their contents bottled by the proprietors of the distillery. Bottling runs are frequently short, as is the life of the label. Where the Directory considers that such things are significant, it includes them. Where it does not, it does not. For advice about them, do as you would with a private bottler: try established whiskies from the same stable first. Once you know these, try the specials. Then ask yourself whether the (invariably more expensive) special bottling is an improvement. Some are; some most certainly are not.

## Private Bottlings

The desire of the blender to eliminate unusual casks from his or her blend has created an opportunity for the private bottler, who can bottle and market the contents of small parcels of whisky or, in many cases, single casks. Private bottlers create another problem for the Directory. The number of privately bottled malts is very large and most of the bottling runs are very short indeed. Even if the Directory were to include them all, the exercise would be futile since stocks of the whiskies listed would be exhausted by the time the Directory was published. To omit privately bottled whiskies altogether would be improper, though, both because some of the bottlings are undoubtedly significant and because of the seminal part which private bottlers have played in the rise of malts from the obscurity in which they lay for over a century. A number of the more prominent private bottlers have been invited to submit whiskies for inclusion in the Directory. Each has been asked to eschew the temptation to show only the very best; rather to select two or three whiskies which the proprietor regards as typical of his or her bottlings. That is not an enviable task, nor one whose execution can be entirely satisfactory. But it is the best that can be done in the circumstances. The reader who seeks advice from the Directory on a privately bottled whisky is advised to look for reports on whiskies from the same bottler, from which he or she may infer something about the type and quality of others of the bottler's whiskies. Chapter 3 lists all of the owners whose products are represented in the Directory.

## Whiskies in Duty-Free

You will find lots of whisky offered in airport duty-free shops which you will see nowhere else. The prices are not excessive because no duty is paid – though they are high enough to yield huge profit margins. The duty-free shops in airports are a dripping roast for people who sell liquor, tobacco and perfume. Jet-lagged travellers are perfect targets for misleading or irrelevant packaging. The Directory does not try to cover special labels for duty-free, on the good ground that nobody who is seriously interested in whisky is going to buy a bottle they have never heard of, just because it has a gaudy label and seems relatively cheap. If you are unfortunate enough to have to travel in aeroplanes and you feel you must buy liquor for your mother, buy her gin, or a whisky brand you know. The ten-year-old malt which gets little shelf space is likely to be at least as good as the glamorously packaged stuff which gets a lot.

## Blended Whiskies

Blended whiskies take up by far the greater part of the Directory. That's only fair: they are drunk by the greatest number of people. The Scotch Whisky Association – which is the trade body of which most brand proprietors are members – publishes a list of its members and their principal brands. The latter numbered 562 at the last count, most of which were blends. In addition to these, there are all the brands belonging to firms which are not members of the SWA. The dimensions of the Directory's problem will be obvious.

In approaching blended whiskies, the Directory uses the same criterion of *significance* which it applies to malts. Significance among blends is not easy to define. Obviously, the brands which sell in the largest numbers are highly significant, and all of these are included. There are, however, reasons other than numbers for including a brand of blended whisky. Some brands are historically important; others are notable for their flavour, their history or their market position.

Many blenders use a few basic blends, which they bottle under different labels. An image which appeals in one market will not do in another, though the whisky is equally appealing to drinkers in both. In Chapter 3, the Directory lists brand owners and the main brands belonging to each. While it is not possible to tell the reader which blend goes into which brand, a perusal of several of a blender's brands will give a fair idea of what to expect from others of the same provenance. The Directory has therefore asked each of the blenders to whom this observation applies to supply for tasting a representative selection of his or her blends. Most have complied, so the blends listed can on the whole be taken as typical.

## How to Use the Directory

The main use for the Directory will be the most obvious one: if you wish to know what a whisky tastes like, you look up its flavour profile in the Directory. The flavour profile tells you about the sensations reported by the Directory's tasters. This is not necessarily how the whisky will taste to you (since everyone's taste is different) but you can use the Directory to correlate your sensations with those of the tasters. We suggest that your best course is first to look up whiskies which you know well, or of which you have samples to hand and compare your taste sensations with those reported by the Directory. The flavour signature will show you what flavours the Directory tasters found in the whisky and you can calibrate your own responses accordingly.

In addition, the five-star rating system (in which five stars indicates a truly outstanding whisky) will provide you with a basic guide to quality. Please see 'The Five-Star Rating System' on page 107 for a detailed explanation of how these stars were apportioned.

If you wish to find out how a specific whisky will taste, look it up in the Whisky List, in which whiskies are listed alphabetically by brand name. If the whisky does not appear in the Whisky List, you should look for it in Chapter 3.

Chapter 3 lists all of the owners of all of the principal brands. If your whisky is a blend from one of the larger firms, it will appear together with a number of other blends, all of which are produced by or for the brand owner. Most distillers and bottlers actually produce only a small number of whiskies, bottling the same whisky under different brand names. Those included in the Directory are highlighted. Try others of the same category from the same owner: the chances are that your whisky is identical to one of them. If it differs, it won't be by much.

If your whisky is a malt, there is a greater likelihood of variation. The Directory covers all of the more important malts, but does not attempt to include every malt whisky. Remember that over 80 per cent of the flavour of a malt comes from the cask in which it is matured. Remember also that only a few malts get star treatment as regards casks: the great majority are put into refill casks of no distinction whose ability to impart serious flavour is very limited, so there are a great many malts which don't differ much, one from another. You *may* find a great malt which is not in the Directory, but only if you are lucky enough to come upon the product of a really fine cask. Such things are so individual that no Directory could hope to include them and they don't last long, so make the most of them and don't bother with a mere book.

Most of the distillers are continually bringing out new products, so you will sometimes find bottles whose label does not appear in the Directory. Treat such things as you would a blend. Look at other whiskies from the same stable. If it is a good stable whose horses are front runners, it's a fair bet the new one will be a goer. If, on the other hand, your whisky comes from a portfolio which contains lots of gimmicky whiskies, you should form your judgement accordingly.

# PART ONE

# INFORMATION

# SCOTCH WHISKIES

There can be few readers of *The Scotch Whisky Directory* who don't know what Scotch whisky is. However, the definition, which is well known, is quite brief and will bear repeating. Besides, definition will lead us into matters which may not be so apparent to the reader.

Scotch whisky is hard liquor made in a small, cold, wet country called Scotland. It acquired a definition as the result of a legal case brought by, of all people, the London Burgh of Islington in the year 1905 against two wine and spirit merchants for selling blended whisky as 'Scotch whisky', contrary to the Burgh's claims that only single malts could be classed as genuine Scotch. In fact, Islington had been put up to it by Scottish malt distillers who, because the whisky trade was in one of its periodic recessions, had large stocks of single malts to get rid of. They thought that their market would improve if they could prevent the sale of grain whisky, and blends of grain and malt whisky, as Scotch. They lost, and Scotch whisky was found to be simply any whisky made in Scotland and matured for at least three years in an oak cask. This judgment clearly relied on a fixed definition of the word 'whisky', so a Royal Commission in 1909 produced the unsurprising (and inelegantly expressed) conclusion that 'whiskey is a spirit obtained by distillation from a wash saccharified by the diastase of malt'. In other words, you brew an ale using barley malt and you distil the ale to get whisky, which you then leave in wood for at least three years. How you make the ale is up to you – provided you use some barley in the malt – and if you make the stuff in Scotland, you can call it Scotch whiskey. (Sticklers for the spelling of 'whisky' may care to note that as late as 1909, 'whiskey' was a perfectly OK usage in respect of Scotch. The orthographic distinction between Scotch and other whiskies is of fairly recent origin.)

The Royal Commission's definition of Scotch whisky has been the accepted one ever since. From that definition follow the three main divisions of Scotch: malts, grains and blends.

## Malt Whiskies

Malt whiskies are whiskies made from a mash which consists of nothing but malted barley and water, fermented with yeast and distilled in a copper pot-still. The barley provides both starch and the enzymes that are to convert the starch into sugars, which are to be fermented to alcohol. It is how ales have been made since time immemorial. Scotch ales have long been renowned for their sweetness. Or rather, they *were* renowned for their sweetness until the brewers grew so large and industrial that they took to making the ale on an industrial scale by industrial methods. Then the ale became gassy and horrible. Much of it still is, but nowadays, thanks to the influence of the Campaign For Real Ale, there again is good ale in the land. You can't make silk purses out of pigs' ears: no more than you can make good whisky from bad ale. Whisky today is a lot better than whisky was 50 years ago, and it begins with the making of good ale.

The pot-still is essential to the production of well-flavoured whisky. It is the onion-shaped copper still beloved of picture books about distilleries. The shape is purely traditional and functional: if you need to distil liquor and the best material you have to hand is copper, then you will inevitably end up with something which looks more or less like a whisky still. It needn't look so elegant as the stills in the distilleries and if you use a peat fire to heat it, it will soon be black instead of coppery, but the essentials of shape and material remain the same. There are many photographs of illicit stills: they are usually misshapen-looking objects and all pretty dirty, but they are recognisable ancestors of the beautiful shiny stills of the modern whisky distilleries.

Both the material and the shape of the still are essential to the flavour of malt whisky. The business of distilling is not simply a matter of separating alcohol from a mixture of alcohol and water, as it is in the chemistry classroom: the components of the whisky-to-be participate in complex reactions in the still, many of which reactions are catalysed by the copper. The result is a set of extremely complex compounds whose flavour is a component of good malt whisky.

*Single malt* whisky is whisky from a single distillery. The use of the term 'single' is historical: it was used to distinguish malt whisky, which was the product of a single distillery, from vatted malt, which was a blend of malt whiskies from different distilleries (see below). 'Single' in the context of malt whisky does not denote a whisky from a single cask. A single malt is usually the result of a bottling of malt from a number of different casks. The bottle label will normally carry an age statement which tells you how old the malt whisky is – which means how long it has been in cask. The age of the whisky in bottle is of no significance, since whisky, unlike wine, does not mature in bottle. (At least, it is of no significance for whisky drinkers: people who collect whiskies are a different sort of person and their values are not the concern of the Directory.) Where a whisky carries an age statement, the spirit in the bottle must have been in cask for at least the time specified in the age statement. In practice, the whisky is usually quite a lot older than the stated age. The more scrupulous of the distillers go to a great deal of trouble when assembling casks for bottling, blending the contents of casks whose age may be much greater than that stated in order to maintain a standard of quality.

Some malt whisky bottlings are of the contents of a single cask. Single-cask bottling was the invention of the Scotch Malt Whisky Society in 1983. The object was to obtain the flavour characteristics of a particular cask, something which is lost in the normal, multi-cask bottlings. Casks vary greatly in quality and character and so long as you can procure particularly good ones, single-cask bottling is greatly to be desired.

Single-cask bottlings are usually at natural strength of about 60 per cent alcohol and the whisky does not need to be chillfiltered. Scotch whisky is traditionally bottled at 40 per cent or 43 per cent. When you dilute whisky from its natural strength, it will often throw a haze, as dissolved solids precipitate out of the whisky. The solids are removed by putting the whisky through a very fine filter at low temperature. The process clears the whisky, but at the price of removing some of the flavour components. So, all other things being equal, an unfiltered whisky is to be preferred to a filtered one.

It is worth bearing in mind, however, that the excellence of single-cask whiskies does not derive from the mere fact of their being from a single cask, but from the excellence of the particular cask. In the early days, when none of the distillers were interested in (or even aware of) the contents of their warehouses, one could pick up really fine casks for the going rate for the alcohol. Nowadays, most distillers are only too aware of the value of good and old whisky and, being naturally keen to maximise their benefit from their stocks, reluctant to part with their best. The chances of a private bottler obtaining really top-rate casks are proportionately reduced. The best single-cask bottlings nowadays tend to come either from the distillers themselves or from old-established firms such as Cadenhead or Gordon & MacPhail, who long ago laid down new whiskies in casks of ascertained quality. (Adelphi is an exception to this rule, as is evident from the flavour profiles of its whiskies.) Because single-cask whiskies are so individual, it is impossible to generalise about them, and the advice on private bottlings in the Introduction applies to all single-cask bottlings.

'*Vatted malt*' is the expression used where the contents of the bottle are malt whisky from more than one distillery. Toward the end of the long ascendancy of blended whiskies, vatted malts gained something of a following in Scotland and, to a limited extent, elsewhere. They have rather faded from view with the fashion for single malts, though a good many are represented in the Directory. Single-malt enthusiasts tend to look down on vatted malts, mainly because they do not exhibit the characteristic flavour of the single malt, the discernment of which is a source of self-congratulation to the malt buff. Since for most people this discernment is illusory, it follows that the disparagement of vatted malts is unjustified. As can be seen from the flavour signatures, most of the vatted malts are pretty good and some are very good indeed.

The term 'pure malt' was sometimes used to indicate a vatted malt. Indeed, it still is: if you see a Scotch whisky described on its label as pure malt, you can be pretty sure that the liquor in the bottle is a mixture of several different single-malt whiskies.

## Grain Whiskies

To qualify as a Scotch whisky under the Royal Commission's definition, a liquor need not be made from malted barley only. The bit about 'a wash saccharified by diastase of malt' means that the enzymes which convert the starches in the wash must come from malted barley. Where the starches come from is up to the distiller. Grain whisky is whisky distilled from a wash in which a small proportion of the starch comes from barley. The rest comes from whatever grain is cheapest: wheat, maize and rye are all acceptable. Some of the best Scotch grain whisky being made at present is made mostly from maize imported from France.

There is nothing in the definition which says that Scotch whisky must be made in a traditional pot-still. Nowadays, all grain spirit is distilled in a patent-still, which is an industrial process more akin to that of an oil refinery than it is to the copper still in the heather of popular imagination. Technologically, the pot-still is out of the Ark. It belongs to an era and a society in which neither time nor labour were of significance. It is an awkward shape; it is difficult to work with; it uses a discontinuous process which is absurdly expensive. It is fine for an agrarian, feudal society, but wildly unsuited to an industrial one.

Lowland Scotland was at the forefront of the technological revolution of the late eighteenth and early nineteenth centuries. The iron and steel, steam engines and shipbuilding which we think of as constituting the Industrial Revolution were built on the base of an earlier industry, mainly textile production. With textiles went chemical production and as part of the latter came advanced techniques of distillation. The 1820s saw a lot of what we now call technology transfer and whisky-making got continuous distillation in the form of the patent-still.

There were several versions of this: Mr Coffey's still did not grow from an unfertilised ground. The patent-still had what the pot-still did not: the capacity for continuous operation. You put mash in one end and you got alcohol out of the other – and you did not have to stop to refill it as you could keep shoving the mash in at the same time as you drew the liquor off. The result was a relatively pure form of alcohol which could be sold very cheaply to the labouring masses, whose numbers were then growing rapidly and who had to be kept from protesting their condition by any means possible. The patent-still therefore served economic and political purposes which were approved by polite society, however much it might deplore what it saw as the moral effects.

The distinction between malt and grain whiskies today turns on the axis of malted barley/pot-still against other grain/patent-still. It should be noted that this is a relatively modern distinction. For several decades in the early nineteenth century, things were much more mixed up and any expedient was adopted which produced cheap alcohol. Pot-stills were devised which were capable of being worked off remarkably rapidly: at the most extreme, 90 times in 24 hours. These stills were weird, distorted things with enormously widened bases so as to present as large an area as possible to the fire. The whisky they produced must have been pretty vile, but it would be just as potent in pure alcohol terms as its better brother. Malt-only washes were sometimes distilled in patent-stills and the resulting whiskies were probably of a quality superior to the output of the industrial pot-stills.

Bizarre whisky stills in the late eighteenth and early nineteenth centuries were a technological response to the Byzantine provisions of the Excise laws. Those laws were responsible for the belief – which persists to this day – that there is some essential difference between Lowland and Highland whiskies. There was once, because Highland whisky-making was taxed on the output of spirit, whereas Lowland distillers paid duty at a rate calculated on the capacity of the still. The result was that Lowland whisky-makers had a strong incentive to work their stills hard, while Highland distillers did not. The Highland whisky naturally had much the better flavour.

This snippet of history is of relevance to the Directory in two ways. First, to squelch the myth put about by coffee-table books on whisky that there is a significant difference between Highland and Lowland malt whiskies. It has long been believed that one can usefully classify Scotch malts into Highland, Island and Lowland whiskies on the grounds of characteristic flavour. This is false: there is no significant regionally derived flavour difference. Most island whiskies are peaty, but only because most island distilleries use a lot of peat in drying their malts. Highland or Lowland whiskies which choose to use similar levels of peating obtain similar flavours. Island whiskies which use little peat taste like Highland or Lowland. The distinction between Highland and Lowland whiskies was once significant, but only because of the quality difference engendered by different stills and distillation techniques.

A second and more important point concerns the issue of the quality of grain whisky. The malt/pot-still and grain/patent-still distinction became established by the mid-nineteenth century. When the British drinking public began to rediscover malt whiskies in the 1970s, and to ask for something better than the diet of blends on which hitherto they had supped, they soon came to see grain whisky as the villain of the piece. Their view was that malt tasted nice and gave blended whisky its flavour, and grain whisky tasted nasty and made profits for distillers. (The latter proposition was certainly true.) It required but a short chop of logic to draw the inference that all malt was good and all grain was bad. This was to become the credo of malt enthusiasts worldwide. The elision was facilitated by the inability of most Scotch whisky distillers (or rather of the guys who ran the companies – not the same thing at all) to see the thing coming. When, in the 1980s, the malt whisky revolution was in full flow, the blenders' response showed neither courage nor intelligence. Nobody got up and said their blends were great and capable of standing against any old malt whisky. No, they continued to plug brand values as if nothing had happened. They still do. The consequence has been a market in which malt and blended whiskies are still miles apart, despite the convergence which is apparent in some of the flavour profiles of the Directory.

## Blended Whiskies

Twenty years ago, the chairman of a major whisky company explained to the compiler of the Directory why blended whiskies were to be preferred to malt: 'Malt whiskies are too individual in taste and require blending with grain spirit to produce a drinkable whisky.' Now, to anyone who knows anything about whisky in the early twenty-first century, that is patently untrue. Yet, for well over a century, it was the credo of both the whisky industry and the drinking public.

There is reason to think that when blending began 150 years ago, the statement may have been true, certainly of some and probably of most malt whiskies. Some distillers undoubtedly produced very fine whisky – we have the word of Elizabeth Grant of Rothiemurchus and the taste of King George IV for that – but they were probably in a minority. The bucolic myths about old-time distilling which are the stuff of brand heritage are mostly just that: myths. There were hundreds of malt whisky distilleries, few of which controlled materials and processes as tightly as distillers do today. Peat was widely used for drying malt, so much of the spirit would have been wildly phenolic. The larger part of the spirit run was utilised, so the whisky would have contained foreshots and feints which the modern stillman excludes from his spirit receiver. There was no legal requirement that malt should be matured in cask and the casks which were used to contain whisky would have been whatever barrels the distiller could procure. Sherry casks were used because there were a lot of them around and they were cheap. Failing sherry casks, any other wood would do. The main requirement of a cask was that it should hold water; if it didn't leak it was OK. The result must have been the presence in the marketplace of some pretty wildly flavoured malt whisky. Patent-still grain spirit would have seemed mild and palatable by comparison.

When, in the 1860s, Scotch whisky found a mass-market south of the border, it did so by means of brand marketing. The identity of a brand required that the whisky which was sold under the brand name should be as uniform as possible. The variability of the produce of even a single-malt whisky distillery meant that it wasn't easy to achieve uniformity of flavour. Obviously, the less flavour the whisky had, the easier it would be to iron out differences. Enter grain whisky: it supplied the alcohol while diminishing the flavour of the malt and so was a natural component of a whisky blend. Since grain whisky was a lot cheaper to make, blending was one of those natural conjunctions which so pleased the Victorians and convinced them that God was on the side of the entrepreneur: the product best-suited to the market was that which yielded the biggest profit.

For more than 100 years, blended whiskies had a captive market in which customers were more concerned with the fictional values of the brand than they were with the flavour qualities of the whisky. The rise of malt whisky was led by consumers who, knowing that really fine whisky existed, demanded access to it. This mystified the whisky companies, most of whose people owed allegiance to their company's brands and believed the propaganda by means of which the brand was promoted. As malts came to be more widely marketed, there arose a widening gap between the flavours of malts and those of blends. Malt whiskies were a very small part of the total market but their supporters were vociferous, the noise they made being out of all proportion to their numbers. The effectiveness of the malt whisky advocates' message lay in its novelty and its simplicity: they said malt whiskies *tasted* nice.

Big companies are like supertankers: they are extremely powerful and go very well in straight lines, but are not so good at turning. The corporate owners of the larger whisky blends were slow to respond to the rise of malts but, when they did, they sought, typically, to grab as large as possible a share of the market. The results of this have, on the whole, been beneficial as far as the drinking public is concerned. The industry now generally seeks much higher standards in both malt and grain whiskies than its predecessors did. The quality and hence the flavour of blended whiskies has improved markedly in the last 20 years. Big companies now bottle most of their malts as single-malt whiskies and warehouses have been scoured for old and unusual casks, whose contents are marketed at a premium. If there is a downside for the cognoscenti, it is that the prices of such products are very high indeed. Gone are the days when you could pick up a cask of world-class liquor for the price of its alcohol content. In fairness, though, one must admit that this is a regret to only a tiny number of people: the great majority have benefited – and if they have to dig deep in their pockets to buy the stuff, at least there is now the possibility, where before there was none. (In this context, praise must be given to Macallan. When they bottled lots of old stock in their Fine and Rare range, at prices ranging from a few hundred to many thousands of pounds a bottle, Macallan put some of it in miniatures. If you can afford to drink malt whisky and you have sufficient interest, then you can taste the stuff without mortgaging your mother.)

The greatest good for the greatest number in all this has undoubtedly been the improvement in the quality of blended whiskies. The malpractices of whisky blenders used to be legendary; today, all of the major producers exercise the closest control at every stage of production and blending. As a result, the quality of blended whiskies is probably higher than at any time in history. There has been such an improvement in the flavour of blends that in some cases blended whiskies are overtaking malts, as the Directory demonstrates. If we compare the profiles of malts and blends, it is apparent that some of the better blends are more flavoursome than many malts.

It remains the case that a well-matured malt exhibits a range and a subtlety of flavour which no blend can match, but the disdain with which many malt aficionados regard blended whiskies is unjustified.

# BRAND IMAGES:
## HOW WHISKIES ARE
### PRESENTED TO THE PUBLIC

We all know what whisky brands are: they are the names we recognise on whisky bottles and in adverts; they are how we tell which whiskies we like and which we don't. We have freedom of choice, or so we believe. We may think that other people derive most of their values from media dominated by brand advertising and hence that this freedom is illusory, but each of us has the agreeable conviction that his or her choice is an authentic expression of his or her unique personality. Perhaps occasionally, we may have doubts, when there is a worm in the soup or we see our burger-eating progeny become obese; but, on the whole, brands are our companions and our guides.

I mentioned in the Introduction that the Directory is a rational guide to choice in whisky. Rationality is the enemy of most brands. Some brands represent really good stuff, but it is their misfortune and ours that there is no way of telling, from advertising alone, which is good and which is not, which suits our taste and which does not. That is what the Directory is for: it strips whisky brands of irrelevant verbiage and allows us to discover how the whisky tastes. If you are to make best use of the Directory, it will help if you know a little about Scotch whisky brands, which is what this chapter is about.

A brand is a symbol by means of which we identify the things the market has to offer us. The symbol may be expressed in words or in signs, or usually in both. Obviously, the sign and the name must mean something to us, otherwise they would convey no message at all. Most whisky brands began their existence with a name which stood for a whisky whose taste people enjoyed. Over time, the importance of flavour tended to decline and the brand accumulated associations of other sorts, for people can be induced to buy by considerations which have nothing to do with flavour. In the longer term, a brand can acquire a penumbra of associations, so that both name and symbol become remote from their origins.

Johnnie Walker is a good example. In 1908, John Walker & Sons approved Tom Browne's sketches for an advertising campaign based on a striding figure and the slogan 'Johnnie Walker whisky – born 1820, still going strong'. The firm had a reputation for whisky of high quality, but it was losing market share to Dewar's and Buchanan's. The advert emphasised the antiquity and continuity of the brand and it did so by reference to a highly distinctive image. This image was the striding man which we still recognise today. It was instantly identifiable to the people of the time as being an antique English sporting gentleman in top hat, monocle, frock coat, boots and britches. In the minds of early twentieth-century consumers, this image carried lots of associations which were favourable to the whisky. There is some irony in the fact that Johnnie Walker is no longer sold in the United Kingdom, which is the only country in which the image might still be recognised, though by very few. To consumers in Japan or Brazil in the twenty-first century, the walking man logo has none of its original significance. But that is of no concern, for the brand image no longer needs that association: its meaning is whatever message the local advertisers choose to hang on it. The brand stands as a sign which evokes ideas associated with the product. Initially, those ideas are usually to do with product quality; later, they can be any ideas at all which induce the consumer to purchase the product.

Until the eighteenth century, most whisky drinkers in Scotland consumed the local produce. Every substantial house had the right to distil whisky from its own barley for domestic use and some whiskies became locally famous. But there were whiskies whose names were a guarantee of quality far beyond the confines of their immediate district. The whisky which the Forbes family had distilled in the barony of Ferintosh in Ross-shire since the later seventeenth century had a high reputation. It also had the unique commercial advantage of being free of the imposition of Excise duty, thanks to an exemption granted in 1690 by the Parliament of Scotland as reward for the proprietors' loyalty to the Protestant succession in the turbulent events of 1688. The name of the whisky and its association with excellence of flavour were known as far away as rural Ayrshire, where the ending of the exemption in 1795 moved an impecunious exciseman by the name of Burns to write:

> Thee, Ferintosh! O sadly lost!
> Scotland laments frae coast to coast!

In fact, the whisky wasn't lost: it merely had to pay tax, the same as all the other whiskies. Presumably this meant that it wasn't as cheap as before.

Branding in Scotch whisky really begins with Glenlivet and the King's visit in 1822. The story is well known, but it is germane to our subject and will bear retelling. By 1822, apart from a hurried visit by Charles I, no king of Britain had set foot in Scotland since James I and VI journeyed south to take up the throne which Elizabeth's death had vacated. When, two centuries later, George came into his inheritance and announced his decision to visit his northern kingdom, there was great excitement. The Scottish establishment exerted itself to give the King the warmest possible reception. This extended to supplying his wants in the matter of drink and it was with some dismay that the committee learned that the King's favourite tipple was Glenlivet whisky. The dismay was because, as far as the law of the land was concerned, Glenlivet produced no whisky. Spirit of superlative quality was distilled illegally by Captain George Smith at his farm at Upper Drumin and its fame had spread far and wide despite its illegitimacy. Since Captain Smith's distilling was carried out with the collusion of his landlord, the Duke of Gordon, the distiller was in no danger of being surprised by the Revenue. But making and selling the whisky was nonetheless illicit and supplies of it could not lawfully be procured by members of the public. Happily, one of the committee set up to arrange the King's welcome, a minor chieftain of Clan Grant by the name of

Sir John Grant, announced that in his house in Badenoch he had ample supplies of the Glenlivet, from which the King's wants could be supplied. His daughter Elizabeth takes up the story:

> My father sent word to me – I was the cellarer – to empty my pet bin, where was whisky long in wood, long in uncorked bottles, mild as milk, and the true contraband gout in it . . . the whisky and fifty brace of ptarmigan all shot by one man, went up to Holyrood House, and were graciously received and made much of, and a reminder of this attention at a proper moment by the gentlemanly Chamberlain ensured to my father the Indian judgeship.

The point of this story is not how the poor Indians got their judges, but the fact that the quality of Glenlivet was so well known by 1822 that, despite its being illegally distilled, the head of state apparently drank little else. The name 'Glenlivet' had such strong associations with quality in whisky that most of the distilleries on the Upper Spey, and many far beyond it, later hyphenated their names with Glenlivet as a boast of quality. Andrew Usher & Co. even used the name to sell a vatted malt which contained a little Glenlivet and a lot of other Speyside whiskies as Old Vatted Glenlivet – and did a roaring trade. The name 'Glenlivet' had become a powerful brand: people seeing 'Glenlivet' on a label bought the whisky in the conviction that the contents of the bottle would be of appropriate gustatory quality. They still do – a fact of which the new owners of the brand appear to be aware.

By the time Ushers were selling their OVG, Glenlivet was part of a much bigger brand, namely Scotch whisky. From having been the drink of the lower classes of a small, poor nation, Scotch whisky had risen to be the preferred potation of the masters of the world. It was this association which allowed Scotch whisky branding to depart from its connection with flavour quality and to rely on its association with power and status. Advertisements for whisky over the second half of the nineteenth century demonstrate this trend: the earlier ones announce the quality of their spirit while the later rely on the association of whisky with imperial power.

This departure was useful to the distillers in the early years of the twentieth century. The early whisky barons had travelled the world, selling their whisky on the excellence of its flavour. But within two or three generations individual owners and family firms had given way to joint-stock companies for which the personal connection and guarantee of quality were of less importance than the maximisation of profit. This was fortunate, for the whisky companies had become the victims of their own success. They had created an international mass-market. The lower orders, which previously had drunk gin or other native spirits, now wanted whisky. Stocks of top-quality whisky sufficient to supply this market did not exist, and even if they had, they could not have been sold profitably at the prices such customers were able to pay. The blenders squared the circle by taking the product downmarket and selling blends which were mostly grain spirit. They were able to do so because of the power of the brand names: both the generic brand which was Scotch whisky and the particular brands within that category. To return to Johnnie Walker: the creation of Johnnie Walker Red Label in the early twentieth century allowed the company to compete in the new marketplace. The proportion of aged malt in the blend was reduced, permitting the new brand to be sold for less than the old. (As will be apparent from the Directory profiles, this is no reflection on the quality of Johnnie Walker in the twenty-first century, which is very high indeed.)

In its maturity, a brand is an artificial identity. It is the sum of all the associations which the commodity has acquired over the years in the minds of all of the people who have any knowledge of it. It is a kind of intellectual property which, though intangible, is nonetheless real. The reality is demonstrated in its market value: when brands change hands, they often do so for very large sums of money. This is because the mass-awareness which is the core of a brand makes it possible to sell large quantities of whatever carries the brand name. (Brand counterfeiting in whisky is rife, especially in India, and liquor companies spend large sums of money in defending their brands against interlopers.) Each brand publicises its product according to a set of criteria – brand values, as they are known – which define not only the product but the target consumer. Some brand values are related to the nature of the product, but most refer to the values of whichever sector of society the brand is aimed at. Naturally, brand values often differ between one country and another, as owners or distributors seek to recommend their whisky in terms of the values of different societies. Some companies employ brand ambassadors, representatives whose business it is to promote the brand by recommending the product to bartenders, retailers and influential consumers. The use of brand ambassadors marks something of a return to earlier modes of promotion, since much of the brand ambassador's job is to invite people to taste the whisky he or she represents. Obviously, the whisky has to be agreeable for this approach to work.

Scotch whisky is a highly flavoured spirit. Even the blandest whisky is strong-tasting stuff compared with vodka or gin. It follows that the marketing of whisky must take more cognisance of flavour than does that of other spirits. By the later 1970s, whisky appeared to have lost its way and brand managers, with the myopia of their tribe, seemed to have forgotten about flavour in the pursuit of their brands' dominant values, most of which had little to do with taste.

A decade or so ago, the people who are paid to promote tourism in Scotland came up with a new idea. This was a great event, for such folk don't have a lot of new ideas, and so they celebrated it accordingly. The idea was to promote the notion of Scotland itself as a brand, under the less-than-enticing slogan of Scotland the Brand. The name, if lacking in romantic association, did at least have the advantage of being transparent to the meanest understanding. It sought to restore an asset which was once important but had atrophied, namely the idea of Scotland. Scotland had all but disappeared from the mental landscape of most of the world's population. Surveys demonstrated that even in Europe, few folk knew where the country was. Asked to associate the name, some said 'men in skirts' but most said 'whisky'.

Scotch whisky branding is like one of those little Russian dolls, each of which opens to reveal a smaller one inside. Inside the Scotland brand there was the Scotch whisky brand, and inside that the whisky brand name. The crisis in Scotch whisky sales coincided with a low point in respect of (and for) Scotland. There has since been something of a renaissance in both. Scotland has re-established an identity in the last few decades in order to assert herself as a small but lively nation and a minor partner in the great European enterprise. That is a better platform for selling her goods than being a junior partner in a defunct imperial power. (This is not a criticism of the union with England – something of the sort has happened to England as well, to her benefit.) The reinvention of Scotch whisky has run in parallel. Whether there is a causal connection is impossible to say but the contemporaneity of the two developments together with the foregoing argument suggests that there is.

Increased concern for quality on the part of distillers and blenders has played a large part in the revival. The renewed interest in the flavour of whiskies has, of course, been led by malts. In the '60s, Glenfiddich led the way in marketing single malts, with a product whose flavour was closer in character to that of blended whiskies than it was to some of the other malts. It found a market, though, and other bottled single malts soon followed it. Gradually, in the '70s, more highly flavoured malt whiskies were bottled as singles: Macallan and Glenfarclas, Laphroaig and Bowmore. With the advent of the Scotch Malt Whisky Society in 1983, the appreciation of flavour in malt whiskies came of age, with the discovery by a small section of the public of the wild flavour spectrum which whiskies exhibit when taken undiluted from a single, fine cask after ten or more years' maturation.

Blended whiskies followed suit, if slowly. The Famous Grouse established a reputation for excellence, in Scotland initially and thereafter beyond the Scottish border. This reputation was gained by producing a whisky which claimed to be no more than a standard blend and was priced accordingly, but contained a higher proportion of single malts than other blends in its market sector. (And, one suspects, because most of the malts in the blend came from the very high-quality Edrington stocks.) Grouse first chased and then overtook Bell's as Scotland's preferred dram. After some time, Bell's responded, with a rebranding (which gave the bottle an age statement for the first time) and greatly improved contents. Other blended whiskies followed suit. As a result, standard blended Scotch whiskies are probably of higher quality today than at any time in the last 100 years.

The last 20 years have seen the disappearance of a great many Scotch whisky brands, as smaller companies have been taken over by the big corporations. A glance at the brand names listed in the next chapter and a comparison with what is available in the shops will show just how many brands have gone. But what we have lost on the swings of blended whisky, we have gained on the roundabouts of malts. Well over half of all the malt whiskies are now available in proprietary bottlings as single malts and those which are not bottled by their owners can be found among the stocks of any of the leading private bottlers.

Those blended whisky brands which have survived have been built into much bigger entities than ever before. Ballantine's, Johnnie Walker, J&B, Whyte & Mackay, Chivas and others are major international brands, whose whiskies are known and respected by millions. The contents of the brand identity may change from state to state, but on the whole the whisky is the same worldwide and the brand stands as guarantor of quality.

In establishing themselves as brands in recent times, malt whiskies followed the path which blends took more than a century ago: they relied on their flavour as their main selling point. The names of malt whiskies became established as brands in their own right and the brand referred to the characteristic flavour of the malt. There even arose a species of amateur expert which claimed, almost always falsely, to be able to identify particular malts by flavour alone. (This is easy enough in the case of a few, but virtually impossible for the great majority of malt whiskies.) The flavour of the malt whisky became the most important element in the brand identity.

The last ten years have seen a dilution of this pristine purity. It began with an awareness on the part of increasing numbers of consumers that the flavour of a malt was not something fixed, but varied with age and maturation. (Independent bottlers were influential in this, since they bottled malts which tasted very different from and often better than the proprietary version.) The owners of malt whisky brands naturally resisted the trend but, seeing it unstoppable, made the best of it by bringing out bottlings of their malts at different ages. It was a small step from there to present their malt whisky at a given age, but matured in bourbon or sherry casks. This was natural enough, since most distillers had both sorts of cask in their warehouses and the whisky matured in the one was very different from that matured in the other. What was perhaps not so natural was to buy unusual casks, with the intention that the whisky matured in them would find a small but lucrative niche market on account of its difference (and deemed superiority) of flavour. Alas, this has been a slippery slope which has landed us with whisky from port pipes and Madeira casks, sherry casks of all sorts, rum barrels and wine casks.

And if that were not bad enough, we have malt whisky finishes. 'Finish' is a term which was coined by Bill Lumsden of Glenmorangie to describe some interesting experiments he made back in the '80s. Bill had a number of casks which were unsuitable for the standard Glenmorangie malt, which is matured in ex-bourbon casks. It would be a long wait to find out what the Glenmorangie would be like matured in such casks, so Bill decided to try the effect of storage of mature Glenmorangie for a few years only in different wood. Some maturations were a success and some were not, but there were enough of interest and quality to warrant trying them in the marketplace. So were the famous Glenmorangie cask finishes born. They grew to constitute a sub-brand within the Glenmorangie brand. The ten-year-old bourbon-cask Glenmorangie, which was the starting point, was good stuff in the first place and the tightest controls ensured that those finished whiskies that made it into bottle were of satisfactory quality. But alas, there is no copyright on a good idea. Gadarene marketing managers throughout the Scotch whisky industry followed suit, so today we have malt whiskies of indifferent original character claiming a tiny market share on account of their having been 'finished' in all sorts of bizarre ways. There is a strong impression of someone somewhere having lost the script. 'Finishes' have become an underhand way of applying extraneous flavours to Scotch whisky and thereby evading the rules which specify that the only permitted ingredients are water, yeast and malted barley. The Directory has included examples of only the more permanent and important of these finished whiskies.

The emergence of malt whisky finishes is only one example of what is known in the trade as portfolio marketing. The conglomerative trend of the last 50 years has led to a few big whisky companies owning more and more different malt whisky distilleries and blended whisky brands. While this leads to improved profits (the reason for conglomerates forming in the first place), it brings marketing problems. In a static market, the success of one brand takes market share from another. If both brands are owned by the one company, the net result may be a reduction in overall profits, since the spend on promoting one brand competes with the spend on another. This problem was particularly acute for United Distillers (as it then was) in the late '80s. Then, as now, by far the biggest of all the whisky corporations, it owned about half of all the malt whisky distilleries, only a few of which were marketed as single malts. The company took a close look at the Scotch Malt Whisky Society, which by then was successfully selling lots of malt whisky bottlings under the one label, and decided that the same could be done with some of its whiskies. The outcome was the Classic Malts: six of the UD malt whiskies, good enough but not outstanding, sold as a single brand and backed by the promotional resources of a major corporation. The Classic Malts have been an outstanding success and have gained a large following, mostly among consumers new to malt whisky.

Private bottlers were well placed to create portfolio brands and of course were not restricted to any group of malt whiskies. Cadenhead and Gordon & MacPhail were long-established firms which held huge stocks of malts, some of them of real antiquity. They and other smaller bottlers established portfolio brands or collections of malt whiskies. Energetic new entrants such as Signatory were able to acquire and lay down stocks of good whisky, establishing a reputation for quality which allowed them to sell whiskies of different ages and provenance under a single label.

There has been a convergence in branding between malt and blended whiskies. The blenders copied the methods of the malt distillers in returning to flavour as an important brand value. This approach had direct and indirect results. Directly, it opened new markets among more discerning drinkers and made up for the declining influence of traditional values. Indirectly, it enabled the brands to be exploited as portfolios, but on the basis of age as the differentiating factor. A look at the lists in Chapter 3 will reveal the extent of the aged bottling of blended whiskies. A few blenders have even sought to follow the malt distillers down the route of finishing and we have seen even first-class brands such as The Famous Grouse endanger their core values by selling inferior liquor as 'finished' versions of the blend.

The consequence of all this activity has been a Scotch whisky market which, while generally buoyant, is in a state of some confusion. Brand owners have gained useful additions to their profits by introducing new products, but at what cost to their core brands is not yet known. Fashions come and go. Cognac and Armagnac are liquors as good as Scotch malt whisky and they have been struggling for years. While they are presently showing some signs of recovery, their decline from a once-dominant position in the high-class liquor market should be a warning to the Scotch whisky industry.

# SCOTCH WHISKY BRANDS
# AND THEIR OWNERS

There are literally hundreds of registered Scotch whisky brands. In many cases, the same whisky is sold under many different brand names. If you wish to ascertain the flavour of a whisky which is not in the Whisky List, you should look at other brands which are owned by the same company.

## Owners

The names of brands whose flavour profile is included in the Directory are highlighted in blue below. The brands and distilleries are listed under the name of the operating company. If the operating company is wholly owned by another company or another company has a majority holding of the stock, that company is shown as the owner. Where no owner is indicated, it means that the operating company is not owned or controlled by any larger company. Most conglomerate companies are the owners of whisky companies which at some time in the past have been taken over. Where such company names are well known, they are listed below, with an entry indicating their owner.

Named whisky brands are listed under the company which owns the brand name and normally the distillery, if the brand is a malt. Where malt whiskies are bottled by anyone other than the owner, the Directory indicates the fact alongside the brand heading.

## Nomenclature

As mentioned in Chapter 1, Scotch whisky brands fall into three main categories: grains, blends and malts. In the last ten years or so, Scotch whiskies have been marketed in an increasing variety of guises, so that a more precise definition is required. The Directory therefore proposes to describe whiskies as follows.

## Grains

There is no problem with these and the term 'grain' is adequate. Very few single grain whiskies are marketed and, in every case, the grain is from a single distillery and the bottling is from a number of casks.

## Blends

Blended Scotch whisky is a mix of malt whisky with grain whisky. The number of malts in a blend varies greatly, some having only two or three, others having dozens. If there is an age statement on the bottle, the youngest whisky in the mix has been in cask for at least as long the stated age. In practice a blend, especially a de luxe blend, will often contain whiskies much older than stated. No inferences may be drawn from the list of the owner's distilleries about the malts in its blends, since distillers commonly trade whiskies.

For many years, the industry has used three designations for blended whiskies: 'standard' , 'premium' and 'de luxe'. These are marketing terms only and are attributed by the brand owner with a view to persuading prospective buyers. They do, however, indicate an ascending order of quality, with the superior varieties generally being of greater age and possessing a higher proportion of malt to grain whiskies in their mix.

## Malts

Until recently, there were two sorts of malt whisky: single malts and vatted malts. 'Single' referred to the produce of a single distillery – as opposed to vatted malt, which was a mixture of malts from more than one distillery. Until the 1980s, very few malt whiskies were bottled at all and all of the available single malts were bottled by their proprietors, or by bottlers working on their instructions, so 'single malt' covered anything other than vatted. With the appearance of malts bottled by persons other than their proprietors, some confusion has arisen.

The situation has not been helped by the vogue for

single-cask bottlings, which in the USA has given rise to 'single single malt'. It is rather a silly expression, but its existence shows the need for a word which describes single-cask bottlings. To add to the confusion, it has become fashionable for distillers to mature malt whiskies so that they owe their flavour to more than one cask. There was a time, not so long ago, when the whisky from a single cask could be described by reference to the previous contents of the cask – usually sherry or bourbon, with occasionally an exotic such as port. There is now a fashion for 'finishes' which involve taking a whisky which has lain ten years or so in one sort of cask and putting it for a period varying from months to years in another sort of cask. The resultant flavour is a mix of the two. At best, when a distiller uses an already mature malt and adds to its flavour by additional maturation in a fresh cask of another sort, the resultant whisky can be very good indeed. But, for some exponents of the technique, finishes are a cheap way of applying some flavour to whiskies which have spent their lives in exhausted casks. At its worst, the practice is a fakery and a device to circumvent the restrictions of the Royal Commission's definition. Where words such as 'French oak' appear after the distillery name, it is safe to assume that the whisky has been 'finished'.

The above remarks do not apply to the long-established practice of mixing sherry- and bourbon-matured whiskies to achieve a pleasing overall character. This has been done for many years and is fully justified by the quality of malts such as Highland Park. For the avoidance of doubt, the Directory will designate malts as follows.

### Single Malt

Malt from one distillery, bottled by or for the proprietor of the distillery. The name of the malt will generally be the name of the distillery. The malt will have come from a number of casks, in which it will have been matured for at least as long as the period indicated in the age statement. Occasionally, the label gives a date of distillation rather than an age. This is usually done for marketing reasons (i.e. it is designed to mislead) and is significant only if the label also tells the date of bottling, since only the age in cask is relevant to the flavour of the whisky. Occasionally, a single malt is bottled by a distiller which does not bear the name of the distillery. For example, William Morton bottles Inchmurrin and Old Rhosdhu, both single malts produced at Loch Lomond Distillery. The distillery has pot-stills of different sorts which make malts of different character, hence the need to use a name other than that of the distillery.

### Single Malt, Private Bottling

This is single malt bottled by someone other than the proprietor of the distillery. The label may or may not bear the distillery name, depending on whether the bottler wishes to risk a legal battle with the owners of the distillery name. Occasionally, the distillery will be indirectly indicated, as in 'From the Ardbeg Distillery', which is clear enough, or 'Leapfrog', an ingenious and amusing homophone for Laphroaig.

### Single Malt, Single Cask

This is single malt that has been matured in cask for the number of years indicated. The bottling is from a single cask, whose contents are unmixed with those of any other. The malt consequently exhibits the characteristics of the particular cask. If the cask is a good one, this is desirable. If not, not. Single-cask bottlings may be by the distillers themselves, or by private bottlers. If the latter, the Directory will indicate the fact.

### Single Malt, Cask Finished

Single malt whose maturation has been finished in a cask of a type different from that in which it began.

### Single Malt, Solera Matured

'*Solera*' is a Spanish term that denotes a method of maturation formerly much used by the makers of sherries. It refers to a tier of casks, each containing sherry wine. Every year, some wine is drawn off from the cask at the bottom of the pile. Only a proportion of the contents of the cask is removed and it is replenished from the cask immediately above it. Each cask in turn is so treated and the topmost cask replenished with new sherry. Once established, the solera will contain no wine younger in years than the number of casks in the tier and some wine (a decreasingly small amount) which is as old as the solera. As a maturation practice, it works fine for sherry and was recommended for whisky a century ago by no less an authority than George Saintsbury. Nonetheless, the only whisky company to adopt the method is William Grant & Sons, for their Glenfiddich whisky. Their maturation vat is as recommended by Saintsbury, but not a true solera. It produces good whisky, though.

### Vatted Malt

This refers to malt from more than one distillery, with no indication as to which distilleries or who owns them. Minimum age in cask is that stated. Where malt is bottled under a name other than that of the distillery, the Directory will assume it to be a vatted malt.

## List of Scotch Whisky Brands and Their Owners

The particulars of ownership given below are believed accurate as at the date of writing. Readers should, however, be aware that the ownership of brands and distilleries changes from time to time, as companies buy and sell both.

### Adelphi Distillery Ltd

3 Gloucester Lane
Edinburgh EH3 6ED
Tel: 0131 226 6670
Fax: 0131 226 6672
Email: james@adelphiwhisky.demon.co.uk
Website: www.adelphidistillery.com

### Brands

Private malt whisky bottlers: various malts under own label.

Adelphi Private Stock – premium blend

Glenlossie 17 Year Old: Adelphi bottling

Linkwood 17 Year Old: Adelphi bottling

## Allied Distillers Ltd

2 Glasgow Road
Dumbarton G82 1ND
Tel: 01389 765 111
Fax: 01389 763 874
Website: www.allieddomecqplc.com

### Owners

Allied Distillers are part of the Allied Domecq Group

### Subsidiaries

Ballantine, George & Son Ltd
Glendronach Distillery Co. Ltd, The
Johnston, D. & Co. (Laphroaig) Ltd
Long John Distilleries Ltd
Stewart & Son of Dundee Ltd
Stodart, Jas & Geo Ltd
Taylor & Ferguson Ltd
Teacher, Wm & Sons Ltd

### Brands

Ambassador de luxe blend
Ballantine's 17 Year Old – de luxe blend
Ballantine's 18 Year Old – de luxe blend
Ballantine's 21 Year Old – de luxe blend
Ballantine's 30 Year Old – de luxe blend
Ballantine's Finest – premium blend
Ballantine's Founder's Reserve 10 Year Old – de luxe blend
Ballantine's Gold Seal – de luxe blend
Ballantine's Purity – vatted malt
Doctor's Special – standard blend
Glendronach 15 Year Old – single malt
Laphroaig 10 Year Old – single malt
Laphroaig 15 Year Old – single malt
Laphroaig Cask Strength – single malt
Long John – standard blend
Long John 12 Year Old – de luxe blend
Miltonduff-Glenlivet 12 Year Old – single malt
Old Smuggler – standard blend
Scapa 12 Year Old – single malt
Stewart's Cream of the Barley – standard blend
Teacher's Highland Cream – standard blend
Tormore 10 Year Old – single malt

### Distilleries

Ardmore

Dumbarton Grain Distillery
Glenburgie
Glendronach
Glentauchers
Imperial
Inverleven
Laphroaig
Miltonduff
Scapa
Strathclyde Grain Distillery
Tormore

## Angus Dundee Distillers plc

Hillman House
79 Marylebone Lane
London W1U 2PU
Tel: 020 7224 2373
Fax: 020 7224 2205
Email: sales@angusdundee.co.uk
Website: www.angusdundee.co.uk

### Brands

Angus Dundee Pure Malt – vatted malt
The Dundee – standard blend
Old Dundee 12 Year Old – de luxe blend
Angus Dundee 25 Year Old – de luxe blend
Angus Dundee 30 Year Old – de luxe blend
Angus Dundee 35 Year Old – de luxe blend
Parkers – standard blend
Parkers Supreme – de luxe blend
Glen Parker Highland Malt – vatted malt
Tomintoul 10 Year Old – single malt

### Distilleries

Tomintoul
Glencadam

## Ballantine, George & Son Ltd

### Owners

Allied Distillers Ltd

## Ben Nevis Distillery (Fort William) Ltd

Ben Nevis Distillery
Lochy Bridge
Fort William PH33 6TJ
Tel: 01397 702 476
Fax: 01397 702 768
Website: www.bennevisdistillery.com

### Owners

Nikka Corporation

### Brands

Ben Nevis Single Highland Malt Whisky – single malt
Dew of Ben Nevis – premium blend
Dew of Ben Nevis 12 Year Old – de luxe blend
Dew of Ben Nevis 21 Year Old – de luxe blend
Dew of Ben Nevis Special Reserve – de luxe blend
MacDonald's Glencoe 8 Year Old – vatted malt

### Distilleries

Ben Nevis

## Berry Bros & Rudd Ltd

3 St James's Street
London SW1A 1EG
Tel: 020 7396 9666
Fax: 020 7396 9677
Email: deborah.hargreaves@cutty-sark.com
Website: www.cutty-sark.com

### Brands

All Malt 12 Year Old – vatted malt
All Malt 17 Year Old – vatted malt
Berry's Best 8 Year Old – de luxe blend
Berry's Best Pure Malt 12 Year Old – vatted malt
Cutty Sark – premium blend
Cutty Sark 12 Year Old – de luxe blend
Cutty Sark 18 Year Old – de luxe blend
Cutty Sark 25 Year Old – de luxe blend
Cutty Sark Golden Jubilee – de luxe blend
Glenrothes 1987 – single malt
St James's 12 Year Old – de luxe blend

## Bruichladdich Distillery Co. Ltd

120 St James' Building
Linwood Road
Paisley
Renfrewshire PA3 3AT
Tel: 0141 842 3000
Fax: 0141 842 3001
Email: vanessa@bruichladdich.com
Website: www.bruichladdich.com

### Brands

Bruichladdich 10 Year Old – single malt
Bruichladdich 15 Year Old – single malt
Bruichladdich XVII – single malt
Bruichladdich Vintage – single malt
Bruichladdich Legacy – single malt

### Distilleries

Bruichladdich

## Buchanan, James & Co. Ltd

### Owners

United Distillers & Vintners Ltd

## Burn Stewart Distillers plc

8 Milton Road
College Milton North
East Kilbride G74 5BU
Tel: 01355 260999
Fax: 01355 264355
Email: enquiries@burnstewart.co.uk

### Owners

CL World Brands, Trinidad

### Brands

Black Bottle – premium blend
Black Bottle 10 Year Old – de luxe blend
Black Cock – standard blend
Black Cock 12 Year Old – de luxe blend
Black Prince Select – premium blend
Black Prince Superior 12 Year Old – de luxe blend
Black Prince 17 Year Old – de luxe blend
Black Prince 20 Year Old – de luxe blend
Black Prince 25 Year Old – de luxe blend
Bunnahabhain 12 Year Old – single malt

Burberry Premium – premium blend
Burberry 12 Year Old – de luxe blend
Burberry 15 Year Old – de luxe blend
Burberry 25 Year Old – de luxe blend
Burberry 15 Year Old – vatted malt
Burn Stewart – premium blend
Burn Stewart 12 Year Old – de luxe blend
Deanston – single malt
Deanston 12 Year Old – single malt
Deanston 17 Year Old – single malt
Glen Blair – vatted malt
Glen Shira – single malt
Highland Rose – standard blend
Highland Rose 12 Year Old – de luxe blend
Ledaig Original – single malt
Ledaig 15 Year Old – single malt
Ledaig 20 Year Old – single malt
Old Royal – de luxe blend
Scottish Castle – standard blend
Scottish Leader – standard blend
Scottish Leader 12 Year Old – de luxe blend
Scottish Leader 15 Year Old – de luxe blend
Scottish Leader 22 Year Old – de luxe blend
Scottish Leader 25 Year Old – de luxe blend
Tobermory 10 Year Old – single malt

### Distilleries

Bunnahabhain

Deanston

Tobermory

### Cadenhead's

172 Canongate
Edinburgh EH8 8DF
Tel: 0131 556 5864
Fax: 0131 556 2527
Email: enquiries@cadenhead.com

### Owners

Cadenhead's is owned by William Cadenhead Ltd, which is wholly owned by J. & A. Mitchell & Co. Ltd

### Brands

Private malt whisky bottlers. A large number of malts under own label.

Lochside 19 Year Old: Cadenhead bottling – single malt, single cask, private bottling

Mosstowie 29 Year Old: Cadenhead's Chairman's Stock – single malt

St Magdalene 24 Year Old: Cadenhead's Authentic Collection – single malt

## Catto, James & Co. Ltd
### Owners
Inver House Distillers

## Chivas Brothers Ltd
West Byrehill
Kilwinning
Ayrshire KA13 6LE
Tel: 01294 551 111
Fax: 01294 558 493
Website: www.pernod-ricard.com
### Owners
The Pernod Ricard Corporation
### Subsidiaries
Campbell Distillers Ltd
Glen Keith Distillery Co. Ltd, The
Glenlivet Distillers Ltd, The
Grant, J. & J. (Glen Grant) Ltd
Highland Bonding Co. Ltd, The
Hill Thomson & Co. Ltd
Longmorn Distillery Ltd, The
Sherriff & Co. (Jamaica) Ltd
Smith, George & J. G. Ltd
Strathisla Distillery Co. Ltd, The
### Brands
100 Pipers – standard blend
Aberlour 10 Year Old – single malt
Aberlour 15 Year Old Double Cask – single malt, finished
Aberlour 15 Year Old Sherry Wood Finish – single malt
Aberlour 1971 Vintage – single malt
Aberlour 100 Proof – single malt
Aberlour a'Bunadh – single malt
Benriach 10 Year Old – single malt
Chairman's Reserve – de luxe blend
Chivas Regal 12 Year Old – de luxe blend

Chivas Regal 18 Year Old – de luxe blend
Clan Campbell – standard blend
Clan Campbell Highlander 12 Year Old – de luxe blend
Clan Campbell Legendary 18 Year Old – de luxe blend
Clan Campbell Pure Malt 8 Year Old – vatted malt
Glenforres – vatted malt
Glen Grant 5 Year Old – single malt
Glen Grant 10 Year Old – single malt
Glen Keith 10 Year Old – single malt
Glenlivet 12 Year Old – single malt
Glenlivet 12 Year Old French Oak – single malt, finished
Glenlivet 18 Year Old – single malt
Glenlivet 21 Year Old Archive – single malt
Highland Clan – standard blend
House of Campbell – standard blend
House of Lords – standard blend
House of Lords 12 Year Old – de luxe blend
Longmorn 15 Year Old – single malt
Passport – standard blend
Queen Anne – vatted malt
Royal Citation – de luxe blend
Royal Salute 21 Year Old – de luxe blend
Something Special – de luxe blend
St Leger – de luxe blend
Strathisla 12 Year Old – single malt
Treasury – de luxe blend
White Heather – standard blend

### Distilleries

Aberlour
Allt a'bhainne
Benriach
Braeval
Caperdonich
Glenallachie
Glen Grant
Glen Keith
Glenlivet
Longmorn
Strathisla

## *Cockburn & Campbell Ltd*

Cockpen House
20–30 Buckhold Road
Wandsworth
London SW18 4AP
Tel: 020 8875 7008
Fax: 020 8875 7009

### *Brands*

Royal & Ancient, The – standard blend
Royal & Ancient, The 28 Year Old – de luxe blend

## *Dewar, John & Sons Ltd*

1700 London Road
Glasgow G32 8XR
Tel: 0141 551 4000
Fax: 0141 551 4030
Website: www.dewars.com

### *Owners*

Bacardi Ltd

### *Subsidiaries*

William Lawson Distillers Ltd

### *Brands*

Aberfeldy 12 Year Old – single malt
Aultmore – single malt
Craigellachie – single malt
Dewar's Ancestor 12 Year Old – de luxe blend
Dewar's Special Reserve 12 Year Old – de luxe blend
Dewar's 'White Label' – standard blend
Glen Deveron 5 Year Old – single malt
Glen Deveron 10 Year Old – single malt
Glen Deveron 12 Year Old – single malt
Glen Deveron 15 Year Old – single malt
King Edward the First – standard blend
Royal Brackla – single malt
Royal Brackla Unaged Malt – single malt
William Lawson's Finest – standard blend
William Lawson's Scottish Gold 12 Year Old – de luxe
   blend

### *Distilleries*

Aberfeldy
Aultmore
Brackla

Craigellachie

Glen Deveron

## The Edrington Group Ltd

106 Nile Street

Glasgow G1 2QX

Tel: 0141 332 6595

Fax: 0141 353 2263

Website: www.theedringtongroup.com

### Owners

The Robertson Trust. Employees of the company have a minor shareholding.

The Edrington Group owns 70 per cent of 1887 Ltd (with William Grant & Sons Ltd), which is the sole owner of Highland Distillers Ltd. The group also owns 50 per cent of the North British Distillery Co. Ltd. While it owns whisky brands directly, the Edrington Group does not own any distilleries save through its ownership of companies which do.

### Brands

Brig O'Perth – premium blend

Capercailzie – standard blend

The Famous Grouse – premium blend

The Famous Grouse Gold Reserve 12 Year Old – de luxe blend

The Famous Grouse Prestige – de luxe blend

The Famous Grouse 15 Year Old – de luxe blend

The Famous Grouse 21 Year Old – de luxe blend

The Famous Grouse Vintage Malt 1987 – vatted malt

Glenturret 12 Year Old – single malt

Glenturret 15 Year Old – single malt

Glenturret 18 Year Old – single malt

Highland Park 12 Year Old – single malt

Highland Park 18 Year Old – single malt

Highland Park 25 Year Old – single malt

Isle of Orkney – vatted malt

Perth Royal, The – standard blend

Ptarmigan – standard blend

Safeways Own Brand – standard blend

Safeways Own Brand 5 Year Old – premium blend

## Fisher, Donald Ltd

**Owners**

United Distillers & Vintners plc

## Glen Catrine Bonded Warehouse Ltd

7 Laigh Road

Catrine

Ayrshire KA5 6SQ

Tel: 01290 551 211

Fax: 01290 551 423

Three family-owned independent distilleries – Glen Scotia, Littlemill and Loch Lomond – are in association under Glen Catrine.

**Brands**

Fraser McDonalds – standard blend

Glen Catrine – standard blend

Glen Scotia – single malt

High Commissioner – standard blend

Inchmurrin 10 Year Old – single malt

Littlemill 8 Year Old – single malt

Loch Lomond – single malt

Old Barrister – premium blend

Old Rhosdhu 5 Year Old – single malt

Scots Earl – de luxe blend

**Distilleries**

Glen Scotia

Littlemill

Loch Lomond

## Glendronach Distillery Co. Ltd, The

**Owners**

Allied Distillers Ltd

## Glen Keith Distillery Co. Ltd, The

**Owners**

Chivas Brothers Ltd

## Glenlivet Distillers Ltd, The

**Owners**

Chivas Brothers Ltd

## Glenmorangie plc

Macdonald House

18 Westerton Road

Broxburn EH52 5AQ

Tel: 01506 852 929

Fax: 01506 855 856

Website: www.glenmorangieplc.com

### Owners

LVMH

### Subsidiaries

Ardbeg Distillery Ltd

The Scotch Malt Whisky Society Ltd

### Brands

Ardbeg 10 Year Old – single malt

Ardbeg 17 Year Old – single malt

Ardbeg 1975 – single malt

Bailie Nicol Jarvie – de luxe blend

Glenmorangie Vintage – single malt

Glenmorangie 10 Year Old – single malt

Glenmorangie 15 Year Old – single malt

Glenmorangie 18 Year Old – single malt

Glenmorangie Madeira Wood Finish – single malt, cask finished

Glenmorangie Port Wood Finish – single malt, cask finished

Glenmorangie Sherry Wood Finish – single malt, cask finished

Glen Moray Chardonnay – single malt, cask finished

Glen Moray 12 Year Old – single malt

Glen Moray 16 Year Old – single malt

Glen Moray Vintage – single malt

Glen Moray Wine Cask 16 Year Old – single malt, cask finished

Highland Queen – standard blend

Highland Queen Majesty – de luxe blend

Highland Queen, Queen of Scots – de luxe blend

James Martin 8 Year Old – de luxe blend

James Martin 20 Year Old – de luxe blend

Martin's VVO – standard blend

Muirhead's – standard blend

### Distilleries

Ardbeg

Glenmorangie

Glen Moray

## Gordon & MacPhail Ltd

George House
Boroughbriggs Road
Elgin
Moray IV30 1JY
Tel: 01343 545111
Fax: 01343 540155
Email: info@gordonandmacphail.com
Website: www.gordonandmacphail.com

Gordon & MacPhail are private bottlers of very long standing. They have a large range of malts and blends. Many of their malts are bottled under the portfolio brand of Connoisseurs Choice.

### Brands

Avonside – de luxe blend

Ben Aigen – standard blend

Ben Alder – standard blend

Benromach 10 Year Old – single malt

Connoisseurs Choice – range of malts

Frasers Reserve – vatted malt

Frasers Supreme – de luxe blend

G & M Reserve – vatted malt

Glen Avon – vatted malt

Glen Calder – standard blend

Glen Fraser – vatted malt

Glen Gordon – vatted malt

Glen Urquhart – de luxe blend

Gordon & MacPhail Cask Strength Malt – single malt

Gordon & MacPhail Rare Old Malt – vatted malt

Highland Fusilier – vatted malt

Immortal Memory – de luxe blend

Inverleven 1985: Gordon & MacPhail bottling – single malt

MacPhail's – vatted malt

MacPhail's Collection – single malt portfolio

Mannochmore 1984 Connoisseurs Choice – single malt

Old Elgin – vatted malt

Old Orkney – de luxe blend

Pride of Islay – vatted malt

Pride of the Lowlands – vatted malt

Pride of Orkney – vatted malt

Pride of Strathspey – vatted malt

Royal Findhorn – standard blend
Spey Cast – de luxe blend
Spey Malt – vatted malt
Spirit of Scotland – vatted malt
Ubique – standard blend
### Distilleries
Benromach

## Grant, J. & G. Ltd
Glenfarclas Distillery
Ballindalloch
Banffshire AB37 9BD
Tel: 01807 500209
Fax: 01807 500234
Website: www.glenfarclas.co.uk
### Brands
Glen Dowan – standard blend
Glenfarclas 10 Year Old – single malt
Glenfarclas 12 Year Old – single malt
Glenfarclas 15 Year Old – single malt
Glenfarclas 21 Year Old – single malt
Glenfarclas 25 Year Old – single malt
Glenfarclas 30 Year Old – single malt
Glenfarclas 105 – single malt
### Distilleries
Glenfarclas

## Grant, J. & J. (Glen Grant) Ltd
### Owners
Campbell Distillers Ltd

## Haig, John & Co. Ltd
### Owners
United Distillers & Vintners Ltd

## Hardie, J. & W. Ltd
### Owners
Tomatin Distillery Co. Ltd, The

## Highland Bonding Co. Ltd
### Owners
Campbell Distillers Ltd

## Highland Distillers Ltd

West Kinfauns
Perth PH2 7XZ
Tel: 01738 440 000
Fax: 01738 628 167
Website: www.themacallan.com

### Owners

Highland Distillers is wholly owned by 1887 Ltd, which is itself owned 70 per cent by the Edrington Group and 30 per cent by William Grant & Sons Ltd. Macallan is owned 75 per cent by Highland Distillers Ltd and 25 per cent by the Suntory Corporation.

### Subsidiaries

Macallan-Glenlivet plc

### Brands

Macallan 10 Year Old – single malt
Macallan 12 Year Old – single malt
Macallan 15 Year Old – single malt
Macallan 18 Year Old 1982 – single malt
Macallan 25 Year Old – single malt
Macallan 30 Year Old – single malt
Macallan 1874 – single malt
Macallan 50 Year Old 1949 – single malt
Macallan 51 Year Old 1948 – single malt
Macallan 52 Year Old 1946 – single malt
Macallan Gran Reserva – single malt
Tamdhu – single malt

### Distilleries

Glenglassaugh
Glenrothes
Glenturret
Highland Park
Macallan
Tamdhu

## Hill Thomson & Co. Ltd

### Owners

Chivas Brothers Ltd

## Ian Macleod & Co. Ltd

Russell House

Dunnet Way

Broxburn EH52 5BU

Tel: 01506 852 205

Fax: 01505 856 434

Email: macleods@gael-net.co.uk

Website: www.ianmacleod.com

### Owners

P. J. Russell & Co. Ltd

### Brands

Black Rooster – standard blend

Black Shield – standard blend

Chieftain's Choice – vatted malt

Cockburn & Murray 'The Seven Stills' – vatted malt

Cockburn & Murray 8 Year Old – de luxe blend

Glengoyne Single Cask – single malt, single cask

Glengoyne 10 Year Old – single malt

Glengoyne 17 Year Old – single malt

Glengoyne 21 Year Old – single malt

Glengoyne Vintage – single malt

Glen Tress – vatted malt

Hedges & Butler – standard blend

Hedges & Butler 8 Year Old – de luxe blend

Hedges & Butler 12 Year Old – de luxe blend

Hedges & Butler 15 Year Old – de luxe blend

Hedges & Butler Malt – vatted malt

Isle of Skye 8 Year Old (Macleod's) – premium blend

Isle of Skye 12 Year Old (Macleod's) – premium blend

Isle of Skye 21 Year Old (Macleod's) – de luxe blend

King Robert II – standard blend

King Robert II De Luxe – de luxe blend

Langs Select 12 Year Old – de luxe blend

Langs Supreme – standard blend

Langs Supreme De Luxe – de luxe blend

Macleod's Single Malt Highland

Macleod's Single Malt Island

Macleod's Single Malt Islay

Macleod's Single Malt Lowland

Macleod's Single Malt Speyside

Mason's – standard blend

Queen's Seal – standard blend

Red Rooster – standard blend
Wm Maxwell – standard blend
**Distilleries**
Glengoyne

## International Whisky Company Ltd

19–20 Grosvenor Street
London W1K 4QH
Tel: 020 7629 0404
Fax: 020 7409 7778
Email: export@royalsilk.co.uk
**Brands**
Royal Silk Reserve Rare – standard blend

## Inverarity Vaults Ltd

12 Napier Road
Edinburgh EH10 5AY
Tel: 0131 229 3972
Fax: 0131 229 4217
Email: ronnie.martin@talk21.com
Website: www.inverarity-vaults.com
**Brands**
The Countryside Spirit – premium blend
Inverarity – standard blend
Inverarity Single Malt 10 Year Old
Inverarity Ancestral 14 Year Old – single malt
Inverarity Speyside Malt – single malt
Inverarity Island Malt – single malt

## Invergordon Distillers Ltd, The
**Owners**
Whyte & Mackay Ltd

## Inver House Distillers Ltd

Moffat Distillery
Airdrie
Lanarkshire ML6 8PL
Tel: 01236 769 377
Fax: 01236 769 781
Email: enquiries@inverhouse.com
Website: www.inverhouse.com

## Subsidiaries

Blairmhor Ltd

James Catto & Co. Ltd

## Brands

An Cnoc 12 Year Old – single malt

Balblair Elements – single malt

Balblair 33 Year Old – single malt

Balmenach – single malt

Blairmhor 8 Year Old – vatted malt

Catto's Deluxe 12 Year Old

Catto's Rare Old Scottish Highland Whisky – standard
blend

Catto's 21 Year Old – premium blend

Catto's 25 Year Old – premium blend

Coldstream Guard – standard blend

Diplomat – standard blend

Dougherty's – standard blend

Glen Drummond – vatted malt

Glen Flagler – vatted malt

Glen Mavis – standard blend

Glen Nicol – vatted malt

Glen Orson – standard blend

Golden Glen – standard blend

Hankey Bannister – standard blend

Hankey Bannister 12 Year Old – premium blend

Hankey Bannister 15 Year Old – de luxe blend

Hankey Bannister 21 Year Old – de luxe blend

Hankey Bannister Finest – standard blend

Highland Breeze – standard blend

Inver House Green Plaid – standard blend

Inver House Green Plaid 12 Year Old – de luxe blend

Inver House 21 Year Old – premium blend

Inver House 25 Year Old – premium blend

Inver House 35 Year Old – premium blend

Kinsey – standard blend

MacArthur's 12 Year Old – de luxe blend

MacArthur's Select – standard blend

Old Pulteney 12 Year Old – single malt

Pinwinnie Royale – de luxe blend

Speyburn 10 Year Old – single malt

Speyburn 21 Year Old – single malt

**Distilleries**

Balblair

Balmenach

Knockdhu

Pulteney

Speyburn-Glenlivet

## Isle of Arran Distillers Ltd

Enterprise House

Springkerse Business Park

Stirling FK7 7UF

Tel: 01786 431 900

Fax: 01786 431 909

Email: arran.distillers@arranwhisky.com

Website: www.arranwhisky.com

**Brands**

Arran Single Malt – single malt

Eileandour 10 Year Old – vatted malt

Glen Eason – vatted malt

Glen Rosa – standard blend

Island Prince 12 Year Old – de luxe blend

Island Prince 15 Year Old – de luxe blend

Island Prince 21 Year Old – de luxe blend

Loch Ranza – premium blend

Royal Island 17 Year Old – de luxe blend

Royal Island 21 Year Old – de luxe blend

Royal Island 30 Year Old – de luxe blend

**Distilleries**

Arran

## J. & A. Mitchell & Co. Ltd

85 Longrow

Campbeltown

Argyll PA28 6EX

Tel: 01586 552 009

Fax: 01586 553 232

Website: www.springbankdistillers.com

**Subsidiaries**

Springbank Distillers Ltd

William Cadenhead Ltd

## Johnston, D. & Co. (Laphroaig) Ltd

**Owners**

Allied Distillers Ltd

## Justerini & Brooks Ltd

**Owners**

United Distillers & Vintners Ltd

## Laing, Douglas & Co. Ltd

Douglas House

18 Lyndoch Crescent

Glasgow G3 6EQ

Tel: 0141 333 9242

Fax: 0141 333 9245

Email: info@douglaslaing.com

Website: www.douglaslaing.com

**Brands**

77 – standard blend

Ardbeg 25 Year Old: Douglas Laing bottling – single malt

Eaton Special – standard blend

Glen Drum – vatted malt

Glenury 20 Year Old: Douglas Laing bottling – single malt

House of Peers – standard blend

House of Peers 12 Year Old – de luxe blend

House of Peers 22 Year Old – vatted malt

House of Peers Gold Label – standard blend

House of Peers X.O. Xtra Old – de luxe blend

John Player Special – standard blend

John Player Special Rare – premium blend

John Player Special 12 Year Old – de luxe blend

John Player Special 15 Year Old – premium blend

King of Scots – de luxe blend

King of Scots Flagship – de luxe blend

King of Scots Gold Label – standard blend

King of Scots Number Edition – standard blend

King of Scots Proclamation – de luxe blend

King of Scots Rare Extra Gold – de luxe blend

King of Scots 17 Year Old – de luxe blend

King of Scots 25 Year Old – de luxe blend

Langside 25 Year Old – standard blend

McGibbons Golf Club – de luxe blend

McGibbons Masters Reserve Golf Club – ceramic de luxe blend

McGibbons Premium Reserve – standard blend

McGibbons Special Reserve – standard blend

McGibbons 12 Year Old – de luxe blend

Port Ellen 18 Year Old: Douglas Laing bottling – single malt

Rosebank 11 Year Old: Douglas Laing bottling – single malt

Royal Galleon 25 Year Old – de luxe blend

Sir Walter Raleigh – standard blend

Sovereign 25 Year Old – de luxe blend

## Loch Fyne Whiskies

Inveraray

Argyll PA32 8UD

Tel: 01499 302 219

Fax: 01499 302 238

Email: shop@lfw.co.uk

Website: www.lfw.co.uk

**Brands**

Loch Fyne – premium blend

## London & Scottish International Ltd

Meadow View House

Tannery Lane

Bramley

Surrey GU5 0AJ

Tel: 01483 894650

Fax: 01483 894651

Email: office@londonandscottish.co.uk

**Brands**

Glen Torran Single Malt 3 Year Old – vatted malt

Glen Torran Single Malt 8 Year Old – vatted malt

Glen Torran Single Malt 12 Year Old – vatted malt

Northern Isles Single Malt 8 Year Old

Old Bridge 3 Year Old – standard blend

Old Bridge 12 Year Old – standard blend

Old Crofter – standard blend

R & H Blenders Selection 3 Year Old – standard blend

Rory 3 Year Old – standard blend

Scottish Reel 3 Year Old – standard blend

Scottish Reel 8 Year Old – standard blend

## Long John Distilleries Ltd
### Owners
Allied Distillers Ltd


## Longmorn Distillery Ltd, The
### Owners
Chivas Brothers Ltd


## Lundie, Wm & Co. Ltd
11 Fitzroy Place
Glasgow G3 7RW
Tel: 0141 221 0707
Fax: 0141 226 3717
Website: wmlundie@aol.com
### Brands
Award – standard blend
Glen Fruin 10 Year Old – vatted malt
Lismore Finest – standard blend
Lismore Highland Malt – vatted malt
Lismore Pure Malt 8 Year Old – vatted malt
Lismore Select 8 Year Old – semi-premium blend
Lismore Signature – vatted malt
Lismore Single Malt 21 Year Old – vatted malt
Lismore Single Malt 25 Year Old – vatted malt
Lismore Special Reserve 12 Year Old – premium blend
Lismore Special Reserve 15 Year Old – de luxe blend
Lismore Special Reserve 18 Year Old – de luxe blend
Prestige D'Ecosse – standard blend
Prestige D'Ecosse 5 Year Old – standard blend
Royal Heritage 21 Year Old – de luxe blend
Tribute 5 Year Old – standard blend
Tribute 12 Year Old – de luxe blend
Tribute 15 Year Old – de luxe blend
Tribute 20 Year Old – de luxe blend
Tribute 21 Year Old – de luxe blend
Tribute 25 Year Old – de luxe blend
Tribute 30 Year Old – de luxe blend


## MacDonald Greenlees Ltd
### Owners
United Distillers & Vintners Ltd

## Macleod, Ian & Co. Ltd

### Owners

P. J. Russell & Co. Ltd

## Morrison Bowmore Distillers Ltd

Springburn Bond
Carlisle Street
Glasgow G21 1EQ
Tel: 0141 558 9011
Fax: 0141 558 9010
Email: info@morrisonbowmore.co.uk
Website: www.morrisonbowmore.co.uk

### Owners

Suntory Corporation

### Brands

Auchentoshan – single malt
Auchentoshan 10 Year Old – single malt
Auchentoshan 21 Year Old – single malt
Auchentoshan 22 Year Old – single malt
Auchentoshan 25 Year Old – single malt
Auchentoshan Select – single malt
Bowmore 12 Year Old – single malt
Bowmore 15 Year Old – single malt
Bowmore 17 Year Old – single malt
Bowmore 21 Year Old – single malt
Bowmore 22 Year Old – single malt
Bowmore 25 Year Old – single malt
Bowmore 30 Year Old – single malt
Bowmore 40 Year Old – single malt
Bowmore Cask Strength – single malt
Bowmore Darkest – single malt
Bowmore Legend – single malt
Clanroy – standard blend
Clanroy 25 Year Old – premium blend
Glen Garioch 8 Year Old – single malt
Glen Garioch 15 Year Old – single malt
Glen Garioch 21 Year Old – single malt
Islay Legend 8 Year Old – premium blend
King's Pride – de luxe blend
King's Pride 12 Year Old – premium blend
King's Pride 17 Year Old – premium blend
King's Pride 21 Year Old – premium blend

King's Pride 25 Year Old – premium blend
King's Pride 30 Year Old – premium blend
McClelland's 16 Year Old – vatted malt
McClelland's Highland – vatted malt
McClelland's Islay – vatted malt
McClelland's Lowland – vatted malt
Rob Roy – de luxe blend
Rob Roy 12 Year Old – premium blend
Rob Roy 17 Year Old – premium blend
Rob Roy 21 Year Old – premium blend
Rob Roy 25 Year Old – premium blend
Rob Roy 30 Year Old – premium blend
Swords – standard blend

**Distilleries**

Auchentoshan

Bowmore

Glen Garioch

## Macallan-Glenlivet plc

**Owners**

Highland Distillers Ltd, Suntory Corporation

## Murray McDavid Ltd

120 St James' Building
Linwood Road
Renfrewshire PA3 3AT
Tel: 0141 842 3000
Fax: 0141 842 3001
Email: websitemaster@murray-mcdavid.com
Website: www.murray-mcdavid.com

**Brands**

Independent private bottlers specialising in malt whiskies bottled without chillfiltration.

Leapfrog 12 Year Old: Murray McDavid bottling – single malt

Lochside 9 Year Old: Murray McDavid bottling – single malt

Springbank 9 Year Old: Murray McDavid bottling – single malt

## North British Distillery Co. Ltd, The

9 Wheatfield Road
Edinburgh EH11 2PX
Tel: 0131 337 3363
Fax: 0131 346 7488
Email: enquiries@northbritish.co.uk
Website: www.northbritish.co.uk

### Owners

Wholly owned by Lothian Distillers Ltd, which is owned
50 per cent each by UDV and Edrington Distillers Ltd.
The latter is wholly owned by the Edrington Group and
UDV is owned by Diageo plc

### Brands

North British Single Grain – single grain

### Distilleries

North British Grain Distillery

## Oddbins Ltd

31 Weir Road
Wimbledon
London SW19 8UG
Tel: 0800 328 2323
Fax: 0800 328 3848
Email: customer.services@oddbinsmail.com
Website: www.oddbins.com

Mainly retailers, but several own brands.

### Brands

Oddbins Own Brand Single Highland Malt 10 Year Old
Oddbins Own Brand Single Island Malt 12 Year Old
Oddbins Own Brand Single Speyside Malt 25 Year Old

## Praban na Linne Ltd

Eilean Iarmain
Isle of Skye IV43 8QR
Tel: 01471 833 266
Fax: 01471 833 260
Email: gaelicwhiskies@yahoo.co.uk
Website: www.gaelic-whiskies.co.uk

### Brands

Mac Na Mara – standard blend
Poit Dhubh 8 Year Old – vatted malt
Poit Dhubh 12 Year Old – vatted malt

Poit Dhubh 21 Year Old – vatted malt

Te Bheag – de luxe blend

Te Bheag Connoisseurs Blend – Unchillfiltered – de luxe blend

## Raymond Armstrong & Family

Bladnoch Distillery

Wigtown DG8 9AB

Tel: 01988 402 605/402 235

Email: enquiries@bladnoch.co.uk

Website: www.bladnoch.co.uk

### Distilleries

Bladnoch

## Sanderson, Wm & Son Ltd

### Owners

United Distillers & Vintners Ltd

## The Scotch Malt Whisky Society

The Vaults

87 Giles Street

Edinburgh EH6 6BZ

Tel: 0131 554 3451

Fax: 0131 553 1003

Email: smws@wdi.co.uk

Website: www.smws.com

A members' club who are private bottlers of malt whisky at full strength and without chillfiltration.

### Owners

Glenmorangie plc

## Sherriff & Co. (Jamaica) Ltd

### Owners

Chivas Brothers Ltd

## Signatory Vintage Scotch Whisky Co. Ltd

7 Elizafield

Edinburgh EH6 5PY

Tel: 0131 555 4988

Fax: 0131 555 5211

Email: signatory@signatory.demon.co.uk

## Brands

Originally private bottlers, now distillers in their own right. Numerous bottlings under the Signatory label.

Caol Ila 1989: Signatory bottling – single malt

Edradour 10 Year Old – single malt

Glenlivet 1976: Signatory bottling – single malt

Linkwood 1988: Signatory bottling – single malt

## Distilleries

Edradour


## Smith, George & J. G. Ltd

### Owners

Chivas Brothers Ltd


## Speyside Distillers Co. Ltd

Duchess Road

Rutherglen

Glasgow G73 1AU

Tel: 0141 647 4464

Fax: 0141 647 0181

Email: rickychristie@compuserve.com

Website: www.speysidedistillery.co.uk

### Brands

Dew of the Western Isles – standard blend

Drumguish – single malt

Glentromie – vatted malt

McGavins – standard blend

Murdoch's Perfection – de luxe blend

Scottish Prince 30 Year Old – de luxe blend

Speyside 10 Year Old – single malt

### Distilleries

Drumguish


## Springbank Distillers Ltd

85 Longrow

Campbeltown

Argyll PA28 6EX

Tel: 01586 552 009

Fax: 01586 553 232

Website: www.springbankwhisky.com

### Owners

J. & A. Mitchell & Co. Ltd

## Brands

Campbeltown Loch – single malt

Hazelburn – single malt

Longrow 10 Year Old Bourbonwood – single malt

Longrow 10 Year Old Sherrywood – single malt

Mitchell's 12 Year Old – de luxe blend

Springbank 10 Year Old – single malt

Springbank 21 Year Old – single malt

## Distilleries

Springbank

Longrow

## Stewart & Son of Dundee Ltd

### Owners

Allied Distillers Ltd

## Stodart, Jas & Geo Ltd

### Owners

Allied Distillers Ltd

## Strathisla Distillery Co. Ltd, The

### Owners

Chivas Brothers Ltd

## Taylor and Ferguson Ltd

### Owners

Allied Distillers Ltd

## Teacher, Wm & Sons Ltd

### Owners

Allied Distillers Ltd

## Tomatin Distillery Co. Ltd, The

Tomatin

Inverness-shire IV13 7YT

Tel: 01808 511 234

Fax: 01808 511 373

Website: www.tomatin.com

### Owners

Takara, Shuzo & Okura

### Subsidiaries

Hardie, J. & W. Ltd

## Brands

The Antiquary 12 Year Old – de luxe blend
The Antiquary 21 Year Old – de luxe blend
Big T 12 Year Old – de luxe blend
Big T Black Label – standard blend
Big T Gold Label – standard blend
The Talisman – standard blend
Tomatin 10 Year Old – single malt
Tomatin 12 Year Old – single malt
Tomatin 25 Year Old – single malt

## Distilleries

Tomatin Distillery

## Tullibardine Ltd

Tullibardine Distillery
Blackford
Perthshire PH4 1QG
Tel: 01674 862 252
Fax: 01674 862 330
Email: info@tullibardine.com

## Brands

Tullibardine 10 Year Old – single malt

## United Distillers & Vintners Ltd

Edinburgh Business Park
5 Lochside Way
Edinburgh EH12 9DT
Tel: 0131 519 2000
Fax: 0131 519 2001
Website: www.udv.com

## Owners

Diageo plc

## Subsidiaries

Buchanan, James & Co. Ltd
Fisher, Donald Ltd
Haig, John & Co. Ltd
Justerini & Brooks Ltd
MacDonald Greenlees Ltd
Sanderson, Wm & Son Ltd
UDV (Distilling) Ltd
United Distillers (UK) PLC
United Distillers & Vintners (ER) Ltd

United Distillers & Vintners (HP) Ltd

Walker, John & Sons Ltd

White Horse Distillers Ltd

## *Brands*

Abbot's Choice – standard blend

Balmenach – single malt

Baxter's Barley Bree – standard blend

Bell's 8 Year Old – standard blend

Bell's 12 Year Old – de luxe blend

Bell's 21 Year Old Royal Reserve – de luxe blend

Bell's Decanter – standard blend

Bell's Extra Special – standard blend

Bell's Islander – standard blend

Benmore – standard blend

Benrinnes – single malt

Black & White – standard blend

Black & White Select – de luxe blend

Blair Athol – single malt

Brora – single malt

Buchanan's 12 Year Old De Luxe – de luxe blend

Buchanan's De Luxe – de luxe blend

Buchanan's Special Reserve – de luxe blend

Bulloch Lade Gold Label – standard blend

C & J Fine Old – standard blend

Cambus – single grain

Caol Ila – single malt

Cardhu 12 Year Old – single malt

Chequers – standard blend

Clynelish 15 Year Old – single malt

Cragganmore 12 Year Old – single malt

Crawford's *** Special Reserve – standard blend

Dailuaine – single malt

Dalwhinnie 15 Year Old – single malt

Dimple 12 Year Old – de luxe blend

Dimple 15 Year Old – de luxe blend

Dimple Pinch – de luxe blend

Dufftown – single malt

Gillon's – standard blend

Glendullan – single malt

Glen Elgin – single malt

Glen Garry – standard blend

Glenkinchie 10 Year Old – single malt

Glenlossie – single malt

Glen Ord – single malt

Grand Old Parr 12 Year Old – de luxe blend

Haig Gold Label – standard blend

Harvey's Special – standard blend

Heathwood – standard blend

Huntly – standard blend

Inchgower – single malt

J&B Rare – premium blend

J&B Jet – de luxe blend

J&B Reserve – de luxe blend

J&B Ultima – de luxe blend

John Begg Blue Cap – standard blend

Johnnie Walker Red Label – standard blend

Johnnie Walker Black Label – de luxe blend

Johnnie Walker Gold Label – de luxe blend

Johnnie Walker Blue Label – de luxe blend

Johnnie Walker Honour – de luxe blend

Johnnie Walker Premier – de luxe blend

Johnnie Walker Swing – de luxe blend

Johnnie Walker Swing Superior – de luxe blend

King George IV – standard blend

King William IV – standard blend

Knockando 1986 – single malt

Lagavulin 16 Year Old – single malt

Linkwood – single malt

Loch Dhu – single malt

Logan 12 Year Old – de luxe blend

McCallum's Perfection – standard blend

MacDonald's – standard blend

Macleay Duff – standard blend

Mortlach – single malt

Oban 14 Year Old – single malt

Old Angus – standard blend

Old Cameron Brig – single grain

Old Matured – standard blend

Old Parr Elizabethan – de luxe blend

Old Parr Superior – de luxe blend

Old Parr Tribute – de luxe blend

Peter Dawson – standard blend

Pittyvaich – single malt

Port Dundas – grain

President – de luxe blend
Queen Elizabeth – standard blend
Queen's Choice – standard blend
Reliance – standard blend
Robbie Burns – standard blend
Rodger's Old Scots – standard blend
Rosebank – single malt
Royal Household – blend
Royal Lochnagar 12 Year Old – single malt
Royal Lochnagar Selected Reserve – single malt
Sanderson's Gold – standard blend
Sandy Mac – standard blend
Scottish Queen – standard blend
Scoresby – standard blend
Singleton 10 Year Old – single malt
Talisker 10 Year Old – single malt
Usher's Green Stripe – standard blend
Usher's OVS – standard blend
Vat 69 – standard blend
White Horse – standard blend
White Horse Extra Fine – de luxe blend
Windsor Castle – standard blend
Wright & Greig – standard blend
Yellow Label (Robertson's) – standard blend
Ye Monks – standard blend

### Distilleries

Auchroisk
Benrinnes
Blair Athol
Caol Ila
Cardhu
Cameronbridge Grain Distillery
Clynelish
Cragganmore
Dailuaine
Dalwhinnie
Dufftown
Glendullan
Glen Elgin
Glenkinchie
Glenlossie
Glen Ord

Glen Spey
Inchgower
Knockando
Lagavulin
Linkwood
Lochnagar
Mannochmore
Mortlach
Oban
Pittyvaich
Port Dundas Grain Distillery
Strathmill
Talisker
Teaninich

## Walker, John & Sons Ltd

### Owners

United Distillers & Vintners Ltd

## White Horse Distillers Ltd

### Owners

United Distillers & Vintners Ltd

## Whyte & Mackay Ltd

Dalmore House
310 St Vincent Street
Glasgow G2 5RG
Tel: 0141 248 5771
Fax: 0141 221 1993
Website: www.whyteandmackay.com

### Subsidiaries

Invergordon Distillers Ltd

### Brands

Ballochmyle, The – standard blend
Bonnie Scot – standard blend
Buchanan Blend (UK only) – standard blend
Claymore, The – standard blend
Claymore, The 12 Year Old – premium blend
Claymore, The 21 Year Old – de luxe blend
Cluny – standard blend
Cluny 12 Year Old – premium blend
Cluny 17 Year Old – de luxe blend

Cluny 21 Year Old – premium blend
Crawford's \*\*\* Special Reserve – standard blend
Crawford's \*\*\*\*\* – de luxe blend
Dalmore 12 Year Old – single malt
Edinburgh Castle – premium blend
Edinburgh Castle 12 Year Old – premium blend
Findlater's Finest – premium blend
Findlater's Mar Lodge – vatted malt
Glen Clova – standard blend
Glendrostan – standard blend
Glenfairn – vatted malt
Glen Foyle – standard blend
Glen Lyon – standard blend
Glen Salen – vatted malt
Glen Sloy – vatted malt
Glen Stag – standard blend
Glen Union – standard blend
Highland Pride – standard blend
Highland Supreme – standard blend
Invergordon Single Grain 10 Year Old – grain
Inverness Cream – standard blend
Jamie Stuart – premium blend
Jock Scott – standard blend
John Barr – standard blend
Jura 10 Year Old– single malt
Legacy – premium blend
Majority – de luxe blend
Northern Scot – standard blend
Old Fettercairn 10 Year Old – single malt
Old Mac – standard blend
Old Mull – standard blend
Original Mackinlay 5 Year Old – standard blend
Original Mackinlay 8 Year Old – premium blend
Original Mackinlay 12 Year Old – de luxe blend
Pig's Nose – standard blend
The Real Mackenzie – standard blend
Regal Scot – standard blend
Scots Club – standard blend
Scots Club 5, 10, 15 Year Old – de luxe blend
Scots Grey – premium blend
Scots Poet – vatted malt
Sheep Dip – vatted malt

Stewart's Finest Old Vatted — standard blend
Tamnavulin 12 Year Old — single malt
Tayside — standard blend
Tomintoul 10 Year Old — single malt
Twelve Pointer — standard blend
Whyte & Mackay — standard blend
Whyte & Mackay 12 Year Old — de luxe blend
Whyte & Mackay 15 Year Old — de luxe blend
Whyte & Mackay 18 Year Old — de luxe blend
Whyte & Mackay 21 Year Old — de luxe blend

## Distilleries

Dalmore
Fettercairn
Invergordon Grain Distillery
Isle of Jura
Tamnavulin-Glenlivet

## William Grant & Sons Ltd

Customer Service Centre
Phoenix Crescent
Strathclyde Business Park
Bellshill ML4 3AN
Tel: 01698 843 843
Fax: 01698 844 788
Websites: www.glenfiddich.com; www.thebalvenie.com

## Brands

Balvenie 15 Year Old — single malt
Balvenie Doublewood 12 Year Old — single malt, finished
Balvenie Founder's Reserve 10 Year Old — single malt
Balvenie Portwood 21 Year Old — single malt, cask-finshed
Black Barrel — grain
Clan MacGregor — standard blend
Glenfiddich Ancient Reserve 18 Year Old — single malt
Glenfiddich Cask Strength 15 Year Old — single malt
Glenfiddich Classic — single malt
Glenfiddich Excellence — single malt
Glenfiddich Heritage Reserve — single malt
Glenfiddich Solera Reserve 15 Year Old — single malt
Glenfiddich Special Reserve 12 Year Old — single malt
Glenfiddich Superior Reserve 18 Year Old — single malt
Glenfiddich 50 Year Old — single malt
Gordon Highlanders, The — standard blend

Grant's Royal – de luxe blend

Robbie Dhu 12 Year Old – de luxe blend

William Grant's Family Reserve – standard blend

William Grant's Classic Reserve 18 Year Old – de luxe blend

William Grant's Heritage Reserve 15 Year Old – de luxe blend

William Grant's Old Gold 12 Year Old – de luxe blend

William Grant's Superior Strength – standard blend

William Grant's 21 Year Old – de luxe blend

### Distilleries

Balvenie

Girvan Grain Distillery

Glenfiddich

Kininvie

## William Lawson Distillers Ltd

### Owners

John Dewar & Sons Ltd

## William Morton Ltd

137 Shawbridge Street

Glasgow G43 1QQ

Tel: 0141 649 9881

### Brands

Inchmurrin

Loch Lomond – single malt

Old Rhosdhu

# THE FLAVOUR OF WHISKY

We said in the Introduction that what matters about whisky is that it tastes nice, and the Directory is intended as a guide to how different whiskies taste. Most of us don't give much thought to the taste of whisky: we know what we like, and we purchase accordingly. But when it comes to assessing whiskies with a view to telling people about their flavour, we require a means of distinguishing one from another, and of describing the difference. This we do by analysing the flavours.

For some hundreds of years, the only experts in the analysis of flavours were perfumers. (Perfumers know about scent rather than flavour, but since smell is by far the larger part of taste, we begin with that.) Originally a skill learned only through a long apprenticeship, the perfumer's craft first came under scientific scrutiny in the nineteenth century. It was realised that nearly every scent was compounded of a number of elementary aromas and an experienced parfumier could often deduce the composition of a competitor's perfume. Since fashionable perfumes fetched a high price, there was strong pecuniary motive behind analysis – in the days before patents, a perfume that could be analysed could be copied.

It happened that the centre of the perfume industry was in France, a country which by the 1860s took great pride in both the excellence of its wines and the development of its sciences. Science in France carried much higher social status than it did in Britain (it still does) and there were few forms of human endeavour that were not subjected to scientific scrutiny. Wine production was a peculiarly fertile field and one which yielded Louis Pasteur some of his most important discoveries in the field of what is now known as microbiology. Gradually, through the work of Pasteur and his followers, it came to be understood that the flavour of wine was a complex thing, made up of lots of elementary flavours and aromas. The techniques employed for training perfumers were adapted to teaching wine tasters. A cabinet *du vin* made its appearance, modelled on the cabinet *du parfum* used to train perfumers – a small chest with dozens of tiny drawers, each of which contained a sample of a particular aroma.

As far as Scotch whisky was concerned, this was all Gallic nonsense and not the kind of thing that the British went in for. As a result, it took 100 years before whisky tasters came to adopt the organoleptic analysis which wine producers used to judge their wines. That they did so, had something to do with the hiatus which the whisky industry experienced in the crisis at the end of the 1970s. The rise of consumerism was a factor too, for customers were beginning to ask for better-flavoured whiskies. The Scotch whisky producers set up a research station at Pentland, just outside Edinburgh, with a brief to investigate scientifically, for the first time, the sources of flavour in whisky. That enterprise has been extremely fruitful and we now know that the flavour of a Scotch whisky may be made up of literally hundreds of different compounds.

To say that there are lots of sources of flavour isn't of great practical help as regards our present aim, which is to tell people how different whiskies taste. Our requirement is for some simple labels which we can attach with confidence and which will allow us to classify whiskies in a way which makes sense to the consumer. Happily, the work of the Pentland laboratory and its successor, the Scotch Whisky Research Institute, has enabled us to do just that. It is possible to classify the most significant of the flavours found in a Scotch whisky under 15 different heads. If we can identify all of those, we shall be able to rate whiskies so as to produce a classification which will be meaningful to any discerning consumer. The Directory tasters have therefore analysed each of the whiskies included in the Directory for the presence and strength of each of those 15 flavours. We will now give a brief account of each of the flavours. Any such account inevitably falls far short of the idea of each flavour. Acquiring a mental image of a flavour is something you must do for yourself. We can only guide you.

The 15 flavours fall into three main categories: nice ones, nasty ones and those which may be nice or nasty, depending on concentration and/or on the individual's preference. The nice ones are easy: they are flavours whose presence is always desirable, no matter how high the concentration. This is not to say that they could never be displeasing, merely that they never occur in whisky at concentrations sufficiently high to render them so. There are five flavours in this class: floral, fruity, vanilla, caramel and nutty.

Ambiguous flavours form by far the largest category: sweet, smoky, cereal, aldehydic, woody, resinous, sulphurous and sour. Of these, smoky flavours will be the most easily recognised – and the most controversial, for some people love them and others can't abide them. All of the other flavours in the group may or may not be pleasing, depending on how strong the flavour is and how it relates to other flavours present. Soapy and musty flavours, the third category, are almost always disagreeable in other than very low concentrations. It helps to think of the flavours arranged in three columns.

| NICE | NICE/NASTY | NASTY |
| --- | --- | --- |
| floral | sweet | soapy |
| fruity | smoky | musty |
| vanilla | cereal | |
| caramel | aldehydic | |
| nutty | woody | |
| | resinous | |
| | sulphurous | |
| | sour | |

This arrangement is to some extent subjective. People who are fond of smoky whiskies will of course list smokiness in the first column. Ditto for folk who like their whisky sweet or woody. Lovers of old whisky will probably put woodiness at the head of the first column, for such people appear to prize the tannins which make old whisky bitter above all other flavours. (At least, that is suggested by the daft prices some people pay for very old whiskies.)

Floral and fruity flavours are almost invariably desirable in Scotch whisky: those light, airy, delicious flower-scents which can be so elusive but are so pleasing, are possibly to be sought above all other flavours. They are the aromas which are characteristic of well-made, ten-year-old malts and are to be found in blended whiskies which contain high levels of those malts. The type of cask doesn't seem to matter so much – both bourbon and sherry casks will yield floral aromas – possibly because the primary source of the aroma is the fermentation of the wash, and what is required of the maturation is that the cask should not act in such a way as to obscure the floral scents. It is never the case that fruity aromas are found to excess in Scotch whiskies. That should not blind us to the principle that any flavour can be present to excess: bourbon whiskies are commonly so floral that they would be better if less so.

Fruity aromas and flavours are more varied and more complex than floral ones, though also mainly the product of fermentation. Some, such as the flavour of pears, are quite common and, subjectively at least, related to the ester-based aromas of flowers. Others are harder to assign origins: the dried-fruit flavours which may or may not accompany the lighter ones and which are characteristically to be found associated with nuts and caramel in some very fine sherry-cask whiskies. Some of the older Macallans spring to mind in this connection. Dried-fruit flavours are more often to be found in bound form, as part of more complex aromas and tastes: when a whisky tastes like fruit cake, for example, dried-fruit flavours are an important component.

Vanilla is the one sure exception to the rule that any flavour can, if excessive, be disagreeable. As anyone knows who keeps a jar of vanilla sugar in the kitchen, there is a threshold above which the sensation of vanilla does not increase, no matter how much its cause is augmented. Vanilla is often found in association with fruity flavours and caramel. Indeed, so often are vanilla and caramel found together, that most people have difficulty in telling the one from the other. There is a school of thought which maintains that there is in fact no difference and that when we think we perceive caramel, all we are smelling is sweetness and vanilla. If caramel is added in excess (as it sometimes is as a permitted colouring), we detect it as a bitter flavour, which suggests that the two are not identical, despite their common origin (additives apart) in the lignin of the cask wood.

Vanilla can also be produced as a by-product of fermentation. So are nutty flavours, though they, too, owe most of their presence to compounds derived from the oak of the cask. Nutty aromas such as coconuts and almonds are happily quite common, especially in malt whiskies. Combined, as they usually are, with vanilla, they make a delightful addition to the flavour of almost any whisky. Like vanilla, nutty flavours are never present in excessive amounts. Sweetness, on the other hand, is a debatable quality in a whisky and ought perhaps to be allocated to the second column. Both Aberlour and Glenrothes are very sweet whiskies. Most people love them for that reason, though there are a few austere souls who find them sickly.

If evidence were needed of how differently people perceive and appreciate flavours, smoky tastes provide it. People who like whisky seem to be equally divided as regards smoky aromas: some love them and some hate them, and there are few who are indifferent. That said, it is possible to acquire the taste. There are plenty of instances of people who on first acquaintance were unable to understand how anyone could drink such stuff, but gradually come to see first the interest and then the pleasure of peaty whiskies. The smoky aroma comes from the peat which is used to dry the malted barley – not, as is commonly believed, from the brown, peaty water which some distilleries use for brewing. We generally call such flavours smoky because that is the obvious reference, but phenolic flavours in whisky may as readily be perceived as being fishy. Indeed, one of the commonest comparisons is made with smoked fish, which has both. 'Medicinal', too, is commonly cited as a referent, though not, one suspects, by anyone under 50 – that being a generation to which phenolic antiseptics are unknown.

While smoky flavours may commend themselves to folk who like woodsmoke or fish or carbolic, that is not their only claim to our attention. For the same whiskies will often be found to exhibit much more delicate flavours, which can be discerned only once the first sensation of smoke or fish has worn off. Bizarrely, the odour of violets is not uncommonly found in smoky whiskies. The compounds which make the whisky smoky will, with the alteration of only a few atoms, produce the scent of violets. Happily, such compounds are to be found in whiskies whose peat content is not discernible as a smoky or fishy smell: they provide the justification in terms of flavour for using low levels of peating. All but one of the malt whiskies use some peat, though many employ very little. Glengoyne alone uses completely unpeated malt.

Beyond smokiness, we find that most of the flavours require to be present at low levels for the whisky to be acceptable. Cereal and aldehydic flavours are possible exceptions to this rule and there are good whiskies which have them in appreciable quantity. Neither of these flavours is easy to describe, nor is the one readily to be distinguished from the other. They do, however, represent two distinct groups of flavours. Cereal aromas are to be found in wheat and vegetables, yeast and bran, baked potatoes and meat. Not exactly an easy lot among which to find something in common – but once you know what you are looking for, you will recognise it. Aldehydic odours are those associated with leather and tobacco, wax and plastic. Think of a good fino sherry. The characteristic aroma is quite delightful and it comes mainly from aldehydes. Aldehydic odours in whisky are produced in the course of distillation, toward the end of the spirit run. Feints are high in aldehydes.

Woody aromas in whisky come mainly from tannins which the spirit acquires as it ages in the cask. The tannins are extracted from the oak wood, just as they are by wines, and the longer you leave the spirit in the wood, the more tannins it absorbs. Old whiskies are almost always heavily tannic. For those whisky drinkers who have more money than sense or palate, tannins have become an indicator of quality. At low levels, the harshness of tannins can form a pleasing counterpart to some of the more luscious flavours, just as they do in a good old red wine. But, as in wine, too much is too much. To see tannins at their best, look at some very old Bowmore, or Glenfarclas or Macallan: all are bottled by scrupulous distillers who choose to show only those old whiskies in which tannins are at acceptable levels.

Occasionally, confusion arises as to what is meant by the term 'woody'. Used of whisky, this generally refers to the presence of tannins. The more aromatic smell of new wood is sometimes found in whiskies, which are described as being resinous. Everyone who has worked with softwoods knows what this means. It is the scent of newly released resins and, at low levels, is quite delightful. At high levels, it has the flavour we associate with some disgusting Greek wines. The latter were originally treated with resin as a means of preservation in the days before cheap bottles. The use of resin continues as tradition, but it is not to be recommended as a flavouring.

Sulphurous aromas are to be found in some very fine whiskies. They contribute to the flavour of the whisky in the same way as asafoetida contributes to the flavour of some Indian cuisine. Sulphur occurs naturally in some of the proteins in barley and somewhat less naturally in the sterilising of sherry casks by means of sulphur candles. Very faint whiffs of sulphurous compounds are nice, but anything more is absolutely disgusting. You will know it if you smell it.

Sourness, too, is desirable and quite common, at low levels. In some of the very richest, sherry-cask-matured whiskies, a slight acidity is a desirable component of a complex flavour. Above a low level it is nasty, but thankfully very rare.

If soapy and musty aromas can be detected, they are displeasing to almost every taste. They are almost always only smells: if strong enough to be detected in the mouth they would be quite revolting. Soapy flavours arise during fermentation. They are, curiously, made of exactly the same atoms as the lovely floral aromas, but in a different arrangement. Think of soap, detergent and stale fat and you will have a rough guide. Musty odours can have many different sources, all of them reflecting shoddy materials or practices. Again these are difficult to describe but, once experienced, they are not soon forgotten. If you are unfortunate enough to smell something really nasty in a whisky, like damp sacks rotting in a cellar, you have probably hit mustiness. As you spit the liquor out, you can console yourself that you have made an addition to your olfactory vocabulary. If soapiness and mustiness are very faint, they are tolerable and contribute to the complexity of a good whisky. But above a very low level they are serious faults and any whisky which has them must be judged bad. Happily, they very rarely make an appearance at high levels in the Directory, reflecting the generally high quality of Scotch whisky.

**5**

# THE TASTING:
# WHO DID IT AND HOW

The use of tasting notes to describe whisky is not new. The practice arose about 20 years ago at the Scotch Malt Whisky Society, which required to devise a way of telling its members about the flavour of Society bottlings of single-cask whiskies. Wine tasters' vocabulary was adopted and adapted to describe whisky, with some remarkable results. Verbal descriptions of whisky have now become widespread and inevitably some people are less scrupulous than others. As in wine, so in whisky: the most extravagant tasting notes are often appended to some very ordinary whiskies – and because such things are essentially subjective, you can't call the perpetrators liars. Which is not to say that all tasting notes are mendacious; merely that it is hard to tell which are, and which are not.

In any attempt to describe the flavour of whisky there are two main obstacles: first, in establishing some agreement about the subjective experience of flavour, and second in devising a way of presenting that experience so as to make it public and intelligible. As regards the first, the Directory is indebted to the staff of the Scotch Whisky Research Institute, who have made available some of the results of several decades' research into the flavour characteristics of whisky. The 15 classes of flavour that the Directory uses to describe the taste of whiskies lean heavily on that research. Those flavour categories can be recognised by anyone who has experience of tasting Scotch whiskies, as they cover most of the gustatory sensations most people are likely to have when tasting whisky. The Directory asked four highly experienced tasters to classify all of the whiskies in the Directory according to those flavours. Their judgements were analysed statistically, so that the results as presented in the Directory are about as close as you can get to an objective – or at least an inter-subjective – assessment of whisky flavours.

The solution of the second problem, the presentation of the data, is the Directory's own. The flavour profiles are unique, though simple. Each type of flavour is presented as a bar on a chart and the strength of the flavour rated on a scale of zero to ten: the higher the bar, the stronger the flavour. The unique flavour profile of each whisky – its flavour signature – shows a shape against two axes which immediately tells you how the whisky tastes. Like any other tool, you have to learn how to use it, but once learned, the technique is perfectly simple.

The Directory is greatly indebted to the people who did the tasting. To them fell the greater part of the work. Each had to taste about 300 whiskies, recording the flavour sensations produced by each whisky. (There were more whiskies tasted than are represented in the Directory, for around 50 were duplicates. These allowed us to check the consistency of each taster's judgements. Happily, all were within respectable limits.) All of the whiskies were tasted blind and in different random orders. There follow a few notes on those heroic souls who, for the enlightenment of a benighted public, sacrificed their time and their livers.

## Jim McEwan

Jim is an Ileach. That is, a native of the island of Islay. (The word is pronounced 'eelach', with the 'ch' sounded gutturally, as in 'Bach'.) He began work in Bowmore Distillery in 1963 at the age of 15 as an apprentice cooper, making, remaking and mending whisky casks for the distillery. The Scotch whisky industry in which Jim got his first job was still a very traditional industry and his career trajectory was more common then than it is now. Jim worked his way up through the distillery, eventually becoming distillery manager. In between, he did every job in the distillery which had anything to do with making, maturing and bottling whisky – and quite a few which had nothing to do with any of these.

Then, as now, most of the produce of the distillery was

destined for use in making blended whisky. It was as blender that Jim's talents in the matter of tasting whiskies first came to the company's notice, for it became clear that he had an unusually acute nose. What was more unusual, though this did not become apparent until later, was that Jim also had the ability to put names to the flavours he detected, and to communicate both his knowledge of the whiskies and his enthusiasm for them. The owners of the company eventually realised what an asset they had, and Jim was translated from his beloved Islay to the wider world, to become a brand ambassador for the company's whiskies. For years he travelled the world, telling people about the Bowmore whiskies. 'Ambassador' is actually a poor term for what Jim became; 'evangelist' is probably closer. He came to be known around the world as one of the finest speakers on whisky and an ambassador for Scotland as well as for its spirit. He gained a string of awards, most recently being voted by his peers Distiller of the Year.

In December 2000, Jim joined forces with independent bottlers Murray McDavid, whose managing director, Mark Reynier, had assembled a group of investors to buy the then-mothballed Bruichladdich Distillery. This they did, and Jim became the production director of the Bruichladdich Distillery Company. He now has a challenge worthy of his talents and energies: the building of a market for a single malt until recently unknown to all but a few. It is one of the world's great liquors and in Jim it has found its ideal propagandist.

## Richard Paterson

When, in 2001, a management team organised Scotland's biggest-ever management buy-out of JBB (Greater Europe) Ltd from Jim Beam Brands, its American owners, it did so in what merchant bankers call an asset-financed operation. What this meant was that the bankers were prepared to lend money because the company being bought had some very valuable capital assets. The assets were things like whisky distilleries such as Dalmore and Jura, great blended-whisky brand names like Whyte & Mackay, and profitable companies like Invergordon. There can be little doubt that one of the assets included in their calculations was of a different sort, namely Richard Paterson.

Richard was a director of Whyte & Mackay Brands and one of the leading luminaries of the Scotch whisky industry. He brought to the new company not only his abilities as master blender but also a trail of glittering prizes from the liquor industry over the previous two decades. Richard came of a family of whisky blenders. His father and his grandfather before him had been in the business. Richard began his working life in whisky blending but quickly became expert in wines and cigars. In 1970 he joined Whyte & Mackay and five years later became their master blender, at 26 the youngest master blender in Scotland. He was appointed to the board of the company some 19 years

later, having gained in the mean time a host of awards and accolades. Thanks to his efforts, the company proceeded to collect more and more laurels, some for Richard personally, some for the whiskies which he produced.

This sort of career as a consummate industry insider might suggest that Richard is more at home with fellow-professionals than with the ordinary whisky drinker. Nothing could be further from the truth. He is one of the best communicators the industry has produced and is known and respected worldwide by amateurs and professionals alike.

Time has not dulled Richard's enthusiasm, nor has it slowed the flow of accolades. In the first few months of 2003, Richard was voted Blender of the Year by *Whisky Magazine*'s Whisky Academy and the Cuban Whisky Cigar Festival presented him its highest prize for both malt and blend: for the Dalmore and for the Whyte & Mackay 21 Year Old.

## David Robertson

It is one of the strengths of the Scotch whisky industry that it draws on different sorts of people to produce and promote its spirit. David is representative of a new wave of distillers. Young, a technocrat with a degree in brewing and distilling from Heriot-Watt University, he joined United Distillers in 1990 as a management trainee at Benrinnes Distillery. There he learned the craft of Scotch whisky production before moving to UD head office as process chemist two years later. In the UD laboratory, he dealt with issues of spirit quality and investigated process efficiency – two conflicting requirements of any modern distilling plant which can be reconciled only through a scientific understanding of the techniques of production.

The rhetoric of Scotch whisky marketing is mostly about craft and tradition, and illustrations tend to show old men with beards and barrels. What this misses is the fact that the scientific revolution happened early in Scotland, so there is a long scientific tradition for the industry to draw on. David is an example: his father was a distillery manager before him and his grandfather had an Edinburgh University doctorate in science. Small wonder that an ambitious, scientifically inclined young man should look to the whisky industry.

In 1994, David joined Macallan as distillery manager and within two years had been promoted to chief whisky maker. At Macallan, he found himself in one of the most demanding production and maturation regimes in the industry. Not only is Macallan renowned for the quality of its spirit, but it has a policy of rigorous control of the type and quality of casks used for maturation of the spirit. Naturally, a policy of this sort makes great demands on the company staff, but its corollary is that the staff are extremely well qualified to promote the whisky. While retaining his chief whisky maker role, David was appointed in 2002 to the post of global marketing manager, in which capacity he travels the world, presenting the Macallan to trade and public. He is expert in both the technology and the craft: a remarkable ambassador.

## David Stewart

William Grant & Sons is the largest and most important family-owned, independent Scotch whisky maker. The company owns the Glenfiddich, Balvenie and Kininvie malt whisky distilleries and the Girvan Grain Distillery. They produce and market both malt and blended whiskies, of which the leader is Glenfiddich: the first single malt in modern times to be marketed beyond the Scottish border. This is the company which David Stewart joined as an apprentice in 1962 – an apprenticeship which was to last for 12 years! In 1974, David was appointed master blender at William Grant & Sons, a position which he has held ever since.

In his 40 years with the company, David has seen Glenfiddich become the world's biggest-selling single malt and the other whiskies he produces gain prizes galore. He introduced the use of different woods for maturation with the Balvenie Doublewood and a solera-type maturation which has been used to finish Glenfiddich and which is bottled as their Glenfiddich Solera Reserve 15 Year Old. (It is assessed in the Whisky List below.)

David is also responsible for the quality of William Grant's Family Reserve, which is the fourth-bestselling Scotch whisky in the world. That a family-owned firm should achieve such a thing in a world dominated by supranational conglomerate corporations, must owe a lot to the man who made the blend.

**6**

# FLAVOUR PROFILES
# AND HOW TO USE THEM

### How to Read the Flavour Profiles

The barchart below each whisky listed in the Directory shows a flavour profile of the whisky. Each bar stands for one of the flavour categories described in Chapter 4, and the height of the bar (on a scale of one to ten) shows the strength of each flavour. The flavours are always in the same order, beginning with the five flavours which are always nice, then the eight which may be nice or nasty, and ending with soapy and musty which are generally unpleasant.

Each whisky shows a different pattern of bars. This unique combination is the whisky's flavour signature. The distillers and blenders try to maintain a constant flavour signature for each of their whisky brands. This is no easy matter, for, as we have seen, the flavour of a whisky is strongly influenced by the cask in which it is matured and there is a lot of variation among casks. The blending of a well-known brand of blended whisky is a high-volume operation involving a great many casks of fairly uniform nature, so the greater part of the blender's work consists of the detection of flavours which vary from a standard. If necessary, though, he or she can vary the composition of the blend. This option is not open to the bottler of a single malt, who may use only the one whisky and whatever casks are available. In practice, though, variation is reduced by a distillery policy of using a particular type of cask and by controlling the type and quality of the cask prior to filling with new whisky. At its most extreme, this control extends as far as Jerez in Spain, where some distillers are closely involved in the sherry trade, purely in order to secure their supply of sherry casks.

Different types of whisky show different characteristic flavour signatures. A single malt whisky made from lightly peated malt will, after ten years in a moderately active cask, show a flavour profile which is high in the first five or six bars, then tails away steeply and shows little or nothing in the final five or six. There are lots of desirable flavours and enough in the intermediate group at low levels to add to the interest of the whisky.

A heavily peated Islay malt of similar age and provenance will show much the same profile, but with a high bar in the middle, indicating smokiness.

A whisky which is very old but nonetheless in good condition will have a profile which will probably be low in floral notes but high in fruit, vanilla, etc. It will have a spike indicating woodiness, but not so high as to render the whisky offensive, and possibly a bit of sulphur.

A whisky which is over the hill will show a very high woodiness bar and probably other high bars in the later part of the barchart.

A good-quality blended whisky can be expected to have moderately high bars to begin with, declining in the second section and fading away in the last.

A cheap blend will tend to show very low bars in the first and most of the intermediate sections, with perhaps some highish bars in the latter part – but not always, for, as the Directory shows, some cheaper blends have very respectable flavour profiles.

## How to Use the Flavour Profiles

The first thing that strikes most people about the flavour profiles is the simple interest of the thing. First, you look through them to see the profile of the whiskies you know well. Then you begin to wonder whether you would give them quite the same ratings as did the Directory tasters. Later, you look at whiskies you don't know and try to figure out how they would taste, given the extent and nature of their flavour signature's variation from that of the ones you do know. Alternatively, you flick through the Directory, looking for some really spectacularly high flavour bars (there are some of these) and wonder how those whiskies are going to taste. Be warned: you are then on a slippery slope which will end with you buying lots of whiskies, spending far too much money, endangering important relationships and damaging your liver. The Directory disclaims responsibility for any such consequences.

It *is* interesting to see how some of the whiskies fared. Remember that the tasters were tasting blind – nobody knew the name of any of the whiskies he tasted. There are a few things which leap out. It's likely that most people who buy the Directory will be malt-whisky enthusiasts. It will interest them to see how the malts fared relative to the blends: what is surprising, is how lowly some of the malts score on all the flavours and how highly some of the blends do. For years now, there has been a widely held belief that malts are always better than blends. The Directory shows that this is not the case.

The case for age in cask is made very clearly, up to a point. The older the whisky, the higher the flavour bars. This is almost invariably true up to around 20 years in cask. After this, the correlation breaks down and in some cases, the quality of the flavour declines. Age in heavily peated malts causes a decline in the smokiness of the whisky. This is so marked that the oldest Bowmore tasted scores no higher on that count than do many whiskies which are very lightly peated.

The value of finishes is evident: in most cases, the finished whisky is more flavoursome than the base whisky. An exception to this is the Glenmorangie, but that is because the simple 10-year-old bourbon-cask-matured whisky is so good that it is hard to improve on it.

Some of the private bottlings are quite spectacular. Look at the flavour profiles of the Douglas Laing Glenury or the Adelphi-bottled Linkwood – they are quite amazing. No doubt there will be none of either left by the time the Directory appears, but it does give one reason to seek out others from the same stable.

It is worth spending some time with whiskies you know well, sampling the whiskies and comparing the flavours you find in them with the profiles in the Directory. No two tasters can know that they taste the same thing, for flavour is irreducibly subjective. But we can standardise our sensations, and this is what you can do by comparing what you taste with the flavours reported for a given whisky by the Directory. You can then make a fairly reliable estimate of how whiskies will taste, purely on the basis of their flavour signatures.

There is one catch, though. You should remember that some of the flavour categories used by the Directory represent single flavours and others groups of flavours. The former include vanilla, caramel, sweetness, soapiness and mustiness, and possibly aldehydic flavours. The latter groups each cover a whole lot of different flavours – there are, for example, lots of differently smelling fruits and flowers. There are also, alas, lots of ways in which sulphurous compounds can manifest themselves, most of them disagreeable. That said, whiskies possessing similar flavour signatures are likely to taste broadly similar. This makes it possible to use the Directory to navigate the seas of Scotch whisky in such a way that we shall be able to tell, in advance of sampling it, approximately how a whisky will taste.

The Directory also makes it possible to explore the world of Scotch whiskies in an orderly and rational manner. If you begin with a whisky you know and like, you can discover how a whisky will taste which differs from your standard in one particular, by looking for others whose flavour signatures differ in only that particular. There is no guarantee that you will find a whisky which matches exactly your requirement, but the chances are good that you will find one or more which come pretty close. In comparing whiskies, though, you should always bear in mind that your perception of each flavour is modified by the presence of other flavours and that the overall sensation arises as a result of interactions among the flavours. So merely increasing or decreasing a given flavour may have an unexpected effect. Should you be so inclined, the investigation of such effects can occupy you happily for a very long time.

## Tasting Whiskies

In inspecting whiskies, there are a few elementary rules which should be borne in mind. This topic has been covered by several writers, so we will deal with it briefly.

First, make sure that the tasting conditions are right: that you don't have a cold; that you haven't eaten or drunk anything which makes things taste funny; that you're not downwind of a curry house or a tannery and that the tasting environment is generally free of extraneous influences. Use a proper nosing glass. Dilute the whisky to about 20 per cent alcohol with still, flavour-free water.

Second, pay close attention. You mustn't expect a good whisky to reveal its all on a brief inspection, any more than you would expect to extract all the meaning from a poem on a first reading. Scotch whiskies are the sonnets of the spirit world and they will reveal layer upon layer of significance if approached with attention and diligence.

Third, calibrate your responses to those of the panel. Just as the tasters varied in their perceptions of flavours, so will your judgement differ from that shown by the flavour signature. But the difference should, on the whole, be consistent. Try a few whiskies and note how your judgements differ from those of the Directory. Save in a few exceptional cases, variation will be regular, so you will still be able to judge from the flavour signature how each whisky will taste.

Once you have gained experience in using the Directory, you will be able to judge from its profiles exactly how each of the whiskies profiled will taste to you. You will be able to select for particular flavours, maximising some and minimising others, as described above. Or – which is much more difficult – to select for balances among flavour components. Much of the pleasure in good liquor comes from balance – which really means the relationships among flavour components. This is a very complicated matter and something you can happily spend years investigating: the number of possible combinations of fifteen flavours on a scale of one to ten is so large that it would not be possible to try them all in a lifetime devoted exclusively to drinking whisky.

For those who are practised in assessing the flavour of whiskies, there is a lot of innocent entertainment to be had in comparing what advertisers say about their whiskies with the reality. The Directory recently attended the launch of a new product: a Scotch whisky which was well-known to the Directory but which had not previously been marketed at the given age by its owners. It is a very good whisky indeed, but the new product is an attempt by the owners to sell it younger than its previous bottling by some years – an age at which it is raw and unsubtle, like a green apple. The presentation was by a personable young woman of undoubted loquacity and conviction. Her delivery was hard to fault, though one did wonder how anyone could be so confident about flavours that the Directory knew by long experience were tentative and difficult to discern. This is not to suggest that the presentation was fraudulent, merely that the nature of flavour perception is such that conformist individuals (and that means most of us) can easily and honestly convince themselves of the existence of flavours which are not there. Think on that for a little, and you will see why the whisky was not the only source of merriment on that particular occasion.

## The Five-Star Rating System

The Directory uses a simple five-star rating system as a rough guide to quality. Five stars indicates a totally brilliant spirit in which high levels of pleasing flavours are experienced against a backdrop of ambivalent aromas sufficient to provide variety and interest. The disagreeable flavours are not, or negligibly, present. Since only 20 out of 267 entries make this grade, it represents a pretty rarefied stratum of excellence.

Those whiskies which justify four stars are very good indeed and a glance at them will show that many in this category only just fail to make the five-star level. The four-star group is the largest in the Directory and it is to this segment that Scotch whisky as a whole owes most of its reputation for quality. Three stars indicate lesser, but still good, whiskies. A whisky which warrants only one star is likely to be one which lacks most of the desirable flavours, or in which such flavours are accompanied by lots of the less-agreeable aromas.

When using the star rating, users of the Directory should bear several things in mind. First, that the stars are only a rough guide. The divisions are particular to this guidebook and the variation within each division large. You may find it difficult to discover a disparity in quality between a whisky which just fails to make four stars and one which scrapes into the category by a single point, while the disparity between the whiskies at the bottom and the top of the category may be very evident. There is not a lot anyone can do about this: it is a problem common to all such ratings. A second point to bear in mind is that the star rating indicates levels of flavour: if you like your spirits delicate, you may prefer one with a lowly rating. Third, so great is the variation in individual taste that you may disagree completely with the Directory's judgement. That is your privilege.

The award of stars for quality is, in accordance with the principles on which the Directory is based, as objective as possible. It is made as follows. Each whisky is rated numerically in respect of each of its flavours, as per the flavour profiles. The five pleasing flavours from floral through to nutty have the values of the flavour bars multiplied by two. The five flavours from sweet to woody are valued at one and the remaining flavours – resinous to musty - are valued at minus one. The sum of all of the values is the flavour value of the whisky. For example, the flavour value of the first whisky in the Directory, 100 Pipers, is calculated as $14+14+10+6+6+4+1+1+4+2-2-1-1-2-1=55$. Whiskies which score less than 30 get one star; 30 to 39, two stars; 40 to 49, three stars; 50 to 59 four stars; and 60 and over five stars.

# PART TWO

## EVALUATION

# THE WHISKY LIST

The strength of each whisky is stated in percentage alcohol by volume or ABV. For an explanation of the designations of the types of whisky, see the 'Nomenclature' section in Chapter 3. The owner stated is the operating company. Particulars of that company and of its owners and associates are given in the List in Chapter 3. The stated age of a whisky is the age *in cask* of the youngest whisky in the bottle. Much of the contents may in fact be considerably older than stated.

# 100 PIPERS

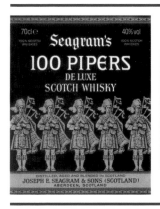

TYPE: standard blend
STRENGTH: 40% ABV
AGE IN CASK: not stated
OWNERS: Chivas Brothers
      Ltd
RATING: ****

A FLAGSHIP FOR ITS OWNERS, CHIVAS BROTHERS, AND RIGHTLY popular in the USA, this blended whisky exhibits a flavour profile which many malt distillers would be happy to produce. In any blind tasting, it would pass for a first-rate single malt whisky.

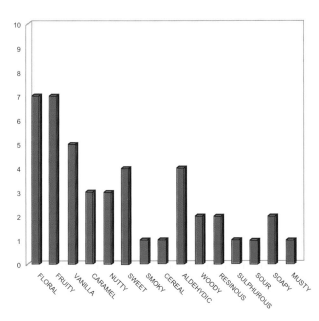

# ABERFELDY
# 12 YEAR OLD

TYPE: single malt
STRENGTH: 40% ABV
AGE IN CASK: 12 years
OWNERS: John Dewar &
         Sons Ltd
RATING: ****

AN EXCELLENT MALT WHICH DESERVES TO BE BETTER KNOWN THAN it is. This profile shows two things: that a high level of aldehydes is not necessarily a defect and that a low level of an otherwise disagreeable flavour can contribute to a great whisky.

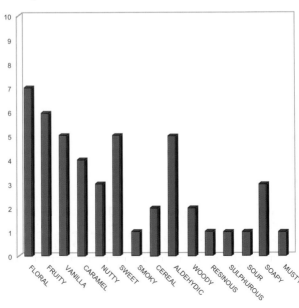

**3**

# ABERLOUR
# 10 YEAR OLD

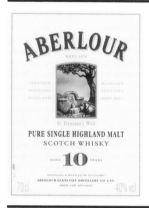

TYPE: single malt
STRENGTH: 40% ABV
AGE IN CASK: 10 years
OWNERS: Chivas Brothers
             Ltd
RATING: ****

A SWEET MALT WITH WELL-DEVELOPED OTHER FLAVOURS, WHICH complement the sweetness. No defects at all – provided you like perfection.

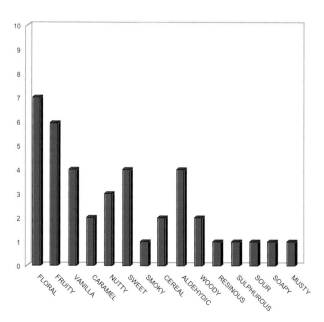

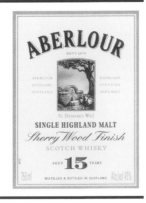

# ABERLOUR
# 15 YEAR OLD
# SHERRY WOOD FINISH

TYPE: single malt, cask
 finished
STRENGTH: 43% ABV
AGE IN CASK: 15 years
OWNERS: Chivas Brothers
 Ltd
RATING: ****

GREATER AGE AND THE SHERRY WOOD HAVE PRODUCED A SPIRIT
more complex than the 10 year old. Higher levels of sweet-
related flavours produce a more rounded whisky, and
stronger – but acceptable – woody and resinous tastes give
it gravitas.

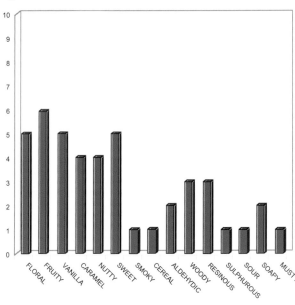

# ABERLOUR A'BUNADH

TYPE: single malt
STRENGTH: 59.9% ABV
AGE IN CASK: not stated
OWNERS: Chivas Brothers Ltd
RATING: ****

RECOGNISABLY FROM THE SAME FAMILY AS ITS PREDECESSORS. The age of the whisky is not stated, nor what casks it was matured in. Very good ones, apparently, for it is well flavoured; old ones, too, for it is quite woody and has other signs of age.

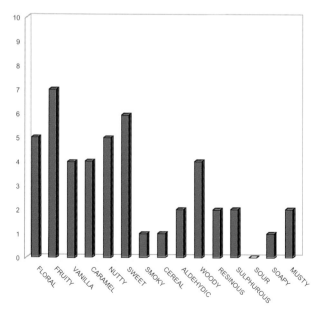

# ADELPHI PRIVATE STOCK

TYPE: premium blend
STRENGTH: 40% ABV
AGE IN CASK: not stated
OWNERS: Adelphi Distillery
        Ltd
RATING: ****

THIS IS ADELPHI'S IN-HOUSE BLEND. IT IS AS GOOD AS YOU WOULD expect from a firm which has access to some brilliant malts. Most malt distillers would be happy to show a 12-year-old single malt as good as this blend.

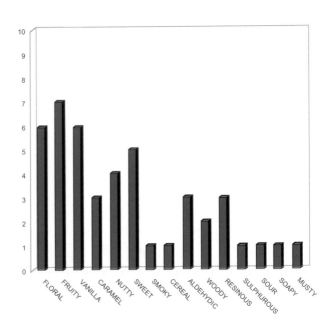

# AN CNOC
# 12 YEAR OLD

TYPE: single malt
STRENGTH: 40% ABV
AGE IN CASK: 12 years
OWNERS: Inver House
          Distillers Ltd
RATING: ****

THE NEW LABEL FOR INVER HOUSE DISTILLERS' KNOCKDHU, THIS IS
a respectable single malt which, if it hits no high spots, also
hits no low and is in consequence a pleasant potation.

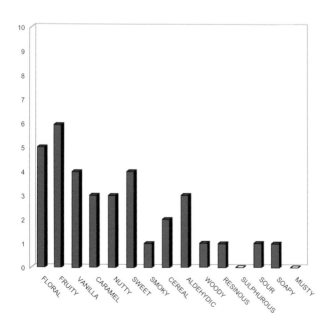

# THE ANTIQUARY
# 12 YEAR OLD

TYPE: de luxe blend
STRENGTH: 40% ABV
AGE IN CASK: 12 years
OWNERS: The Tomatin
          Distillery Co. Ltd
RATING: ***

A GOOD-QUALITY BLENDED WHISKY WITH A DECENT SPREAD OF flavours. Some of the latter show evidence of whiskies in the blend of an age greater than that stated.

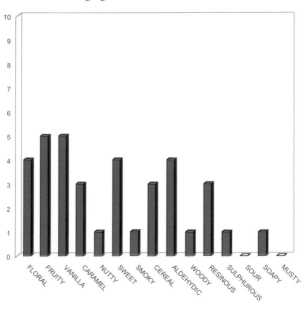

# THE ANTIQUARY 21 YEAR OLD

TYPE: de luxe blend
STRENGTH: 43% ABV
AGE IN CASK: 21 years
OWNERS: The Tomatin
              Distillery Co. Ltd
RATING: ****

GREATER AGE HAS PRODUCED A WHISKY WHICH, CONSISTENTLY more flavoursome than the 12 year old from the same stable, shows no age-related faults. Good stuff.

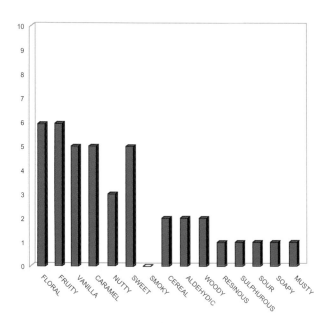

# ARDBEG
# 10 YEAR OLD

TYPE: single malt
STRENGTH: 46% ABV
AGE IN CASK: 10 years
OWNERS: Glenmorangie plc
RATING: ***

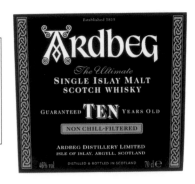

ARDBEG HAS LONG BEEN KNOWN FOR ITS SPECTACULAR phenolics, the consequence of very high peat levels in the malting. The same process also contributes to some of the other flavours which, with practice, one can discern among the smoke.

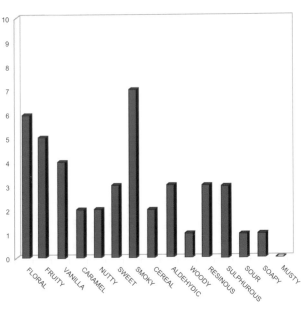

# ARDBEG
# 17 YEAR OLD

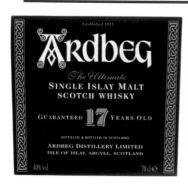

TYPE: single malt
STRENGTH: 46% ABV
AGE IN CASK: 17 years
OWNERS: Glenmorangie plc
RATING: **

PHENOLIC FLAVOURS ARE GENERALLY MUTED BY AGE, AS IS evident in this bottling. So, alas, are the fruity and floral aromas which make the 10 year old so pleasing.

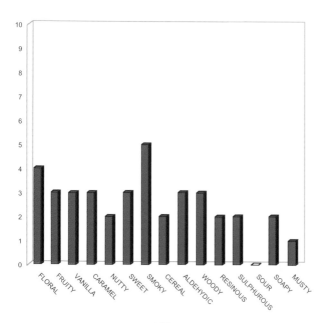

# ARDBEG 1975

TYPE: single malt
STRENGTH: 43% ABV
AGE IN CASK: not stated
OWNERS: Glenmorangie plc
RATING: ***

THIS BOTTLING, FOR WHICH WE ARE GIVEN A YEAR BUT NOT AN AGE – a perfectly pointless exercise in a whisky – is nevertheless a very good whisky. An Ardbeg for those who don't like peaty malts because for some reason – probably age – the smoky flavours are greatly diminished.

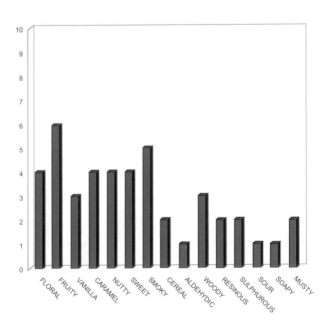

# ARDBEG 25 YEAR OLD: DOUGLAS LAING BOTTLING

SINGLE CASK BOTTLING

DISTILLED AT
ARDBEG DISTILLERY

SINGLE MALT SCOTCH WHISKY

DISTILLED 1975 OCTOBER

BOTTLED 2000 OCTOBER

Aged 25 Years

NO CHILL FILTRATION. NO COLOURING
BOTTLED AT OUR PREFERRED STRENGTH OF 50% ALC/VOL

700ml          50% ALC/VOL

DISTILLED, MATURED AND BOTTLED IN SCOTLAND
DOUGLAS LAING & CO LTD, GLASGOW  G3 6EO
PRODUCT OF SCOTLAND

TYPE: single malt, private bottling
STRENGTH: 50% ABV
AGE IN CASK: 25 years
OWNERS: Douglas Laing & Co. Ltd
RATING: ***

DOUGLAS LAING BOTTLE SOME UNUSUAL WHISKIES. THIS ONE breaks the rules as regards the effects on smokiness of age because, after 25 years, the spirit is still as phenolic as a young whisky. The other flavours are respectable if not remarkable.

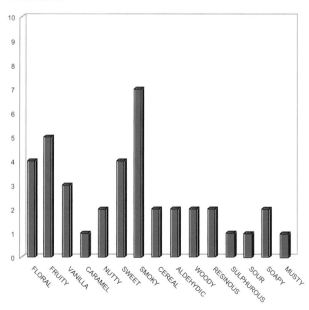

# ARRAN SINGLE MALT

TYPE: single malt
STRENGTH: 43% ABV
AGE IN CASK: not stated
OWNERS: Isle of Arran
        Distillers Ltd
RATING: ***

A unique *Single Island* Malt Scotch *Whisky*

*Arran*

Captures the *Character* of this *Beautiful* Island of *Clear Mountain* water & soft *Sea Air*.

70 cl   *Matured in Sherry Casks*   43%vol.

FROM THE NEW ARRAN DISTILLERY, THIS MALT HAS NO AGE statement for the good reason that, though the distillery has been around for long enough to produce age-legal whisky, it hasn't had time to market a 10 year old. On the showing of this youngster, which is a respectable drop of stuff, it will be worth the wait.

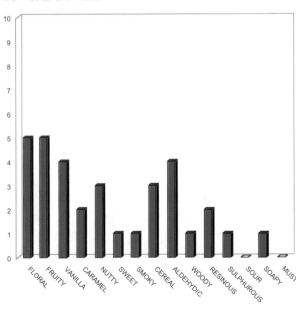

# AUCHENTOSHAN
# 10 YEAR OLD

TYPE: single malt
STRENGTH: 40% ABV
AGE IN CASK: 10 years
OWNERS: Morrison
         Bowmore
         Distillers Ltd
RATING: ✱✱✱

THE REASON FOR THE ODD TASTE OF AUCHENTOSHAN 10 YEAR OLD is apparent in this flavour profile: it is aldehydic as much as it is fruity or floral, and it is as soapy as it is sweet. A lot of folk like it nonetheless.

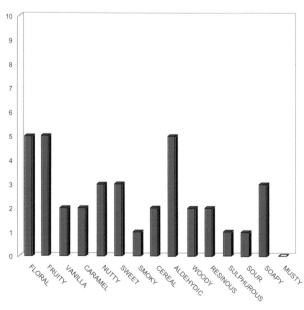

# AUCHENTOSHAN
# 21 YEAR OLD

TYPE: single malt
STRENGTH: 40% ABV
AGE IN CASK: 21 years
OWNERS: Morrison
　　　　Bowmore
　　　　Distillers Ltd
RATING: ****

OLD AUCHENTOSHAN IS JUST AS IDIOSYNCRATIC AS YOUNG – AS CAN
be seen: it is more resinous, which one would expect, and less
aldehydic, which one would not. The rise in sweetness and
caramel-nuttiness makes for a pleasing whisky, though.

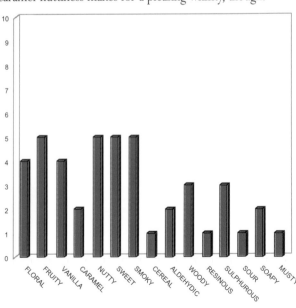

# BAILIE NICOL JARVIE

The BAILIE NICOL JARVIE
→ BLEND OF ←
Old Scotch Whisky.
PRODUCE OF SCOTLAND
Sole Proprietors.
NICOL ANDERSON & CO. LT?
QUEEN'S DOCK
LEITH
VERY OLD RESERVE

TYPE: de luxe blend
STRENGTH: 40% ABV
AGE IN CASK: not stated
OWNERS: Glenmorangie plc
RATING: **

GLENMORANGIE'S ENTRY INTO THE WORLD OF DE LUXE BLENDED whiskies made much less impact than one might have expected, given the prominence of its malts. A very respectable whisky which, apart from a slight soapiness, is delicate and pleasing and could easily be mistaken for a good single malt.

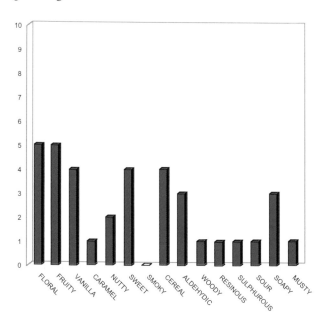

# BALLANTINE'S
# 17 YEAR OLD

TYPE: de luxe blend
STRENGTH: 43% ABV
AGE IN CASK: 17 years
OWNERS: Allied Distillers
Ltd
RATING: ****

FOR MANY YEARS, BALLANTINE'S HAS BEEN A MAJOR BLENDED whisky worldwide. The 17 year old shows the solid profile of a flavoursome, well-rounded blend whose aromas and tastes are integrated into a pleasing whole to which age-related flavours make a significant contribution.

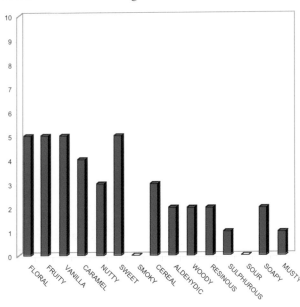

# BALLANTINE'S
# 21 YEAR OLD

TYPE: de luxe blend
STRENGTH: 43% ABV
AGE IN CASK: 21 years
OWNERS: Allied Distillers
        Ltd
RATING: ****

AS WELL FLAVOURED AS ITS YOUNGER SIBLING, BUT SWEETER AND with a touch of woodiness indicating the greater age in cask.

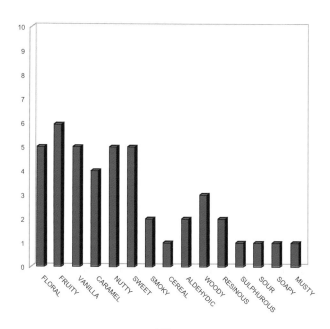

# BALLANTINE'S
# 30 YEAR OLD

TYPE: de luxe blend
STRENGTH: 43% ABV
AGE IN CASK: 30 years
OWNERS: Allied Distillers
           Ltd
RATING: ***

THE PROFILE IS THAT OF A WELL-MADE BLEND MATURED FOR A
very long time, presumably in well-worn casks of fairly low
activity – hence the presence of woody and resinous
flavours without the more disagreeable ones which would
have arisen in an active cask.

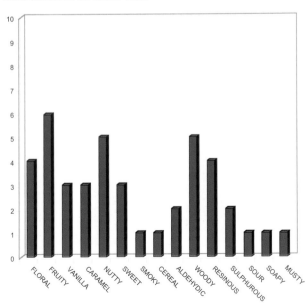

# BALVENIE DOUBLEWOOD 12 YEAR OLD

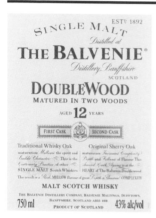

TYPE: single malt, cask finished
STRENGTH: 43% ABV
AGE IN CASK: 12 years
OWNERS: William Grant & Sons Ltd
RATING: ***

THE PRACTICE OF MATURING IN TWO CASKS IS USED TO PRODUCE desirable flavours in a whisky. In this example, it is evidently, if unspectacularly, successful. The profile is not as good as you would get after 12 years in a good and active single cask.

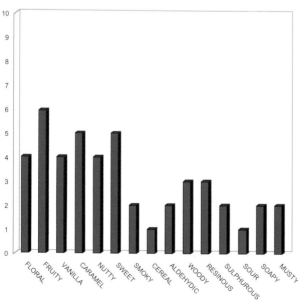

# BALVENIE
# FOUNDER'S RESERVE
# 10 YEAR OLD

TYPE: single malt
STRENGTH: 40% ABV
AGE IN CASK: 10 years
OWNERS: William Grant &
Sons Ltd
RATING: ***

A CURIOUSLY PATCHY PROFILE: SOME MODERATE FLAVOUR BARS, but not enough of any and, overall, insufficient to justify the pretensions of the name.

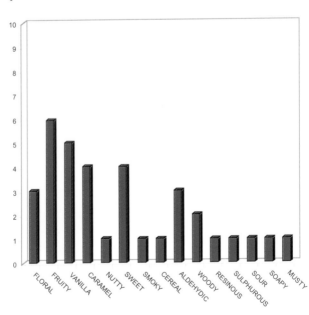

# BALVENIE
# PORTWOOD
# 21 YEAR OLD

TYPE: single malt
STRENGTH: 40% ABV
AGE IN CASK: 21 years
OWNERS: William Grant &
Sons Ltd
RATING: ****

THE USE OF PORT PIPES FOR MATURATION PRODUCES A
noticeable improvement in the Balvenie whisky: floral,
fruity and sweet-related flavours are all present in very
desirable amounts, together with enough of other aromas
to add interest.

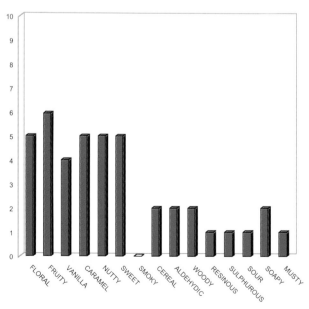

**24**

# BELL'S 8 YEAR OLD

TYPE: standard blend
STRENGTH: 40% ABV
AGE IN CASK: 8 years
OWNERS: United Distillers
& Vintners Ltd
RATING: ***

THIS IS A VERY GOOD FLAVOUR PROFILE FOR A STANDARD BLEND. It fully justifies the UDV's decision some years ago to improve the ordinary Bell's whisky and give it an age statement. There are plenty of single malts on the market which are not as good as this.

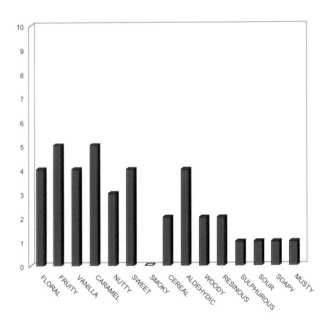

# BEN NEVIS SINGLE HIGHLAND MALT WHISKY

**25**

TYPE: single malt
STRENGTH: 46% ABV
AGE IN CASK: 10 years
OWNERS: Ben Nevis
         Distillery (Fort
         William) Ltd
RATING: ****

A GOOD SINGLE MALT WHISKY WITH ALL OF THE FLAVOURS YOU would expect at acceptably agreeable levels. Some evidence of age in a 10 year old indicates the use of active casks.

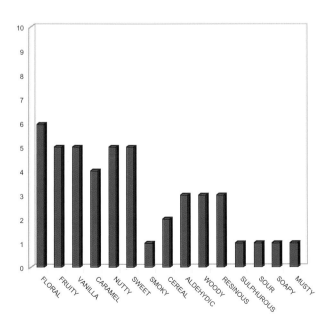

137

26

# BENRIACH
# 10 YEAR OLD

TYPE: single malt
STRENGTH: 43% ABV
AGE IN CASK: 10 years
OWNERS: Chivas Brothers
Ltd
RATING: ***

BENRIACH DISTILLERY
EST.1898
A SINGLE
**PURE HIGHLAND MALT**
Scotch Whisky
Benriach Distillery, in the heart of the Highlands,
still malts its own barley. The resulting whisky has
a unique and attractive delicacy
PRODUCED AND BOTTLED BY THE
# BENRIACH
DISTILLERY C.O
ELGIN, MORAYSHIRE, SCOTLAND, IV30 3SJ
Distilled and Bottled in Scotland
PRODUCE OF SCOTLAND
AGED 10 YEARS
IMPORTED BY THE BENRIACH DISTILLING CO. NY, NY
750 ML.    ALC. 43% BY VOL.

A SPREAD OF FLAVOURS WHICH MAKES FOR AN INTERESTING MALT: fruity and floral with cereal and aldehydic aromas on a sufficient base of sweetish tastes.

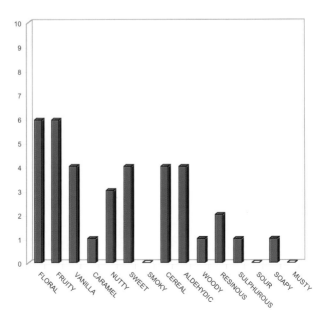

# BENROMACH
# 10 YEAR OLD

TYPE: single malt
STRENGTH: 40% ABV
AGE IN CASK: 10 years
OWNERS: Gordon &
          MacPhail Ltd
RATING: **

RATHER A DISAPPOINTING PROFILE FOR A SINGLE MALT OF TEN
years: not a bad whisky, but not that great either.

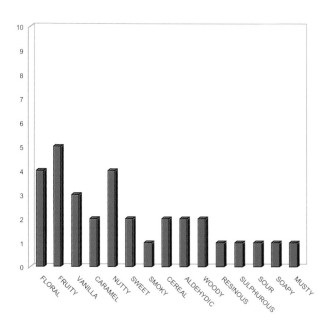

# BLACK & WHITE

TYPE: standard blend
STRENGTH: 40% ABV
AGE IN CASK: not stated
OWNERS: United Distillers
        & Vintners Ltd
RATING: ****

A STANDARD BLEND WHOSE FLAVOUR PROFILE PLENTY OF MALT
distillers would be happy with. Lots of fruit and sweetness,
though some might find the high levels of aldehydes a bit
difficult.

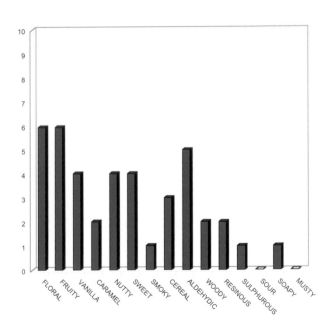

# BLACK BARREL

TYPE: grain
STRENGTH: 43% ABV
AGE IN CASK: not stated
OWNERS: William Grant &
Sons Ltd
RATING: ***

THIS IS WILLIAM GRANT'S SINGLE-GRAIN WHISKY AND THE BASE OF
the blended whiskies from that firm. And a good blending
whisky, too, since it has nothing unpleasant and the flavours
it lacks can be supplied by the malts in the blend.

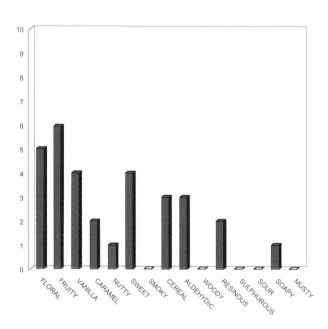

# BLACK BOTTLE

TYPE: premium blend
STRENGTH: 40% ABV
AGE IN CASK: not stated
OWNERS: Burn Stewart
       Distillers plc
RATING: ***

A DECENT PREMIUM BLEND, IN WHICH THE PREDOMINANT flavour is that of sweetness.

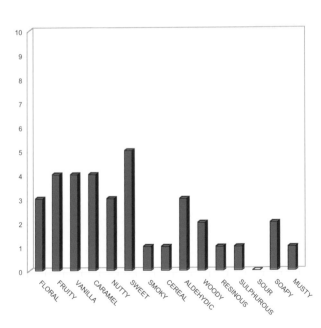

# BLACK BOTTLE
# 10 YEAR OLD

TYPE: de luxe blend
STRENGTH: 40% ABV
AGE IN CASK: 10 years
OWNERS: Burn Stewart
          Distillers plc
RATING: ***

THE SAME NAME AS BEFORE, BUT OLDER MATERIALS ARE USED TO make a more flavoursome whisky. Evidently more peated malt has been used in the blend than is the case with the younger whisky, for smoky flavours are present in some strength.

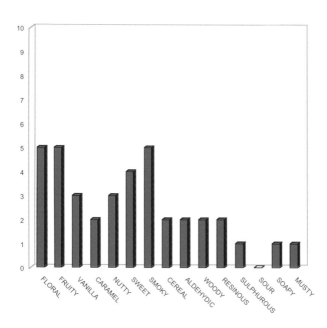

# BLACK COCK

TYPE: standard blend
STRENGTH: 40% ABV
AGE IN CASK: not stated
OWNERS: Burn Stewart
         Distillers Ltd
RATING: ****

A WELL-MADE WHISKY WITH PLENTY OF GOOD FLAVOURS supplemented by some wood. A touch soapy, though.

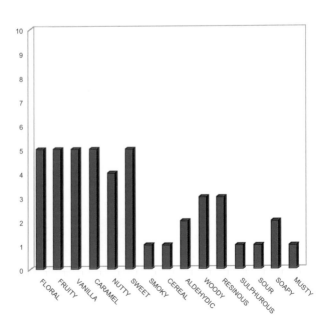

# BLAIRMHOR
# 8 YEAR OLD

TYPE: vatted malt
STRENGTH: 40% ABV
AGE IN CASK: 8 years
OWNERS: Inver House
            Distillers Ltd
RATING: ****

FRUIT AND FLOWERS ARE THE MOST PROMINENT AROMAS IN THIS interesting and flavoursome malt.

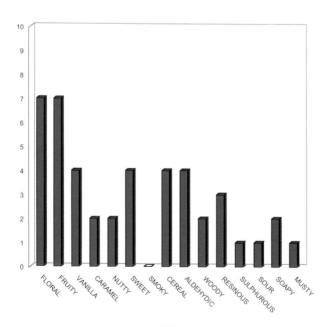

# BOWMORE
# 12 YEAR OLD

TYPE: single malt
STRENGTH: 43% ABV
AGE IN CASK: 12 years
OWNERS: Morrison
        Bowmore
        Distillers Ltd
RATING: ****

A FULL-FLAVOURED MALT WITH ENOUGH OF THE LESSER AROMAS
to give character but not to detract from the overall taste.
Peaty, but not excessively so. A very fine malt indeed.

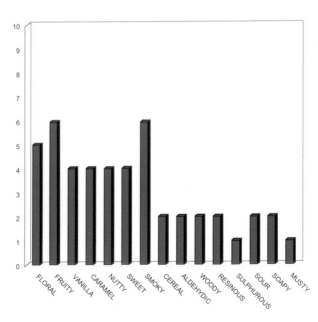

# BOWMORE
# 15 YEAR OLD

TYPE: single malt
STRENGTH: 43% ABV
AGE IN CASK: 15 years
OWNERS: Morrison
         Bowmore
         Distillers Ltd
RATING: ****

UNEXPECTEDLY, THE PHENOLIC FLAVOURS ARE MORE EVIDENT IN this than in the 12 year old. Quality is as the younger whisky, but with a different balance of flavours.

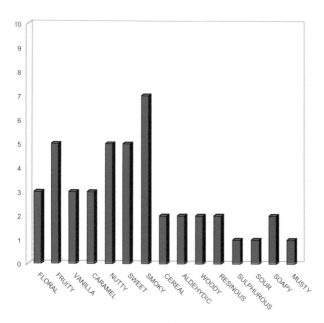

# BOWMORE
# 21 YEAR OLD

TYPE: single malt
STRENGTH: 43% ABV
AGE IN CASK: 21 years
OWNERS: Morrison
          Bowmore
          Distillers Ltd
RATING: *****

SIX YEARS HAVE WROUGHT A GREAT CHANGE IN THE SPIRIT. THE peaty aromas have dwindled until they are barely noticeable. Their decline is, however, more than compensated for by some powerfully delicious flavours from floral to sweet.

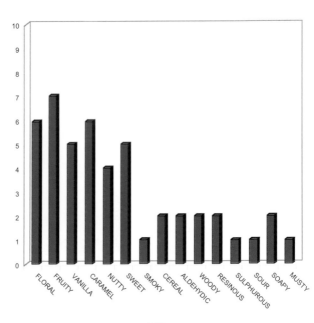

# BOWMORE LEGEND

TYPE: single malt
STRENGTH: 43% ABV
AGE IN CASK: not stated
OWNERS: Morrison
Bowmore
Distillers Ltd
RATING: ****

THE AGE IS NOT STATED, PRESUMABLY BECAUSE THE WHISKY IS younger than the other Bowmore bottlings. Still good whisky, though, with lots of smoke and plenty of other flavours. Surprisingly, it shows as woody, too.

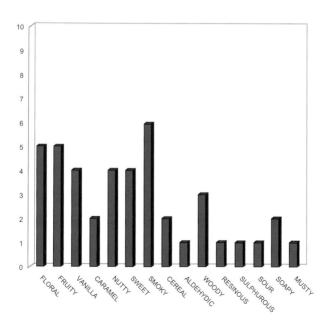

# BRUICHLADDICH
# 10 YEAR OLD

TYPE: single malt
STRENGTH: 46% ABV
AGE IN CASK: 10 years
OWNERS: Bruichladdich
        Whisky Co.
RATING: ****

**BRUICHLADDICH UNDER ITS NEW OWNERS AT LAST SHOWS WHAT IT** is capable of. In all three bottlings, there is a noticeable absence of off-note aromas. The 10 year old is strongly floral, fruity and toffee-like and, surprisingly, it shows cereal and leathery flavours too.

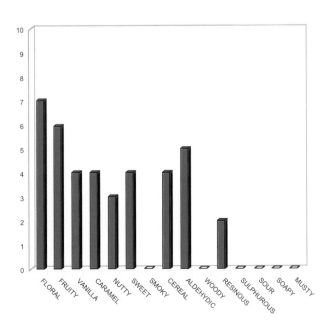

# BRUICHLADDICH
# 15 YEAR OLD

TYPE: single malt
STRENGTH: 46% ABV
AGE IN CASK: 15 years
OWNERS: Bruichladdich
          Whisky Co.
RATING: ****

ANOTHER FIVE YEARS SHOWS THE SAME LOT OF FLAVOURS, BUT with a different distribution. Good stuff, too, but not as strikingly so as the 10 year old.

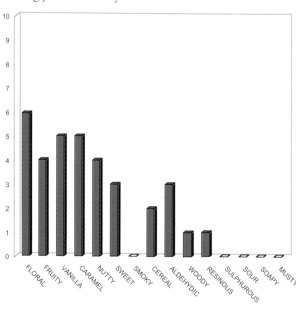

# BRUICHLADDICH
## XVII

TYPE: single malt
STRENGTH: 46% ABV
AGE IN CASK: 17 years
OWNERS: Bruichladdich
       Whisky Co.
RATING: *****

TWO YEARS MORE AND THE SONG IS LOUDER AND MORE TUNEFUL.
Wildly fruity, floral and with lots of vanilla-caramel
sweetness. The flavours in the four later bands add
character and depth.

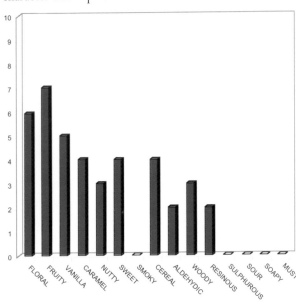

# BUCHANAN'S 12 YEAR OLD DE LUXE

TYPE: de luxe blend
STRENGTH: 40% ABV
AGE IN CASK: 12 years
OWNERS: United Distillers
       & Vintners Ltd
RATING: ****

A VERY CREDITABLE FLAVOUR PROFILE FOR A WHISKY WHOSE makers describe it only as a standard blend and which is accordingly cheap. Higher levels of pleasing flavours than many malts and not really enough of the other aromas to prejudice the overall taste.

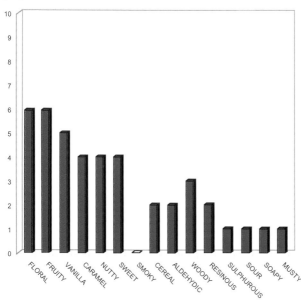

# BUNNAHABHAIN
# 12 YEAR OLD

TYPE: single malt
STRENGTH: 40% ABV
AGE IN CASK: 12 years
OWNERS: Burn Stewart
         Distillers plc
RATING: \*\*\*

A DECENT, BUT NOT BRILLIANT, MALT. HAS NOTHING LIKE THE concentration and balance of flavour of the much cheaper blend at number 41.

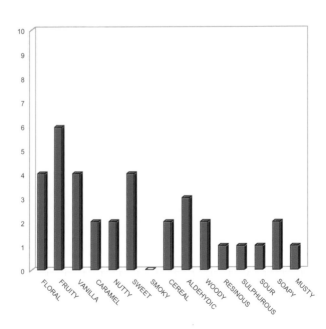

# CAMERON BRIG

43

TYPE: grain
STRENGTH: 40% ABV
AGE IN CASK: not stated
OWNERS: United Distillers
        & Vintners Ltd
RATING: **

AN ODDITY: A SINGLE-GRAIN WHISKY WITH A PRETTY PATCHY profile. Some people (mostly Fifers, in a spirit of local patriotism) drink it by preference, though. It says a lot for the skills of the UDV blenders that they can convert this stuff into some very good blends.

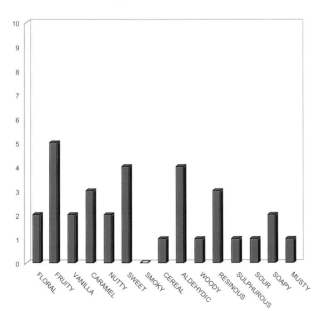

44

# CAMPBELTOWN LOCH

TYPE: standard blend
STRENGTH: 43% ABV
AGE IN CASK: not stated
OWNERS: Springbank
         Distillers Ltd
RATING: ***

A RESPECTABLE IF UNEXCEPTIONAL BLEND IN WHICH THERE IS A wide spread of flavour, though none at high level – and some detectable off-notes at the end.

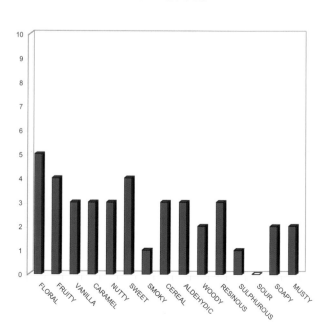

# CAOL ILA 1989: SIGNATORY BOTTLING

TYPE: single malt, private
   bottling
STRENGTH: 43% ABV
AGE IN CASK: not stated
OWNERS: Signatory Vintage
   Scotch Whisky
   Co. Ltd
RATING: ***

A QUITE EXTRAORDINARY FLAVOUR PROFILE: HUGELY PHENOLIC
and very sweet. Fruity and flowery as well. Shows what a
really fine cask and a scrupulous bottler can achieve.

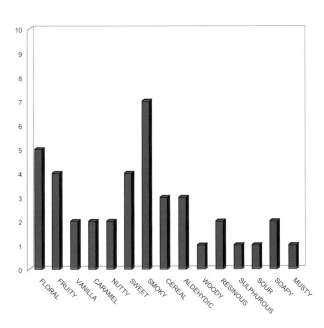

# CARDHU
## 12 YEAR OLD

TYPE: single malt
STRENGTH: 40% ABV
AGE IN CASK: 12 years
OWNERS: United Distillers
       & Vintners Ltd
RATING: ***

NOW A VATTED MALT. THIS, ITS SINGLE-MALT PREDECESSOR, IS OF
no great quality. With UDV's vast resources it ought not to
be too hard to vat a malt which is considerably better.

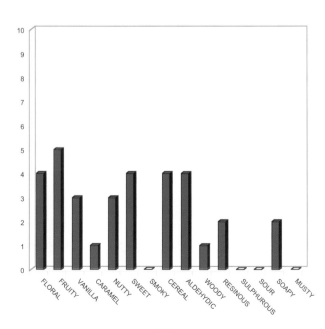

# CATTO'S DELUXE
# 12 YEAR OLD

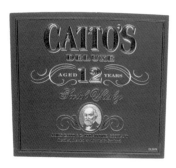

TYPE: de luxe blend
STRENGTH: 40% ABV
AGE IN CASK: 12 years
OWNERS: Inver House
Distillers Ltd
RATING: ***

A GOOD ENOUGH BLEND, BUT LITTLE TO JUSTIFY THE 'DE LUXE' classification.

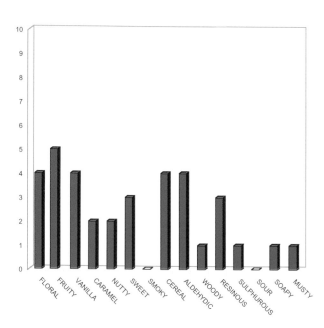

# CATTO'S RARE OLD SCOTTISH HIGHLAND WHISKY

TYPE: standard blend
STRENGTH: 40% ABV
AGE IN CASK: not stated
OWNERS: Inver House
           Distillers Ltd
RATING: ***

A SOLID BLEND WITH A GOOD SPREAD OF FLAVOURS. THE TOUCH OF soapiness does not detract unduly from its pleasing character.

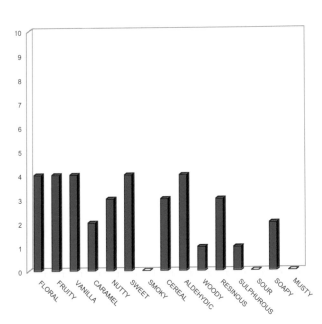

# CHIVAS REGAL 12 YEAR OLD

TYPE: de luxe blend
STRENGTH: 40% ABV
AGE IN CASK: 12 years
OWNERS: Chivas Brothers
Ltd
RATING: ***

THIS IS WHAT A LARGE PART OF THE WORLD THINKS OF AS FIRST-rate liquor. It is, indeed, perfectly good whisky, but not as good as a lot of folk think and as its market position implies.

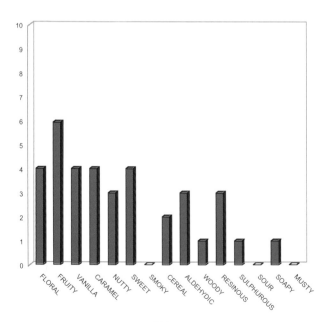

# CHIVAS REGAL
# 18 YEAR OLD

TYPE: de luxe blend
STRENGTH: 40% ABV
AGE IN CASK: 18 years
OWNERS: Chivas Brothers
          Ltd
RATING: ***

MUCH THE SAME COULD BE SAID OF THIS AS OF THE 12 YEAR OLD.
There is nothing wrong with the whisky and the bottle
looks classy. But it is a triumph of appearance over
substance and you are paying a lot for packaging.

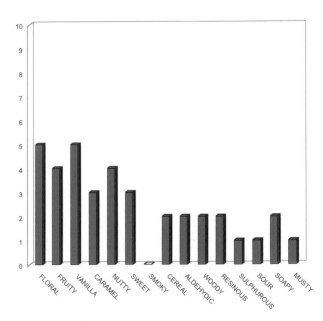

# CLAN CAMPBELL

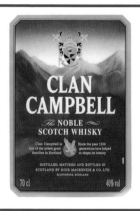

TYPE: standard blend
STRENGTH: 40% ABV
AGE IN CASK: not stated
OWNERS: Chivas Brothers
Ltd
RATING: ****

THERE CAN BE NO DOUBT THAT CHIVAS BROTHERS MAKE GOOD blends, and we should rejoice that the folk who buy their other products do so: they subsidise the production of really good, flavoursome, standard blends such as this.

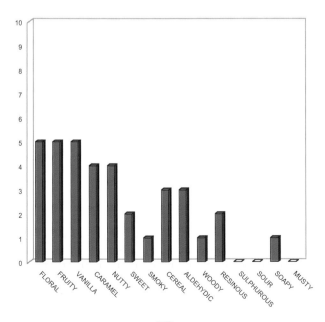

# CLAN CAMPBELL HIGHLANDER 12 YEAR OLD

TYPE: de luxe blend
STRENGTH: 40% ABV
AGE IN CASK: 12 years
OWNERS: Chivas Brothers
              Ltd
RATING: \*\*\*\*

THE DE LUXE VERSION OF THE CLAN CAMPBELL. FOR ONCE, A DE luxe variant justifies the description: the quality of the Clan Campbell standard blend, with even more of what makes it so good.

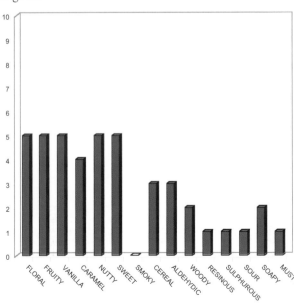

# CLAN CAMPBELL
# PURE MALT
# 8 YEAR OLD

TYPE: vatted malt
STRENGTH: 40% ABV
AGE IN CASK: 8 years
OWNERS: Chivas Brothers
                    Ltd
RATING: ****

A VATTED MALT, AND NOT BAD STUFF IN ANY OTHER COMPANY. BUT sharing a stable with so many fine blends, it inevitably suffers by comparison.

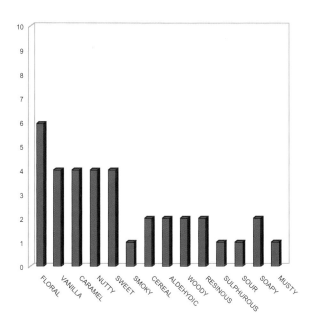

# CLAN MACGREGOR

TYPE: standard blend
STRENGTH: 40% ABV
AGE IN CASK: not stated
OWNERS: William Grant
& Sons Ltd
RATING: ***

A GOOD STANDARD BLEND OF A KIND UNLIKELY TO BE DRUNK BY folk who read whisky directories. It is to be recommended to those who do and who want a simple everyday dram.

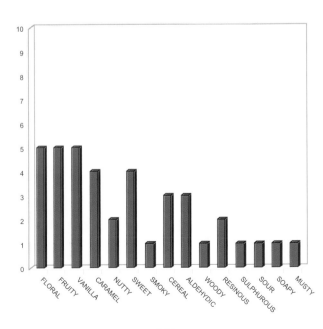

# THE CLAYMORE

TYPE: standard blend
STRENGTH: 43% ABV
AGE IN CASK: not stated
OWNERS: Whyte & Mackay
        Ltd
RATING: ****

A LITTLE-KNOWN BUT VERY RESPECTABLE STANDARD BLEND FROM
Whyte & Mackay. Good value for money.

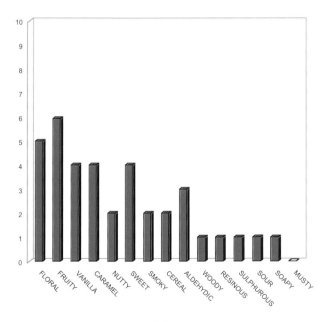

# CLUNY

TYPE: standard blend
STRENGTH: 40% ABV
AGE IN CASK: not stated
OWNERS: Whyte & Mackay
　　　　Ltd
RATING: ***

A STANDARD BLEND FROM THE SAME HOUSE AS THAT WHICH produces the Claymore. Slightly lower strength and lower and more patchy flavours.

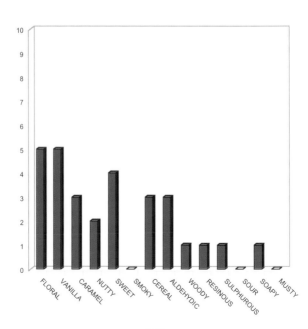

# CLYNELISH
# 15 YEAR OLD

**57**

TYPE: single malt
STRENGTH: 40% ABV
AGE IN CASK: 15 years
OWNERS: United Distillers
& Vintners Ltd
RATING: ****

THIS IS THE SORT OF STUFF WHICH GIVES MALT WHISKY ITS reputation: lots of very fine principal flavours, lots of interesting minor ones and sufficient general excellence for the spirit to be able to absorb a few off-notes without prejudice.

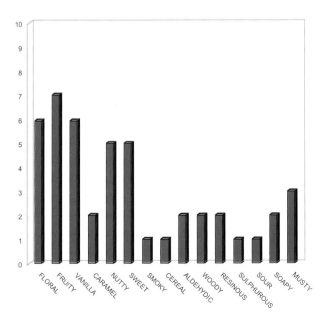

# CRAGGANMORE
# 12 YEAR OLD

TYPE: single malt
STRENGTH: 40% ABV
AGE IN CASK: 12 years
OWNERS: United Distillers
         & Vintners Ltd
RATING: ****

A VERY FINE MALT INDEED AND EASILY THE BEST OF THE CLASSIC
Six. Lots of fruit and flowers backed by nuttiness and
sweetness mixed with cereal and leathery notes. No faults
at all.

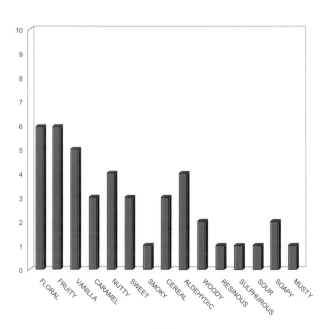

# CRAWFORD'S ✱✱✱
# SPECIAL RESERVE

TYPE: standard blend
STRENGTH: 40% ABV
AGE IN CASK: not stated
OWNERS: Whyte & Mackay
        Ltd
RATING: ✱✱✱✱

AN UNUSUAL WHISKY: ITS FLAVOUR IS CONCENTRATED IN THE caramel-sweet area. Lots of that, but not a lot else. But given that it is one of the cheapest blends on the market, a very creditable performance.

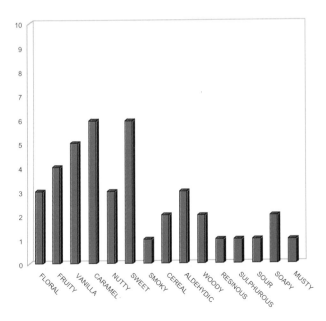

# CUTTY SARK

TYPE: premium blend
STRENGTH: 43% ABV
AGE IN CASK: not stated
OWNERS: Berry Bros &
        Rudd Ltd
RATING: ****

THE LOW LEVELS OF FLAVOUR AND PALE COLOUR OF THIS BLEND are quite intentional, given that it was designed to be taken with mixers. If it has little to offer the aficionado, it has no obvious faults either.

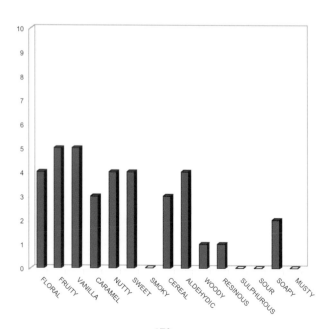

61

# DALMORE
# 12 YEAR OLD

TYPE: single malt
STRENGTH: 40% ABV
AGE IN CASK: 12 years
OWNERS: Whyte & Mackay
Ltd
RATING: *****

WHYTE & MACKAY'S FLAGSHIP MALT, AND WITH SOME justification: the levels and distributions of flavours are those of a first-class malt whisky. Lots of goodies, lots of interest and quite flawless.

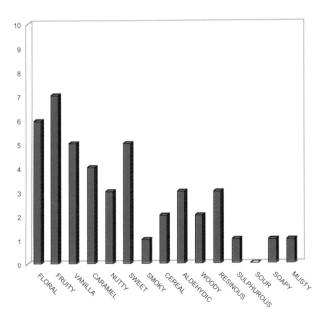

# DALWHINNIE
# 15 YEAR OLD

TYPE: single malt
STRENGTH: 40% ABV
AGE IN CASK: 15 years
OWNERS: United Distillers
        & Vintners Ltd
RATING: ***

A DECENT BUT UNEXCEPTIONAL DRAM WHOSE CHARACTER, OR lack of it, suggests that flavour was not an important consideration for its owners when they selected whiskies for their Classic designation.

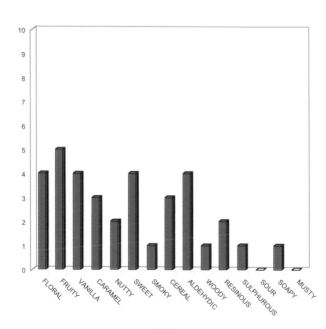

# DEANSTON
# 12 YEAR OLD

| | |
|---|---|
| TYPE: single malt |
| STRENGTH: 40% ABV |
| AGE IN CASK: 12 years |
| OWNERS: Burn Stewart Distillers plc |
| RATING: *** |

A DRINKABLE MALT, BUT NOT ONE LIKELY TO GATHER ANY PLAUDITS. Low levels of flavour and insufficient to counter the slight off-notes.

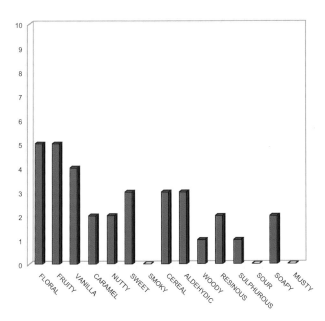

# DEANSTON
# 17 YEAR OLD

TYPE: single malt
STRENGTH: 40% ABV
AGE IN CASK: 17 years
OWNERS: Burn Stewart
        Distillers plc
RATING: ***

PRODUCT OF SCOTLAND

Burn Stewart Distillers

Deanston Mill Built 1785

# DEANSTON

Single Highland Malt
Scotch Whisky

A unique smooth Single
MALT, rich rounded

**17**
YEARS OLD

with a touch of
Amontillado Sherry

40% vol

DEANSTON DISTILLERY DOUNE
PERTHSHIRE

700ml

THE SAME WHISKY AS THE 12 YEAR OLD BUT LONGER IN CASK, SO it has had time to pick up some desirable flavours – of which it has a respectable number.

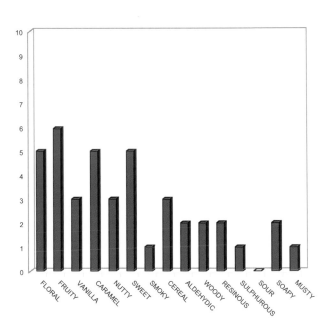

# DEWAR'S ANCESTOR 12 YEAR OLD

TYPE: de luxe blend
STRENGTH: 43% ABV
AGE IN CASK: 12 years
OWNERS: John Dewar &
Sons Ltd
RATING: ***

A LITTLE AGE CAN CONFER A LOT IN THE WAY OF FLAVOUR, AS THIS blend demonstrates. The fruity flavours are at levels which any malt would envy and are matched by sweet, floral aromas. There is enough of interest to make this a dram worthy of long perusal.

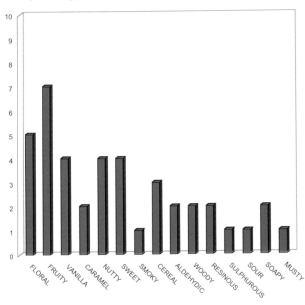

# DEWAR'S SPECIAL RESERVE 12 YEAR OLD

TYPE: de luxe blend
STRENGTH: 43% ABV
AGE IN CASK: 12 years
OWNERS: John Dewar &
　　　　　Sons Ltd
RATING: ****

A PROFILE TO BE PROUD OF: LOTS OF FRUIT AND FLOWERS, BACKED by nutty sweetness and a savoury, resinous base. An excellent whisky in any company.

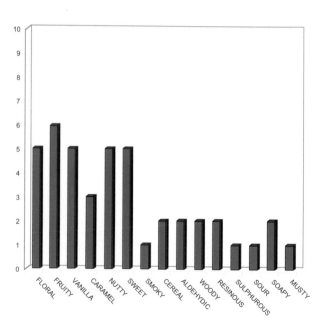

# DEWAR'S 'WHITE LABEL'

**67**

TYPE: standard blend
STRENGTH: 40% ABV
AGE IN CASK: not stated
OWNERS: John Dewar &
             Sons Ltd
RATING: ***

A RESPECTABLE STANDARD BLEND OF LONG STANDING, IT HAS FEW pretensions and so does not disappoint. Perfectly drinkable, inexpensive whisky.

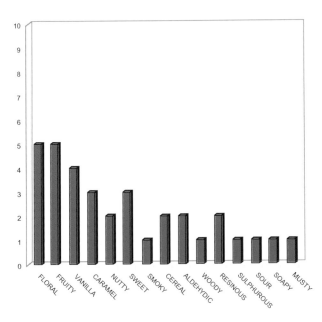

# DEW OF BEN NEVIS

TYPE: premium blend
STRENGTH: 40% ABV
AGE IN CASK: not stated
OWNERS: Ben Nevis
        Distillery (Fort
        William) Ltd
RATING: ****

IT IS DESCRIBED AS A PREMIUM BLEND AND LACKS AN AGE statement. Don't be put off by the latter, for this is good blended whisky. Full-flavoured and without perceptible fault.

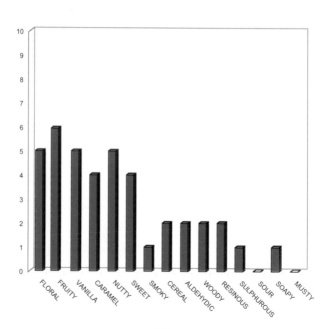

# DEW OF BEN NEVIS 21 YEAR OLD

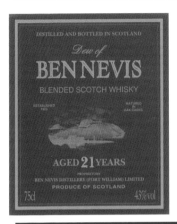

TYPE: de luxe blend
STRENGTH: 43% ABV
AGE IN CASK: 21 years
OWNERS: Ben Nevis
        Distillery (Fort
        William) Ltd
RATING: ****

A LITTLE DISAPPOINTING, GIVEN THE QUALITY OF ITS YOUNGER siblings, and probably not as good a buy as either. But decent stuff, nonetheless.

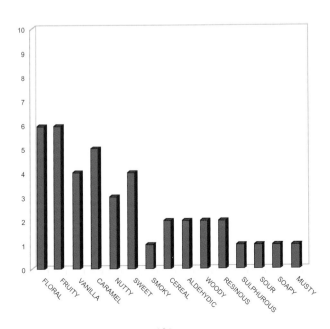

# DEW OF BEN NEVIS
# SPECIAL RESERVE

<table>
<tr><td>TYPE: de luxe blend</td></tr>
<tr><td>STRENGTH: 40% ABV</td></tr>
<tr><td>AGE IN CASK: not stated</td></tr>
<tr><td>OWNERS: Ben Nevis<br>   Distillery (Fort<br>   William) Ltd</td></tr>
<tr><td>RATING: ****</td></tr>
</table>

A CURIOUS BUT PLEASING FLAVOUR PROFILE. FRUITY, CARAMEL and sweet, it is distinctive and unique.

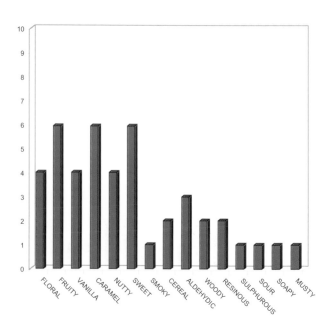

# DIMPLE
# 12 YEAR OLD

TYPE: de luxe blend
STRENGTH: 43% ABV
AGE IN CASK: 12 years
OWNERS: United Distillers
       & Vintners Ltd
RATING: ***

A LONG-ESTABLISHED MEMBER OF THE UDV STABLE. WHILE THE whisky is respectable, it is unremarkable and one suspects the brand's sales (which are mostly overseas) owe more to the distinctive bottle than to anything else.

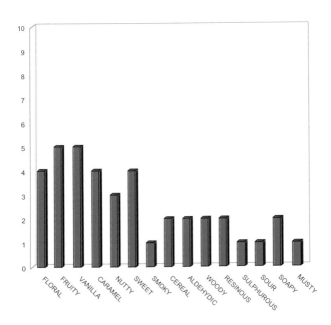

# DRUMGUISH

TYPE: single malt
STRENGTH: 40% ABV
AGE IN CASK: not stated
OWNERS: Speyside
        Distillery Co. Ltd
RATING: ***

A SINGLE MALT WITHOUT AN AGE STATEMENT USUALLY INDICATES A young spirit. The flavour profile of this one indicates the same, having some odd peaks and being rather unbalanced. It looks promising, though, and time will tell.

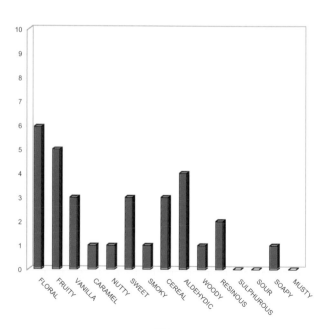

# EDRADOUR
## 10 YEAR OLD

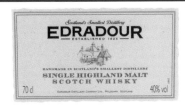

70 cl    40% vol

TYPE: single malt
STRENGTH: 43% ABV
AGE IN CASK: 10 years
OWNERS: Signatory Vintage Scotch
Whisky Co. Ltd
RATING: ****

THIS IS A GOOD MALT SPOILED BY SOME UNFORTUNATE SULPHUROUS
and musty off-notes. For a 10 year old, it is strangely woody.
The problem may be due to lack of attention on the part of
the management, a matter likely to be rectified by Signatory,
the new owners, who have a good track record in such things.

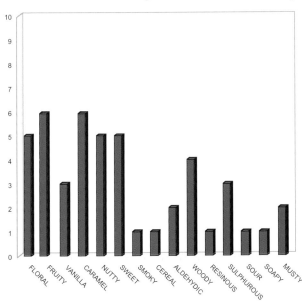

# THE FAMOUS GROUSE

TYPE: premium blend
STRENGTH: 40% ABV
AGE IN CASK: not stated
OWNERS: The Edrington
Group Ltd
RATING: ★★★★

**THIS – RATHER THAN ANY MALT – IS THE WHISKY WHICH SHOWED** Scottish dram drinkers that higher quality whiskies could be produced than were generally available on the market at the time. It is Scotland's biggest-selling whisky. The flavour profile shows why.

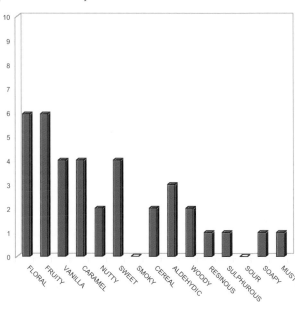

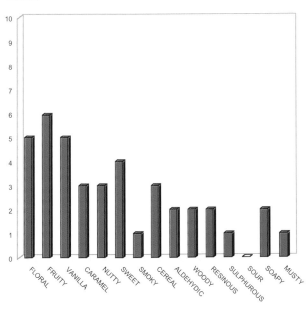

# THE FAMOUS GROUSE GOLD RESERVE 12 YEAR OLD

75

TYPE: de luxe blend
STRENGTH: 40% ABV
AGE IN CASK: 12 years
OWNERS: The Edrington
Group Ltd
RATING: ***

THE SUCCESS OF GROUSE PROMPTED EDRINGTON TO EXPLOIT THE brand name by what in the trade are called line-extensions. This 12 year old, while a perfectly good whisky, is dearer than its more proletarian cousin but not obviously a lot better.

187

# THE FAMOUS GROUSE PRESTIGE

TYPE: de luxe blend
STRENGTH: 40% ABV
AGE IN CASK: not stated
OWNERS: The Edrington
        Group Ltd
RATING: ****

NO AGE STATEMENT ON THIS, WHICH IS SURPRISING, FOR IT IS VERY toothsome stuff and, judging by the fact that it is woody and resinous, has a lot of old malt in it. Not widely distributed but worth seeking out and buying in preference to a lot of malts.

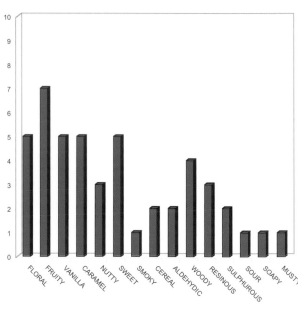

# FINDLATER'S FINEST

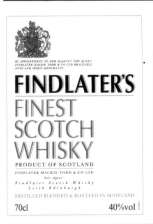

TYPE: premium blend
STRENGTH: 40% ABV
AGE IN CASK: not stated
OWNERS: Whyte & Mackay
Ltd
RATING: ****

ANOTHER VERY FINE BLEND FROM WHYTE & MACKAY. IT HAS A classic flavour profile: high in the first five bars, indicating lots of flavour, with enough low bars to suggest variety. A little soapiness is barely noticeable, being submerged in the overall flavour.

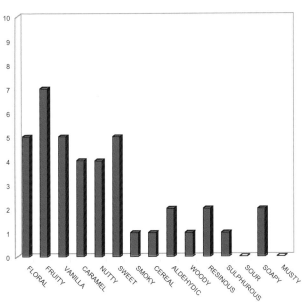

# GLEN DEVERON
# 10 YEAR OLD

TYPE: single malt
STRENGTH: 40% ABV
AGE IN CASK: 10 years
OWNERS: John Dewar &
Sons Ltd
RATING: ****

A GREAT AND UNDERRATED MALT. FLORAL AND LUSCIOUS, BUT NOT excessively so, for it is relatively dry, and there is a base of other, deeper, animal and botanical aromas.

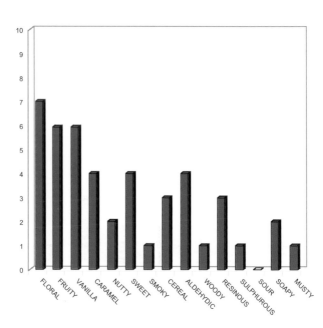

# GLENDRONACH
# 15 YEAR OLD

TYPE: single malt
STRENGTH: 40% ABV
AGE IN CASK: 15 years
OWNERS: Allied Distillers
 Ltd
RATING: *****

**LOOK AT THE LEVELS OF FLAVOUR IN THIS AND THEN CONSIDER THAT** for years the distillery has been mothballed and produces only occasionally. Evidence, if it were needed, that the public's taste is deeply irrational. A great spirit which, matured in good sherry casks, produces first-rate whisky.

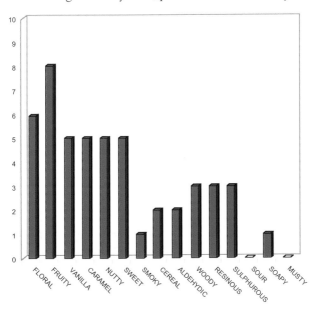

**80**

# GLENFARCLAS
# 10 YEAR OLD

TYPE: single malt
STRENGTH: 40% ABV
AGE IN CASK: 10 years
OWNERS: J. & G. Grant Ltd
RATING: ***

ONE OF THE GREAT CLASSIC (NOTE, NOT *CLASSIC*) SPEYSIDE malts. Lots of the flavours which contribute to a really fine sherry-cask malt whisky. A sulphurous note at the end is sufficient to improve, but not to impair, the taste.

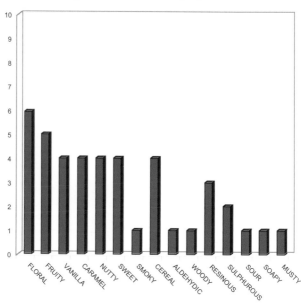

# GLENFARCLAS
# 12 YEAR OLD

81

TYPE: single malt
STRENGTH: 43% ABV
AGE IN CASK: 12 years
OWNERS: J. & G. Grant Ltd
RATING: ****

A LITTLE MORE AGE SIMPLY RAISES THE OVERALL LEVELS OF flavour and, since the sulphurous note gives way to resinous aromas, the character is quite different.

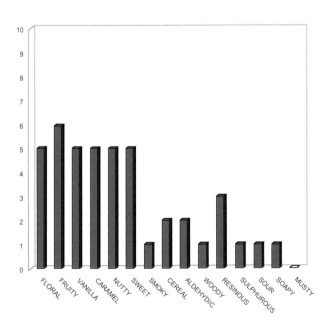

# GLENFARCLAS
# 21 YEAR OLD

TYPE: single malt
STRENGTH: 43% ABV
AGE IN CASK: 21 years
OWNERS: J. & G. Grant Ltd
RATING: ****

MORE FLORAL, BUT NOT OTHERWISE AN IMPROVEMENT ON THE
younger whisky. Shows that when you start with good
casks, age does not necessarily bring improvement.

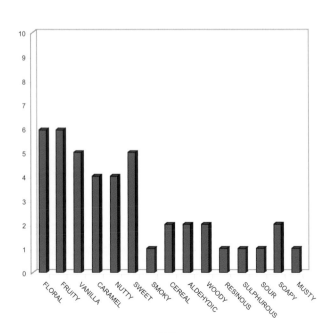

# GLENFARCLAS
# 25 YEAR OLD

TYPE: single malt
STRENGTH: 43% ABV
AGE IN CASK: 25 years
OWNERS: J. & G. Grant Ltd
RATING: ****

AND, BACKTRACKING ON THE PRECEDING PROPOSITION, WE ARE compelled to admit that the 25 year old shows that Glenfarclas when old in wood can produce some very striking flavours. Hugely fruity and floral, the spirit is sweet and nutty as well, and the background aromas are good.

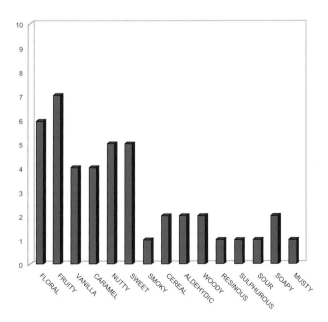

# GLENFARCLAS 105

TYPE: single malt
STRENGTH: 60% ABV
AGE IN CASK: not stated
OWNERS: J. & G. Grant Ltd
RATING: ***

ONE OF THE EARLIEST CASK-STRENGTH BOTTLINGS, THE 105 IS A little disappointing in taste, showing that high alcoholic strength does not by itself imply great flavours. That said, it's good stuff.

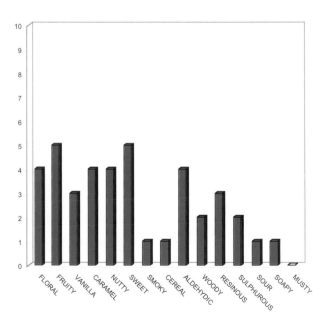

# GLENFIDDICH ANCIENT RESERVE 18 YEAR OLD

**85**

TYPE: single malt
STRENGTH: 40% ABV
AGE IN CASK: 18 years
OWNERS: William Grant & Sons Ltd
RATING: ****

THIS GOES TO SHOW THAT IF GLENFIDDICH IS LEFT IN CASK FOR 18 years, it turns out a very fine malt indeed. Floral and fruity, the whisky when nosed runs through a gamut of flavours. Take it slowly or just drink it: either way the experience will be a pleasurable one.

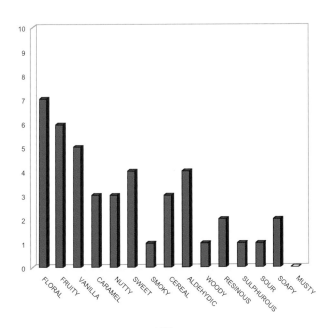

# GLENFIDDICH
# SOLERA RESERVE
# 15 YEAR OLD

TYPE: single malt, solera
matured
STRENGTH: 40% ABV
AGE IN CASK: 15 years
OWNERS: William Grant &
Sons Ltd
RATING: ***

GLENFIDDICH HAD THE SOUND IDEA OF MATURING A QUANTITY OF
spirit in a huge cask, replacing what was drawn off by
younger whisky, as recommended by the late, great George
Saintsbury. Alas, the experiment does not seem to be
justified by the result.

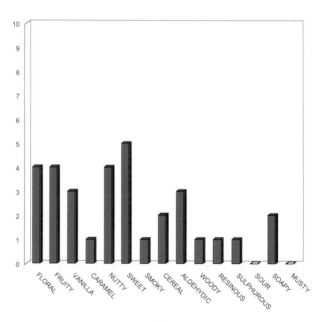

# GLENFIDDICH
# SPECIAL RESERVE
# 12 YEAR OLD

87

TYPE: single malt
STRENGTH: 40% ABV
AGE IN CASK: 12 years
OWNERS: William Grant &
Sons Ltd
RATING: ****

THIS IS THE WHISKY WHICH LED THE MALT REVOLUTION. IT DID SO with a fairly bland malt and eventually found itself overtaken. The owners have recently improved it greatly and given it a minimum age of 12 years. It is a very good malt and excellent value for money, since it continues to be sold quite cheaply.

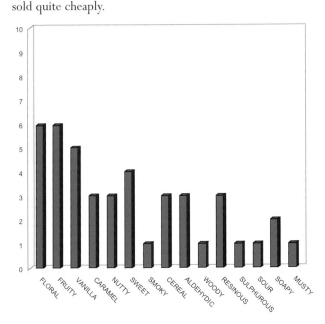

# GLEN GARIOCH
## 8 YEAR OLD

TYPE: single malt
STRENGTH: 40% ABV
AGE IN CASK: 8 years
OWNERS: Morrison
      Bowmore
      Distillers Ltd
RATING: **

GLEN GARIOCH IS A GOOD MALT, BUT EIGHT YEARS IN CASK IS TOO little time for it to develop, as this bottling amply shows. A flavour profile which would be poor in a cheap blend.

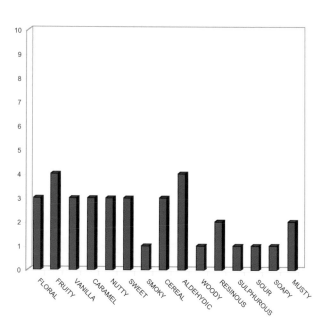

# GLEN GARIOCH
# 15 YEAR OLD

TYPE: single malt
STRENGTH: 43% ABV
AGE IN CASK: 15 years
OWNERS: Morrison
        Bowmore
        Distillers Ltd
RATING: ****

ANOTHER SEVEN YEARS IN WOOD HAVE WROUGHT A MIGHTY change. The whisky is now flavoursome and rounded but, alas, there is something a bit sour and soapy which rather spoils it.

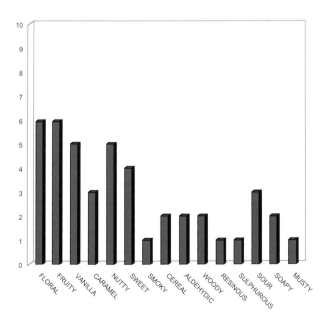

# GLEN GARIOCH
# 21 YEAR OLD

70cl e   Distilled in the heart of the Garioch,
traditionally one of the finest
barley-growing areas in Scotland.   43% Vol

L.583

TYPE: single malt
STRENGTH: 43% ABV
AGE IN CASK: 21 years
OWNERS: Morrison Bowmore
        Distillers Ltd
RATING: *****

**THIS IS A WHISKY WHICH HAS COME OF AGE. IT HAS ACHIEVED HIGH** levels of delicious flavour, having lost the rawness of youth and the unsavoury aromas of adolescence.

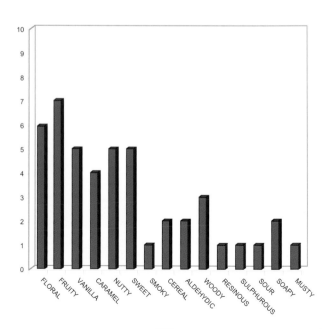

# GLENGOYNE
# 10 YEAR OLD

TYPE: single malt
STRENGTH: 40% ABV
AGE IN CASK: 10 years
OWNERS: P. J. Russell & Co.
        Ltd
RATING: ****

SINCE THE MASH IS MADE FROM UNPEATED MALT, THE FLAVOUR profiles of the Glengoyne score zero for smokiness. They score very well for other flavours, though. The 10 year old has aromas from floral to sweet, with cereal, leathery and resinous notes. Soapy aromas are present but do not intrude.

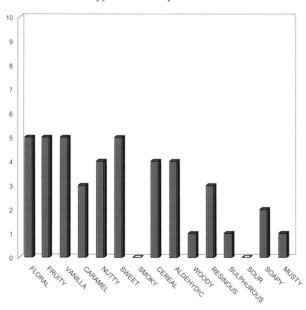

# GLENGOYNE
# 17 YEAR OLD

TYPE: single malt
STRENGTH: 43% ABV
AGE IN CASK: 17 years
OWNERS: P. J. Russell & Co.
Ltd
RATING: ****

ANOTHER SEVEN YEARS HAVE CHANGED THE PROFILE. THE solidity of the principal flavours remains and the others diminish to produce a spirit which, if it is perhaps less interesting to the nose, is rather more delicious overall.

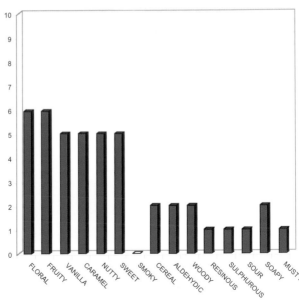

# GLENGOYNE
# 21 YEAR OLD

**93**

TYPE: single malt
STRENGTH: 43% ABV
AGE IN CASK: 21 years
OWNERS: P. J. Russell & Co.
        Ltd
RATING: *****

AGE HAS NOT WITHERED: RATHER, IT HAS DEVELOPED, AND THE whisky combines spring and autumn, flowers and fruit, nuts and vanilla. The woody flavour is that of maturity, not senility.

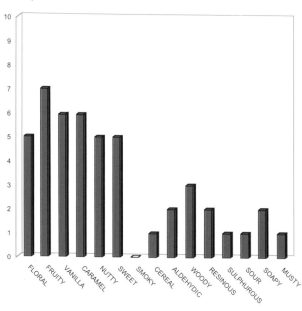

# GLEN GRANT
# 5 YEAR OLD

TYPE: single malt
STRENGTH: 40% ABV
AGE IN CASK: 5 years
OWNERS: Chivas Brothers
        Ltd
RATING: *

IT IS VERY DIFFICULT TO FIND SOMETHING TO COMMEND IN THIS
whisky: it has few good flavours and some bad ones. It sells
in vast quantities in Italy, where it compares favourably with
grappa, though that's not saying much. Five years is much
too young.

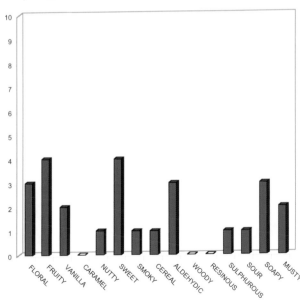

# GLEN GRANT
# 10 YEAR OLD

TYPE: single malt
STRENGTH: 40% ABV
AGE IN CASK: 10 years
OWNERS: Chivas Brothers
Ltd
RATING: ***

DEMONSTRATING THE NEED FOR MATURATION, THE 10 YEAR OLD IS still slightly soapy, but at least there are compensating flavours, lots of flowers and a fair bit of fruit.

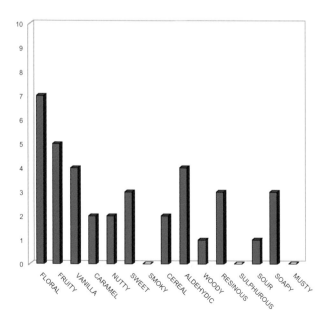

# GLEN KEITH
# 10 YEAR OLD

TYPE: single malt
STRENGTH: 43% ABV
AGE IN CASK: 10 years
OWNERS: Chivas Brothers
Ltd
RATING: ***

A GOOD AND UNPRETENTIOUS MALT. PLENTY OF FLAVOUR IN THE places you would want it and at levels sufficient to make a dram repay attention.

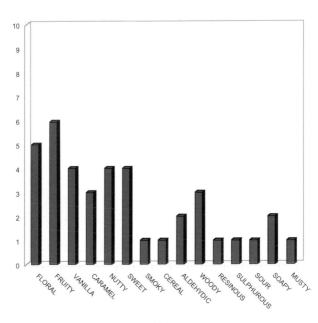

97

# GLENKINCHIE
# 10 YEAR OLD

**GLENKINCHIE**
THE EDINBURGH MALT
*LOWLAND SCOTCH WHISKY*

Glenkinchie Distillery was established in 1837 by
John and George Rate. It is situated beside the
Kinchie Burn in the heart of East Lothian
farmland. Over the gently rolling hills around
Glenkinchie, some of the finest barley is grown.

**10**
YEARS OLD

Glenkinchie Lowland Malt Whisky has a light
delicate nose and a fresh clean aroma; the finish
is smooth, with a subtle hint of dryness. A truly
fine distinctive Single Malt, excellent as a
pre-dinner drink.

43%vol        DISTILLED AT THE GLENKINCHIE DISTILLERY
                      PENCAITLAND SCOTLAND        750ml

TYPE: single malt
STRENGTH: 40% ABV
AGE IN CASK: 10 years
OWNERS: United Distillers & Vintners Ltd
RATING: ****

ANOTHER OF THE CLASSIC SIX, AND A GOOD ONE. LOTS OF
flavours: fruit, flowers, fudge and no faults at all.

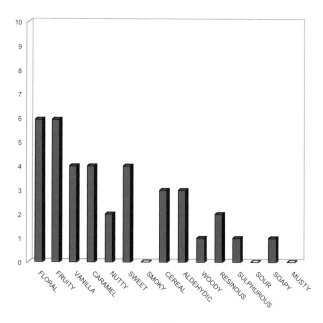

# GLENLIVET 12 YEAR OLD

TYPE: single malt
STRENGTH: 40% ABV
AGE IN CASK: 12 years
OWNERS: Chivas Brothers
Ltd
RATING: ***

**THE GLENLIVET.**

George Smith's Original 1824
Pure Single Malt
Scotch Whisky

AGED **12** YEARS

Aged only in Oak Casks

**GEORGE & J. G. SMITH**

Distilled in Scotland at
The Glenlivet Distillery, Banffshire

PRODUCT OF SCOTLAND

75cl 750ml ℮ 40%vol 40°GL 40% alc./vol.

THE ENTRY-LEVEL GLENLIVET: A GOOD, SUBTLE, MUSCULAR SPIRIT which suffers from its former prominence and is undervalued by aficionados. In consequence it is sold at a price which makes it something of a bargain.

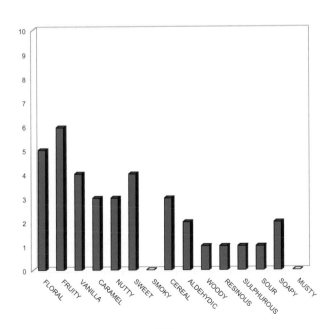

# GLENLIVET
# 12 YEAR OLD
# FRENCH OAK

99

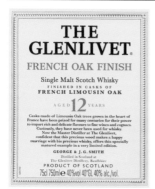

**THE GLENLIVET.**

FRENCH OAK FINISH

Single Malt Scotch Whisky
FINISHED IN CASKS OF
FRENCH LIMOUSIN OAK

AGED *12* YEARS

Casks made of Limousin Oak trees grown in the heart of
France have been prized for many centuries for their power
to impart rich and delicate flavours to fine wines and cognacs.
Curiously, they have never been used for whisky.
Now the Master Distiller at The Glenlivet,
confident that this precious wood makes a happy
marriage with his precious whisky, offers this specially
matured example in a very limited edition.

GEORGE & J. G. SMITH
Distilled in Scotland at
The Glenlivet Distillery, Banffshire
PRODUCT OF SCOTLAND
75cl 750ml ⓔ 40%vol 40°GL 40% alc./vol.

TYPE: single malt, cask
finished
STRENGTH: 40% ABV
AGE IN CASK: 12 years
OWNERS: Chivas Brothers
Ltd
rating: \*\*\*\*\*

WHATEVER YOUR OPINION OF THE PRACTICE OF FINISHING, YOU
can't deny that it perks up some whiskies no end. This, the
same spirit as the previous, has spent some time in a decent
cask instead of the worn-out ex-bourbon casks which most
of the industry uses. The improvement is spectacular.

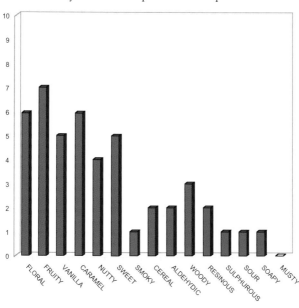

# GLENLIVET
# 18 YEAR OLD

TYPE: single malt
STRENGTH: 43% ABV
AGE IN CASK: 18 years
OWNERS: Chivas Brothers
           Ltd
RATING: ****

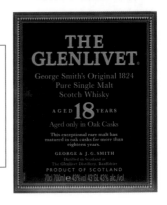

MORE AGE MEANS MORE EXTRACTION OF FLAVOUR, SO A FURTHER
6 years in a standard cask produces a very fine, fruity malt.

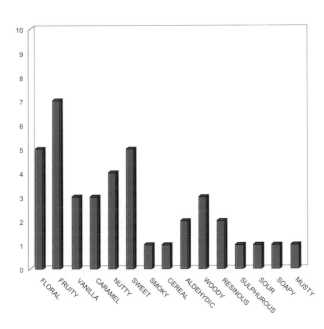

# GLENLIVET 21 YEAR OLD ARCHIVE

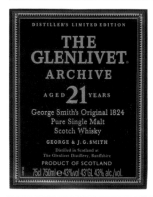

TYPE: single malt
STRENGTH: 43% ABV
AGE IN CASK: 21 years
OWNERS: Chivas Brothers
      Ltd
RATING: ****

ANOTHER THREE YEARS AND YOU GET THE SAME LEVEL OF FRUITY flavours, but floral aromas as well – and lots of caramel-nutty-sweetness to go with them. Woody and resinous, too. And a whiff of sulphur completes the age experience.

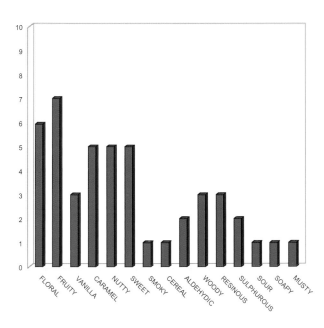

# GLENLIVET 1976: SIGNATORY BOTTLING

TYPE: single malt, private
bottling
STRENGTH: 57.7% ABV
AGE IN CASK: 24 years
OWNERS: Signatory Vintage
Scotch Whisky
Co. Ltd
RATING: *****

SIGNATORY IS ONE OF A HANDFUL OF PRIVATE BOTTLERS WHO somewhat manage to procure really great casks. This is possibly the most spectacularly flavoursome whisky inspected by the Directory. It has everything, and in spades.

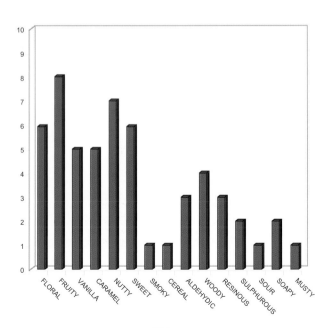

# GLENLOSSIE
# 17 YEAR OLD:
# ADELPHI BOTTLING

103

TYPE: single malt, private
     bottling
STRENGTH: 59% ABV
AGE IN CASK: 17 years
OWNERS: Adelphi Distillery
     Ltd
RATING: ****

A VERY TASTY OFFERING FROM ANOTHER PRIVATE BOTTLER KNOWN for the quality of his casks. It is astonishingly woody for a 17 year old, showing what high levels of flavour are to be got from active casks.

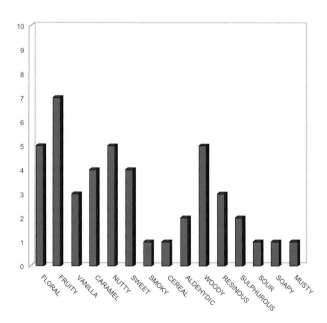

# GLENMORANGIE
# 10 YEAR OLD

TYPE: single malt
STRENGTH: 43% ABV
AGE IN CASK: 10 years
OWNERS: Glenmorangie plc
RATING: ****

GLENMORANGIE'S PRINCIPAL BRANDED MALT AND ALSO ITS cheapest. It is so good that we take it for granted, and the owners find it difficult to produce profit-generating variants which are any improvement. A standard by which other whiskies of the sort – ethereal malt matured in fresh bourbon casks – are to be judged.

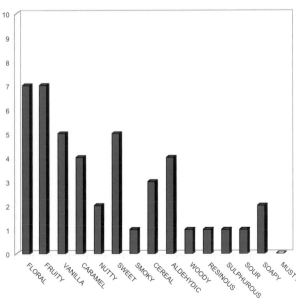

# GLENMORANGIE
# 15 YEAR OLD

TYPE: single malt
STRENGTH: 43% ABV
AGE IN CASK: 15 years
OWNERS: Glenmorangie plc
RATING: ****

A VERY GOOD MALT WHICH IN OTHER COMPANY WOULD STAND OUT;
it suffers alas by the comparison with its younger sibling,
for though quite delicious, it does not achieve the peaks of
flavour of the 10 year old.

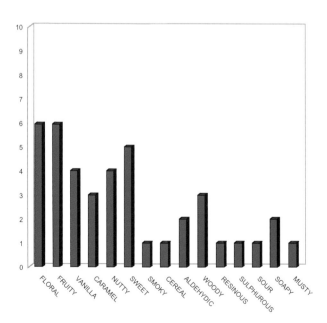

# GLENMORANGIE
# 18 YEAR OLD

TYPE: single malt
STRENGTH: 43% ABV
AGE IN CASK: 18 years
OWNERS: Glenmorangie plc
RATING: ***

CURIOUSLY, THE FLAVOUR LEVELS IN GLENMORANGIE APPEAR TO diminish with age. This is no great shakes as a malt and certainly nothing like as good as it was eight years earlier.

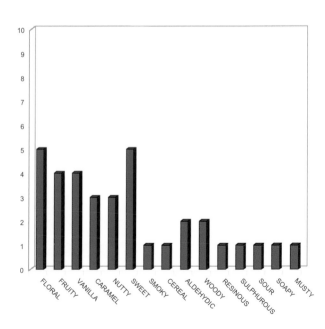

# GLENMORANGIE MADEIRA WOOD FINISH

MADEIRA WOOD FINISH

**GLENMORANGIE**

SINGLE HIGHLAND MALT SCOTCH WHISKY

ESTABLISHED IN 1843    PRODUCE OF SCOTLAND

*Handcrafted by the Sixteen Men of Tain*

*The* GLENMORANGIE
DISTILLERY COY. TAIN, ROSS-SHIRE
BOTTLED IN SCOTLAND

70cl ℮    43% Vol.

TYPE: single malt, cask
        finished
STRENGTH: 43% ABV
AGE IN CASK: not stated
OWNERS: Glenmorangie plc
RATING: ***

GLENMORANGIE WERE THE ORIGINATORS OF CASK FINISHES. HAVING
lots of really fine bourbon-cask whisky, some years ago they
tried putting the 10 year old in different sorts of casks for a
few years. On the evidence of this, though it is a good enough
whisky, the Madeira casks were not an improvement.

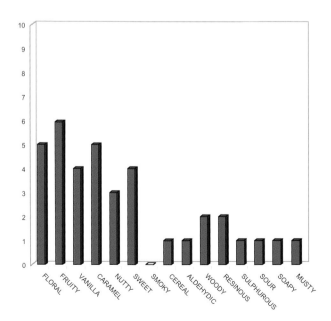

# GLENMORANGIE
# PORT WOOD FINISH

TYPE: single malt, cask
    finished
STRENGTH: 43% ABV
AGE IN CASK: not stated
OWNERS: Glenmorangie plc
RATING: ****

THE PORT CASKS, ON THE OTHER HAND, WERE A HUGE SUCCESS.
To begin with, the whisky wasn't all it might be, but the
term in port wood was judged nicely and the outcome is a
fruity, floral whisky, still recognisable as Glenmorangie, but
with exotic additions.

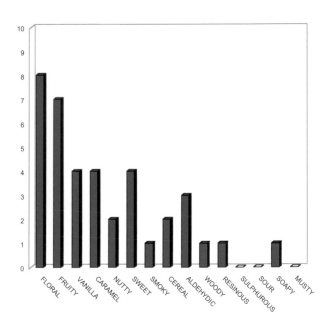

# GLENMORANGIE SHERRY WOOD FINISH

| TYPE: single malt, cask finished |
| --- |
| STRENGTH: 43% ABV |
| AGE IN CASK: not stated |
| OWNERS: Glenmorangie plc |
| RATING: *** |

THE SHERRY CASK FINISH IS MUCH LESS SUCCESSFUL THAN THE port. Poor levels of desirable flavour and insufficient to support the leathery aldehyde aroma.

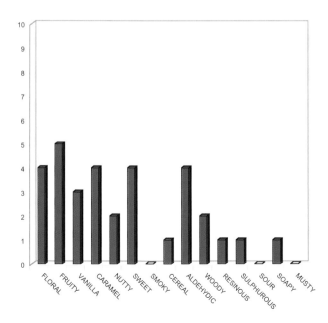

# GLEN MORAY
# CHARDONNAY

TYPE: single malt, cask
    finished
STRENGTH: 40% ABV
AGE IN CASK: not stated
OWNERS: Glenmorangie plc
RATING: **

GLENMORANGIE OWN THE GLEN MORAY DISTILLERY, WHICH PRODUCES
a good, if unremarkable, malt. Since other companies had
copied their finishing experiments, they decided to do
something different with the Glen Moray. Casks of unfortified
wines were used as finishes, with the result which you can see
– and taste, if you have a mind. Given the flavour profile, it is
an experiment you are unlikely to wish to repeat.

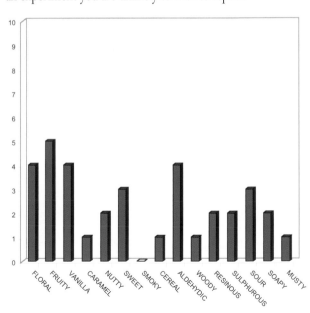

# GLEN MORAY WINE CASK 16 YEAR OLD

TYPE: single malt, cask finished
STRENGTH: 40% ABV
AGE IN CASK: 16 years
OWNERS: Glenmorangie plc
RATING: ***

70cl ℮   AGED   **16**   YEARS   40% vol

*A well-rounded Speyside Malt matured in oak casks and further mellowed in Chenin Blanc white wine barrels for a unique dry taste.*

THIS IS EVIDENTLY OLDER THAN THE CHARDONNAY, THOUGH THE type of wine is not specified. It is an improvement on the Chardonnay, though whether on a simple Glen Moray in a decent bourbon cask is doubtful.

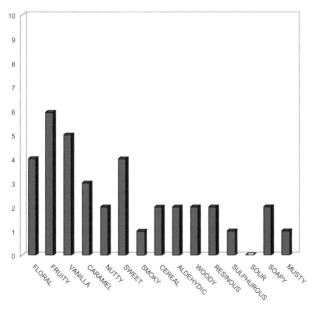

# GLEN ORD

TYPE: single malt
STRENGTH: 40% ABV
AGE IN CASK: 12 years
OWNERS: United Distillers
        & Vintners Ltd
RATING: ****

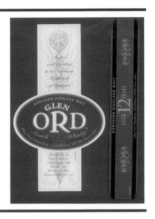

HIGH-QUALITY HIGHLAND MALT: LOTS OF FLAVOUR IN THE RIGHT places, interest as well as delight and very low levels of undesirables.

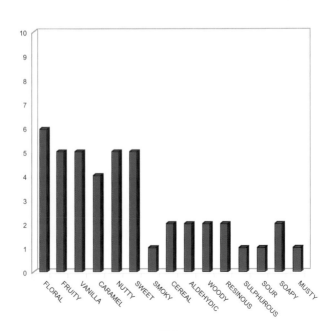

# GLENROTHES 1987

TYPE: single malt
STRENGTH: 43% ABV
AGE IN CASK: 13 years
OWNERS: Berry Bros &
Rudd Ltd
RATING: ***

THIS IS A VERY DRINKABLE 13-YEAR-OLD MALT. ITS OWNERS presumably attach some significance to the year of production, which they state on the label, though what that may be is hard to say. It's a great bottle, though: short and round, with a dimple in the bottom. Worth buying for the bottle alone.

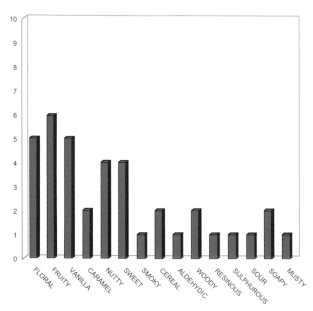

# GLEN SCOTIA

TYPE: single malt
STRENGTH: 40% ABV
AGE IN CASK: not stated
OWNERS: Glen Catrine
        Bonded
        Warehouse Ltd
RATING: ***

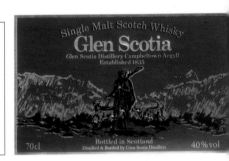

A CAMPBELTOWN WHISKY, FROM THE REVITALISED DISTILLERY OF the same name. The flavour does not contain any suggestion of its origin. A good if unexceptional malt.

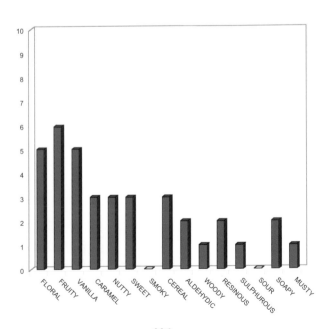

# GLEN SHIRA

TYPE: single malt
STRENGTH: 40% ABV
AGE IN CASK: not stated
OWNERS: Burn Stewart plc
RATING: ****

A SINGLE MALT WHOSE PROVENANCE IS NOT DISCLOSED. LOTS OF flavour and all of it good, with balance and depth. Worth treating with care and a bargain at the price.

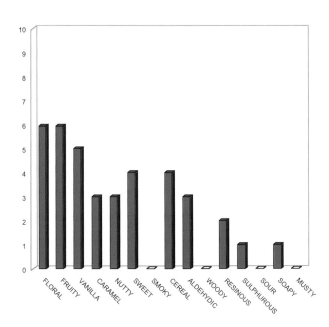

# GLENTURRET
# 12 YEAR OLD

TYPE: single malt
STRENGTH: 40% ABV
AGE IN CASK: 12 years
OWNERS: The Edrington
       Group Ltd
RATING: *

A VERY POOR PROFILE FOR SUCH AN IMPORTANT MALT WHISKY. Some sweetness, but little else of the left (and better) side of the profile; the aldehydes are too prominent and its soapy underwear is left open to view. Nothing like as good as The Famous Grouse of which it is an important component.

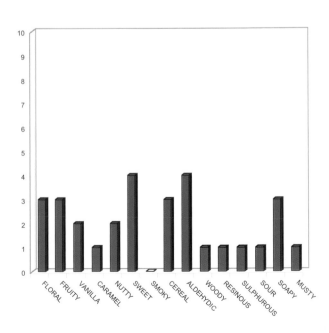

# GLENTURRET
# 15 YEAR OLD

TYPE: single malt
STRENGTH: 40% ABV
AGE IN CASK: 15 years
OWNERS: The Edrington
        Group Ltd
RATING: ****

MORE AGE BRINGS MORE FLAVOUR, AS ONE MIGHT EXPECT – BUT oddly assorted flavours: sweet and fruity, but otherwise somewhat lacking in variety. It just scrapes into the four-star category.

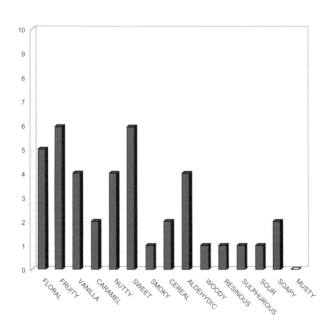

# GLENTURRET
# 18 YEAR OLD

TYPE: single malt
STRENGTH: 40% ABV
AGE IN CASK: 18 years
OWNERS: The Edrington
        Group Ltd
RATING: ***

HOWEVER WE MAY WISH TO BE KIND (REMEMBER THIS IS THE SAME company that makes The Famous Grouse), it has to be said that this is a poor performance for an 18 year old. There are lots of standard blended whiskies in the Directory which have a better profile than that which is shown here.

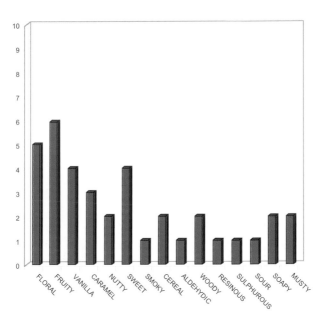

# GLENURY 20 YEAR OLD: DOUGLAS LAING BOTTLING

TYPE: single malt, single cask, private bottling
STRENGTH: 50% ABV
AGE IN CASK: 20 years
OWNERS: Douglas Laing & Co. Ltd
RATING: ****

THIS WHISKY HAS HAD A MERE TWO YEARS MORE IN CASK THAN ITS immediate predecessor in the Directory, but observe the difference: lots more fruit, caramel, nuts and sweetness; wildly woody and as sulphurous as the vents of a volcano. Whether it's a good whisky (it's not, unless you like them funky) is another matter, but at least it has lots of character.

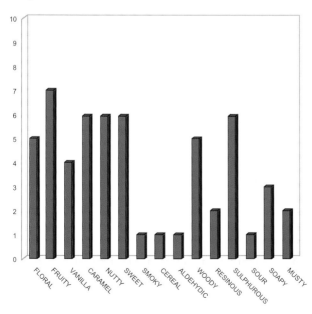

# HAIG GOLD LABEL

TYPE: standard blend
STRENGTH: 40% ABV
AGE IN CASK: not stated
OWNERS: United Distillers
& Vintners Ltd
RATING: ****

A LONG-ESTABLISHED BLENDED WHISKY BEARING A FAMOUS NAME. It is modestly classed as a standard blend – but compare it with the 18-year-old Glenturret, which sells for several times the price. You have to admit that UDV can turn out some good blended whiskies.

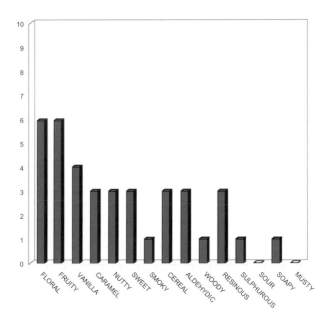

# HANKEY BANNISTER 12 YEAR OLD

TYPE: premium blend
STRENGTH: 40% ABV
AGE IN CASK: 12 years
OWNERS: Inver House
        Distillers Ltd
RATING: ***

THE USE OF AGED MALTS GIVES THIS A BETTER PROFILE THAN ITS standard stablemate: the slope of the profile is characteristic of a very good traditional whisky.

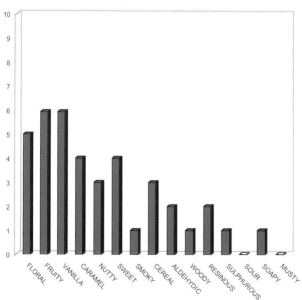

# HANKEY BANNISTER FINEST

TYPE: standard blend
STRENGTH: 40% ABV
AGE IN CASK: not stated
OWNERS: Inver House
          Distillers Ltd
RATING: ***

ANOTHER GOOD STANDARD BLEND, THIS TIME FROM INVER HOUSE.
A respectable cross-section of flavours, strong on the nice
and weak on the not-so-nice, as it should be.

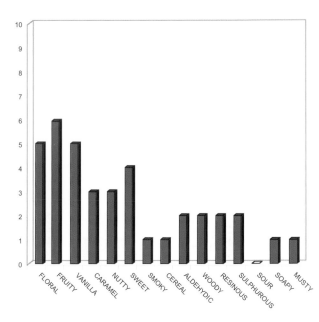

# HEDGES & BUTLER

TYPE: standard blend
STRENGTH: 40% ABV
AGE IN CASK: not stated
OWNERS: P. J. Russell & Co.
Ltd
RATING: ***

A STANDARD BLEND, INGENIOUSLY TITLED, FROM A WELL-KNOWN bottler. It's a better blend than the more famous one to which its label bears more than a passing resemblance.

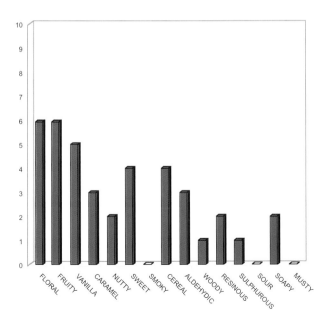

# HEDGES & BUTLER
# 8 YEAR OLD

TYPE: de luxe blend
STRENGTH: 40% ABV
AGE IN CASK: 8 years
OWNERS: P. J. Russell & Co.
      Ltd
RATING: **

INTENDED AS A HIGHER-QUALITY VERSION OF THE STANDARD blend, this, like so many others of its ilk, misses the mark. If you like H&B, stick to the cheaper whisky.

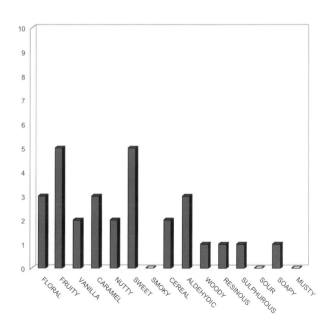

# HEDGES & BUTLER
# 12 YEAR OLD

**125**

TYPE: de luxe blend
STRENGTH: 40% ABV
AGE IN CASK: 12 years
OWNERS: P. J. Russell &
          Co. Ltd
RATING: ****

THE EXTRA AGE GIVES A BETTER PROFILE TO THE 12 YEAR OLD.
It is less striking than the youngest of the three, perhaps,
but more subtle.

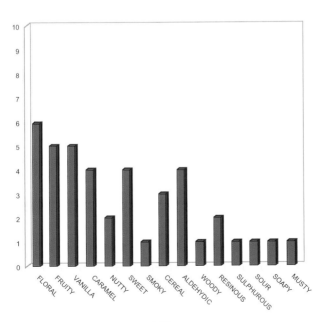

# HIGH COMMISSIONER

TYPE: standard blend
STRENGTH: 40% ABV
AGE IN CASK: not stated
OWNERS: Glen Catrine
        Bonded
        Warehouse Ltd
RATING: **

A CHEAP BLEND FROM GLEN CATRINE. IT'S NOT GREAT BUT IT'S NOT bad, and it's cheap. Nothing wrong with that.

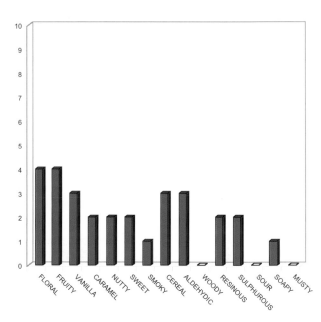

# HIGHLAND PARK
# 12 YEAR OLD

TYPE: single malt
STRENGTH: 40% ABV
AGE IN CASK: 12 years
OWNERS: The Edrington
Group Ltd
RATING: ***

NOW WE COME TO A VERY GREAT MALT. EVERYONE WHO KNOWS whisky knows how good Highland Park can be. By such a criterion, this is a disappointment. A good enough whisky: but good enough isn't good enough for something with the potential of Highland Park.

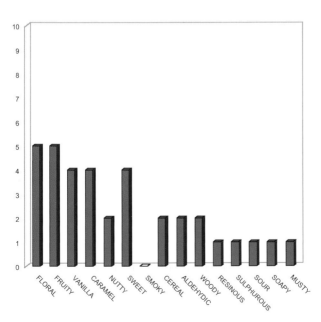

# HIGHLAND PARK
# 18 YEAR OLD

TYPE: single malt
STRENGTH: 43% ABV
AGE IN CASK: 18 years
OWNERS: The Edrington
          Group Ltd
RATING: ****

THIS IS APPROACHING EXPECTATIONS: LOTS OF FLAVOUR IN THE fruity-sweet spectrum. But whence the blast of mustiness which is in a fair way of spoiling it?

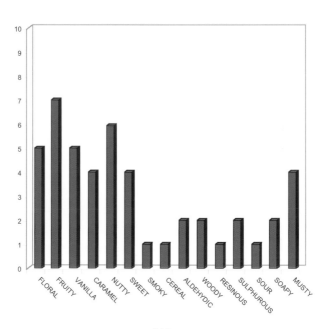

# HIGHLAND PARK
# 25 YEAR OLD

TYPE: single malt
STRENGTH: 53.5% ABV
AGE IN CASK: 25 years
OWNERS: The Edrington
           Group Ltd
RATING: ***

**IF ANYTHING, AN EVEN GREATER DISAPPOINTMENT. WHAT THERE IS,** is fine, but there isn't much of it. And why so little flavour after 25 years? We know that Highland Park is good whisky, so what's going on at Edrington? Is the Macallan getting all the best casks? If so, there should be fairer shares, for Highland Park is as good a spirit as Macallan any day.

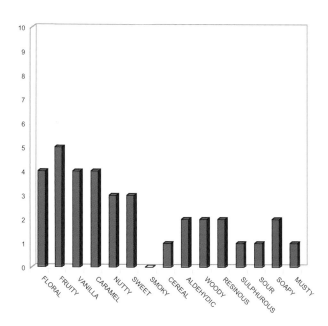

# HIGHLAND QUEEN

TYPE: standard blend
STRENGTH: 40% ABV
AGE IN CASK: not stated
OWNERS: Glenmorangie plc
RATING: ***

AN ANCIENT BRAND, NOW OWNED BY GLENMORANGIE PLC.
Evidently a pot into which goes a lot of fairly young whisky
from well-used wood. Not bad, though, and not expensive.
With a name like that, they should colour it pink and sell it
in San Francisco.

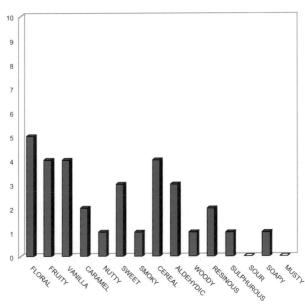

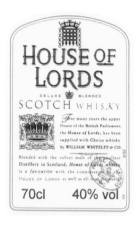

TYPE: standard blend
STRENGTH: 40% ABV
AGE IN CASK: not stated
OWNERS: Chivas Brothers
Ltd
RATING: ****

YET ANOTHER EXCELLENT BLEND FROM CHIVAS BROTHERS. LOTS of flavours in the right places, and subtle with it.

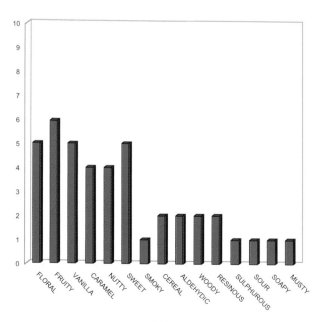

# HOUSE OF LORDS
# 12 YEAR OLD

TYPE: de luxe blend
STRENGTH: 40% ABV
AGE IN CASK: 12 years
OWNERS: Chivas Brothers
        Ltd
RATING: ***

AN AGED EXTENSION OF THE BLEND. AN OK WHISKY, BUT THE
result in terms of taste does not justify the use of aged spirit
on the part of the blender, or the parting with more money
on the part of the consumer.

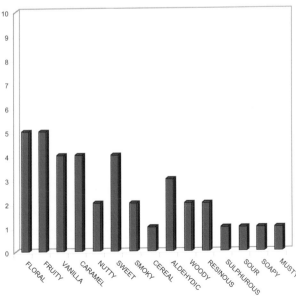

# INCHMURRIN
## 10 YEAR OLD

INCHMURRIN

SINGLE HIGHLAND MALT

SCOTCH WHISKY

Distilled by
THE LOCH LOMOND DISTILLERY
DUNBARTONSHIRE SCOTLAND

70cl℮        40%vol
PRODUCT OF SCOTLAND

TYPE: single malt
STRENGTH: 40% ABV
AGE IN CASK: 10 years
OWNERS: Glen Catrine
              Bonded
              Warehouse Ltd
RATING: **

A NOT-VERY-GOOD MALT FROM GLEN CATRINE. FLAVOUR SPECTRUM
patchy and loaded too much toward the soapy, musty end.

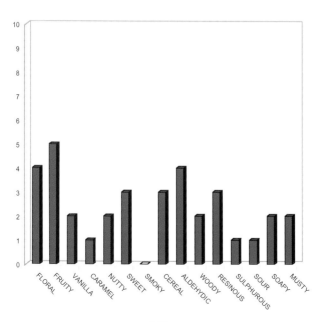

# INVERARITY

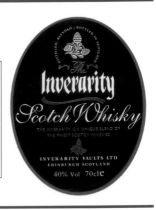

TYPE: standard blend
STRENGTH: 40% ABV
AGE IN CASK: not stated
OWNERS: Inverarity Vaults
    Ltd
RATING: ***

A VERY DECENT STANDARD BLEND FROM AN ENTERPRISING company. Adequate levels of flavour and the different flavours in a desirable relationship: what might be called well-balanced in the wine world.

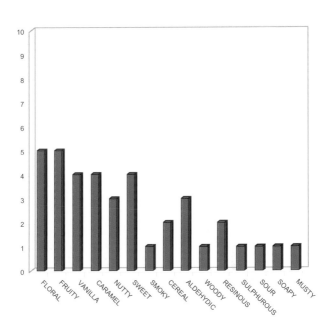

# INVERARITY SINGLE MALT 10 YEAR OLD

RARE SPEYSIDE
**Single Malt**
SCOTCH WHISKY

*The*

# Inverarity

*Aged* **10** *Years*

DISTILLED AND BOTTLED IN SCOTLAND

**INVERARITY VAULTS LTD**
**EDINBURGH SCOTLAND**

40% Vol 70cl℮

---

TYPE: single malt
STRENGTH: 40% ABV
AGE IN CASK: 10 years
OWNERS: Inverarity Vaults
                 Ltd
RATING: ***

---

A BIT COY, THIS: WE ARE TOLD IT IS A SINGLE MALT, BUT NOT where it's distilled – for there is no Inverarity distillery. Its source shouldn't be too hard to identify, though, for that flavour spectrum is pretty individual: its gaps showing like missing teeth. The whisky is like the curate's egg: good in parts.

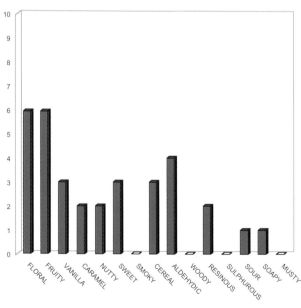

# INVERGORDON SINGLE GRAIN 10 YEAR OLD

TYPE: grain
STRENGTH: 40% ABV
AGE IN CASK: 10 years
OWNERS: Whyte & Mackay Ltd
RATING: ***

**THIS IS THE GRAIN BASE FOR ALL THE WHYTE & MACKAY BLENDS.**
One can see why those blends are so flavoursome, given a base of spirit which many malts would envy. Unusually, a grain whisky which is worth drinking by itself.

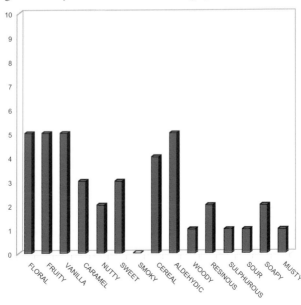

# INVER HOUSE GREEN PLAID

TYPE: standard blend
STRENGTH: 43% ABV
AGE IN CASK: not stated
OWNERS: Inver House
         Distillers Ltd
RATING: ***

A MORE-THAN-RESPECTABLE BLEND. INVER HOUSE CONTINUE TO distinguish themselves, for this is sold as a standard blend and priced accordingly.

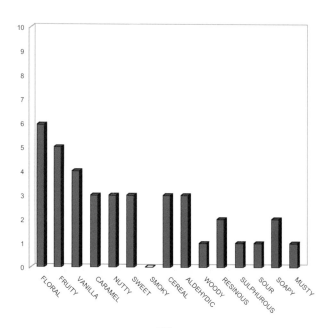

# INVER HOUSE GREEN PLAID 12 YEAR OLD

TYPE: de luxe blend
STRENGTH: 40% ABV
AGE IN CASK: 12 years
OWNERS: Inver House
       Distillers Ltd
RATING: ***

GREATER AGE HAS PRODUCED MORE FLAVOUR PEAKS AND therefore possibly more of interest. Certainly, it is easier to distinguish individual flavours, for they are less well-integrated than in the younger blend.

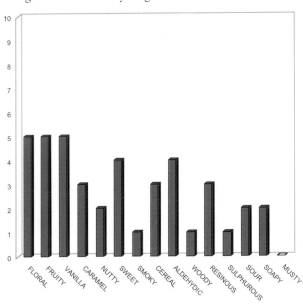

# INVERLEVEN 1985: GORDON & MACPHAIL BOTTLING

**139**

TYPE: single malt, private
bottling
STRENGTH: 40% ABV
AGE IN CASK: not stated
OWNERS: Gordon &
MacPhail Ltd
RATING: ***

ALTHOUGH THIS BOTTLING FROM ONE OF THE PRIVATE STOCKHOLDERS
has too many aromas in the soapy range of flavour to be top-
class, it shows sufficient of fruit and flowers on a leathery base
to be of considerable interest to the aficionado.

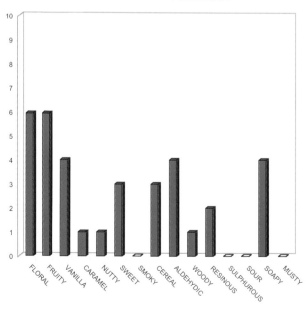

# ISLE OF SKYE
# 8 YEAR OLD

TYPE: premium blend
STRENGTH: 40% ABV
AGE IN CASK: 8 years
OWNERS: P. J. Russell & Co.
         Ltd
RATING: ****

A FAVOURITE TIPPLE IN BARS IN SCOTLAND, ISLE OF SKYE IS ONE OF the best whiskies, malt or blended, in its price and age range. Look at the flavour profile and compare it with a lot of much more expensive single malts and draw your own conclusions.

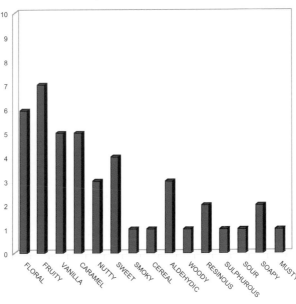

# ISLE OF SKYE
# 12 YEAR OLD

TYPE: premium blend
STRENGTH: 40% ABV
AGE IN CASK: 12 years
OWNERS: P. J. Russell & Co.
Ltd
RATING: ****

A VERY GOOD BLEND BY ANYONE'S STANDARDS, BUT SUFFERS BY comparison with its younger, more glamorous sibling. Age has mellowed and rounded the profile, so that it appeals to a different set of criteria.

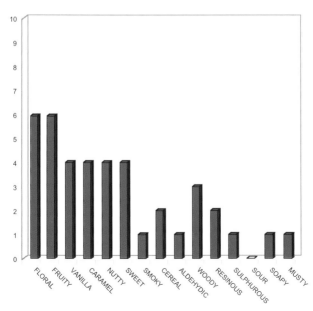

# ISLE OF SKYE
# 21 YEAR OLD

TYPE: premium blend
STRENGTH: 40% ABV
AGE IN CASK: 21 years
OWNERS: P. J. Russell & Co.
       Ltd
RATING: ****

IT CAN'T REALLY BE SAID THAT THIS IS AN IMPROVEMENT ON THE 8 or the 12 year old, though it is a good whisky for all that.

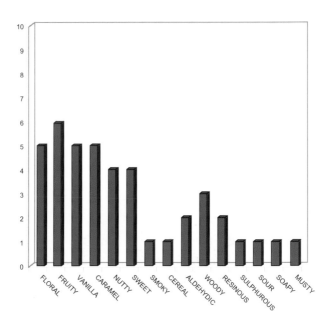

# JAMES MARTIN
# 8 YEAR OLD

JAMES MARTIN

JM

8 Years Old **Malt Scotch Whisky**

Distilled & Bottled in Scotland by James Martin Co. Ltd., Broxburn, EH18 2WU

TYPE: de luxe blend
STRENGTH: 40% ABV
AGE IN CASK: 8 years
OWNERS: Glenmorangie plc
RATING: ***

ANOTHER OF GLENMORANGIE'S FORAYS INTO THE WORLD OF DE luxe blends and not noticeably more successful than the others. While it is a perfectly OK whisky, you would think that, with their resources of great malt, they might come up with something better.

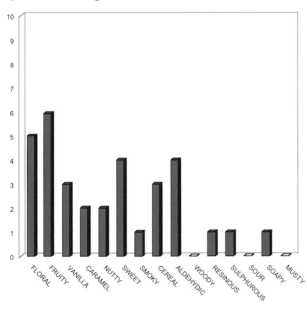

# J&B RARE

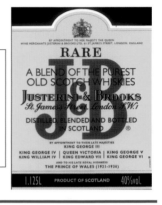

TYPE: premium blend
STRENGTH: 40% ABV
AGE IN CASK: not stated
OWNERS: United Distillers
         & Vintners Ltd
RATING: **

ITS OWNERS CLASS THIS AS A PREMIUM BLEND: CERTAINLY IT IS SO regarded by a huge number of drinkers around the globe. It has to be said that, while there is nothing amiss with it, there is little apparent in its flavour to warrant such a claim.

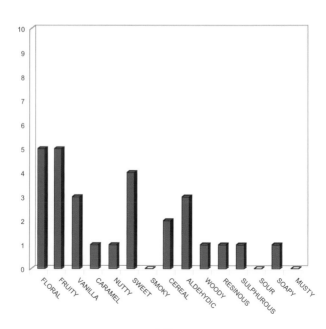

# J&B JET

145

TYPE: de luxe blend
STRENGTH: 43% ABV
AGE IN CASK: 12 years
OWNERS: United Distillers
           & Vintners Ltd
RATING: ***

THIS IS DESCRIBED AS A DE LUXE BLEND, SO PRESUMABLY IS intended to occupy a niche in the marketplace slightly more elevated than that allotted to its Rare compadre. On the evidence of its flavours, there is nothing to justify this.

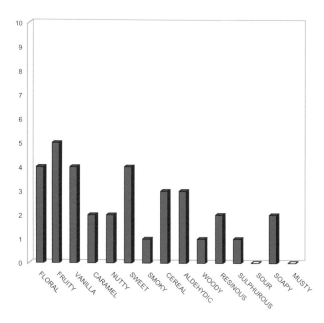

# J&B RESERVE

TYPE: de luxe blend
STRENGTH: 40% ABV
AGE IN CASK: 15 years
OWNERS: United Distillers
& Vintners Ltd
RATING: ****

THIS J&B DE LUXE BLEND IS AN ALTOGETHER MORE SUBSTANTIAL whisky than its stablemates. Hugely floral and fruity, it is both sweet and grassy, with plenty of background flavour as well. A very fine blend indeed.

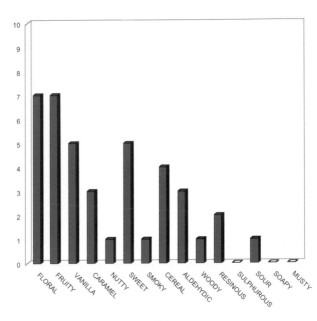

# J&B ULTIMA

TYPE: de luxe blend
STRENGTH: 43% ABV
AGE IN CASK: not stated
OWNERS: United Distillers
        & Vintners Ltd
RATING: ***

'ULTIMA' SUGGESTS PRETENSIONS OF A PRETTY HIGH ORDER.
While it's an OK whisky, it can't be said to live up to them,
nor to the J&B Reserve.

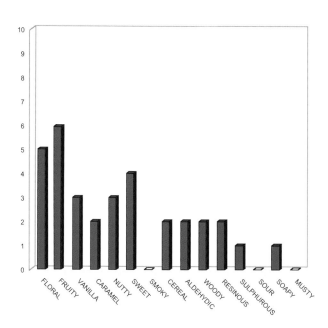

# JOHN BARR

TYPE: standard blend
STRENGTH: 40% ABV
AGE IN CASK: not stated
OWNERS: Whyte & Mackay Ltd
RATING: ****

ANOTHER GOOD, SOLID, STANDARD BLEND FROM WHYTE & MACKAY with plenty of pleasing flavours and low levels of the not-so-pleasing.

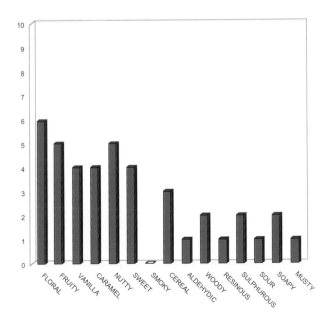

# JOHNNIE WALKER RED LABEL

TYPE: standard blend
STRENGTH: 40% ABV
AGE IN CASK: not stated
OWNERS: United Distillers
           & Vintners Ltd
RATING: ***

ONE OF THE WORLD'S BEST-SELLING WHISKIES, FOR WHICH THE world should be grateful, for it is better than the world deserves. A very good flavour profile for a standard blend: flowers and fruit, sweet flavours in plenty and enough cereal and resin to give body and variety.

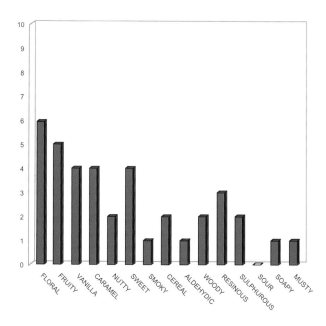

# JOHNNIE WALKER
# BLACK LABEL

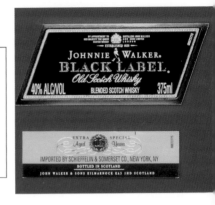

TYPE: de luxe blend
STRENGTH: 40% ABV
AGE IN CASK: not stated
OWNERS: United Distillers
        & Vintners Ltd
RATING: ****

A LAUDABLE EXTENSION OF THE BRAND INTO OLDER WHISKIES AND higher levels of flavour. More of everything and everything there. If you wish to see what a good blender can do, look at that profile.

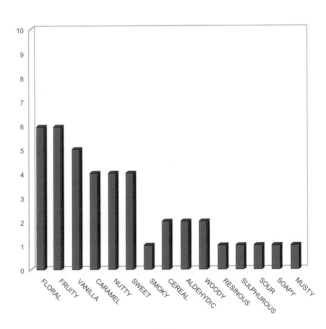

# JOHNNIE WALKER GOLD LABEL

| | |
|---|---|
| TYPE: de luxe blend |
| STRENGTH: 43% ABV |
| AGE IN CASK: not stated |
| OWNERS: United Distillers & Vintners Ltd |
| RATING: ***** |

A REALLY TOP-RATE WHISKY. PERHAPS IT DOES NOT MATCH SOME of the peaks of flavour of which some single malts are capable, but it has all the desirable flavours in high degree, which few malts ever achieve.

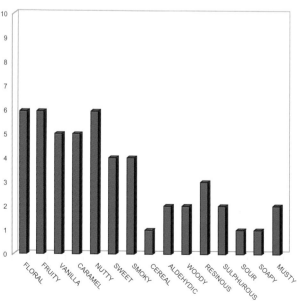

# JOHNNIE WALKER BLUE LABEL

JOHNNIE WALKER
**Blue Label**
A BLEND OF OUR VERY RAREST WHISKIES
BLENDED SCOTCH WHISKY,
DISTILLED, BLENDED & BOTTLED IN SCOTLAND.
JOHN WALKER & SONS, KILMARNOCK
KA3 1HD, SCOTLAND
40% vol     PRODUCT OF SCOTLAND     70cl ℮

TYPE: de luxe blend
STRENGTH: 40% ABV
AGE IN CASK: not stated
OWNERS: United Distillers & Vintners Ltd
RATING: **

SURPRISINGLY, GIVEN THE REST OF THE BRAND'S RANGE, THERE IS a falling-off with the Blue. Not a bad lot of flavours: just not what one would expect from the people who produced the other three in the range and definitely not what you would expect, given the top-end packaging and price.

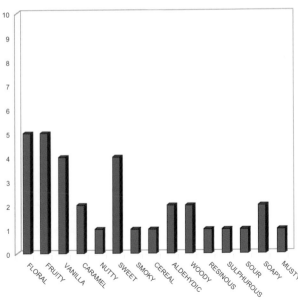

# JOHN PLAYER SPECIAL

TYPE: standard blend
STRENGTH: 40% ABV
AGE IN CASK: not stated
OWNERS: Douglas Laing &
         Co. Ltd
RATING: **

A STANDARD BLEND BY DOUGLAS LAING & CO., THE PRIVATE
bottlers. Not one of their best, for low levels of desirable
flavours have to cope with a number of undesirables whose
incidence is almost as great.

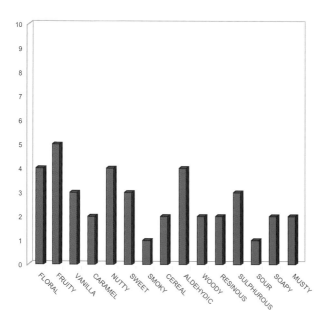

# JOHN PLAYER SPECIAL RARE

| | |
|---|---|
| TYPE: premium blend | |
| STRENGTH: 43% ABV | |
| AGE IN CASK: not stated | |
| OWNERS: Douglas Laing & Co. Ltd | |
| RATING: **** | |

A BIG IMPROVEMENT ON THE STANDARD BLEND OF THE SAME name. It is relatively high in fruitiness and low in almost everything else. This, combined with its vanilla-caramel-sweet nexus, makes for a much more satisfactory whisky than the Special.

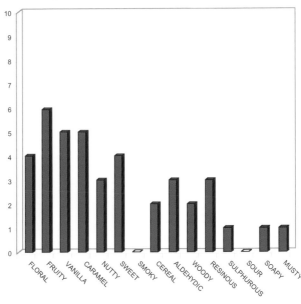

# JURA 10 YEAR OLD

TYPE: single malt
STRENGTH: 40% ABV
AGE IN CASK: 10 years
OWNERS: Whyte & Mackay
Ltd
RATING: **

JURA IS A BIT OF A MYSTERY. WHY WOULD ANYONE WHO MAKES AS good whisky as Whyte & Mackay do want to spend lots of money on promoting this pretty inferior malt? Not only is its flavour profile not up to that of other W&M malts and blends, it doesn't even approach the grain spirit from the same group. One suspects the unique location has proved too tempting for the marketing department.

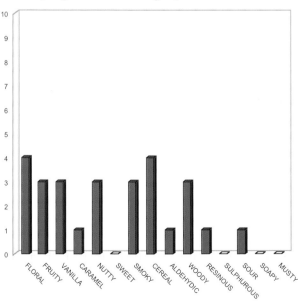

# KING OF SCOTS

TYPE: de luxe blend
STRENGTH: 40% ABV
AGE IN CASK: not stated
OWNERS: Douglas Laing &
         Co. Ltd
RATING: ****

ANOTHER DOUGLAS LAING DE LUXE BLEND: THEY REALLY PULL IT off this time. A spectacular profile heavily weighted toward the left-hand, best end of the spectrum. Lots of everything you might wish to have, and more besides. Deserves to be better known than it is. If you can find it, buy it.

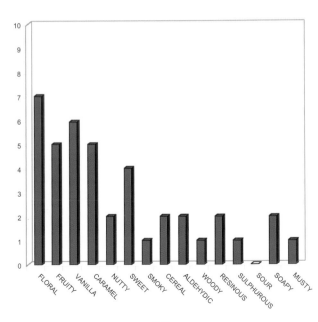

# KING OF SCOTS
# 25 YEAR OLD

The King of Scots

PRODUCT OF · SCOTLAND

700ml · 40% vol

**BLENDED
SCOTCH WHISKY**

DELUXE

DISTILLED, BLENDED & BOTTLED IN SCOTLAND · DOUGLAS LAING & CO LTD · GLASGOW G3 6EQ

TYPE: de luxe blend
STRENGTH: 40% ABV
AGE IN CASK: 25 years
OWNERS: Douglas Laing &
        Co. Ltd
RATING: *****

A TOTALLY AMAZING PROFILE. LOOK AT IT: HUGELY FLAVOURFUL AND all of it nice. Delicate and lovely and big and gutsy all at once. Our remarks about buying apply even more to this: it isn't dear for what it is.

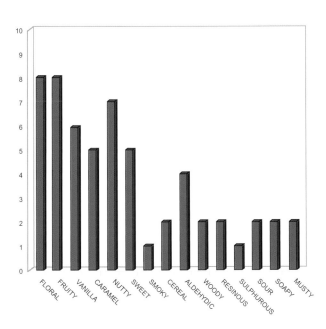

# KING ROBERT II

TYPE: standard blend
STRENGTH: 40% ABV
AGE IN CASK: not stated
OWNERS: P. J. Russell & Co.
Ltd
RATING: ***

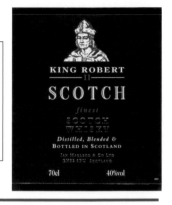

A DECENT ENOUGH STANDARD BLEND FROM P. J. RUSSELL. OK: NOT
a lot to say.

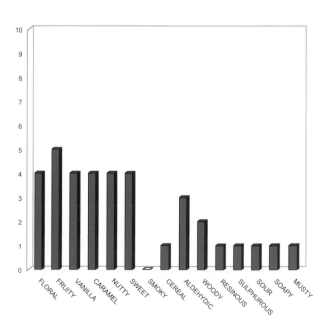

# KNOCKANDO 1986

TYPE: single malt
STRENGTH: 40% ABV
AGE IN CASK: 12 years
OWNERS: United Distillers
       & Vintners Ltd
RATING: ★★★★

A DECENT ENOUGH MALT, BUT NOTHING SPECIAL. NOT IN THE SAME league from the same company which precede it in the Directory. Malt buffs take note.

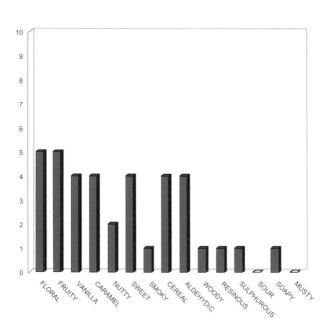

# LAGAVULIN
# 16 YEAR OLD

LAGAVULIN
SINGLE ISLAY MALT WHISKY
16
SCOTCH WHISKY

| TYPE: single malt |
| --- |
| STRENGTH: 43% ABV |
| AGE IN CASK: 16 years |
| OWNERS: United Distillers & Vintners Ltd |
| RATING: *** |

THE ISLAY REPRESENTATIVE OF THE CLASSIC SIX. AS YOU CAN SEE from the profile, it has lots of peat and lots of fruit and not a lot of anything else, which makes it a bit two-dimensional and lacking in substance.

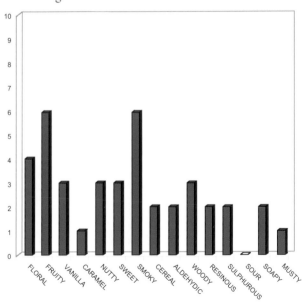

# LANGS SUPREME

161

TYPE: standard blend
STRENGTH: 40% ABV
AGE IN CASK: 5 years
OWNERS: P. J. Russell & Co.
           Ltd
RATING: **

RUN-OF-THE-MILL BLENDED WHISKY. NOT BAD STUFF, AND NOT expensive.

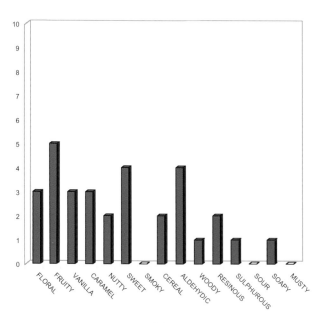

273

# LAPHROAIG
## 10 YEAR OLD

TYPE: single malt
STRENGTH: 43% ABV
AGE IN CASK: 10 years
OWNERS: Allied Distillers
        Ltd
RATING: ***

**LAPHROAIG®**

SINGLE ISLAY MALT
SCOTCH WHISKY

**10**
*Years Old*

The most richly flavoured of
all Scotch whiskies

ESTABLISHED
**1815**

DISTILLED AND BOTTLED IN SCOTLAND BY
D. JOHNSTON & CO., (LAPHROAIG), LAPHROAIG DISTILLERY, ISLE OF ISLAY.

1.14 litre ℮       43% vol
                                 L00719

PRODIGIOUSLY PHENOLIC, THE SPIRIT SHOWS A BIT OF FRUIT BUT not a lot of flavour otherwise – which is surprising, given that its owners have made it their only heavily peated brand, having sold off the rather superior Ardbeg some years ago. The soapy flavours which the profile shows are usually, but not always, obscured by the smoke.

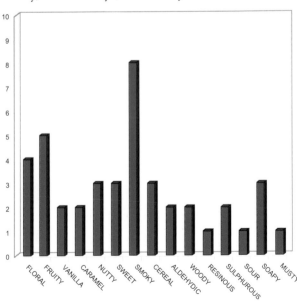

# LAPHROAIG CASK STRENGTH

TYPE: single malt
STRENGTH: 57.3% ABV
AGE IN CASK: 10 years
OWNERS: Allied Distillers
Ltd
RATING: ****

A BETTER FLAVOUR PROFILE ALTOGETHER. THE ABSENCE OF chillfiltration accounts for some of the improvement but does not explain the altered shape of the profile. Presumably Allied Distillers select better casks for the cask strength bottling. Certainly a much better whisky than the straight 10 year old.

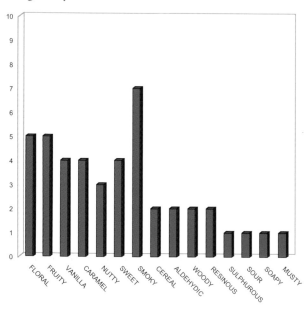

# LEAPFROG 12 YEAR OLD: MURRAY McDAVID BOTTLING

TYPE: single malt, private
    bottling
STRENGTH: 46% ABV
AGE IN CASK: 12 years
OWNERS: Murray McDavid
    Ltd
RATING: ***

THE NAME IS THE PRIVATE BOTTLER'S AMUSING WAY OF AVOIDING infringing Allied Distillers' trademark while bottling their spirit. The whisky isn't as superior as one might expect from an independent who can be selective about the casks he chooses for a small bottling run.

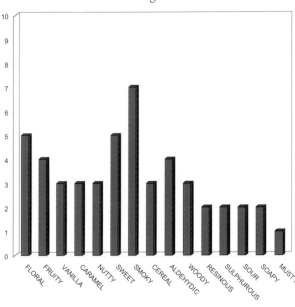

# LEDAIG
# 15 YEAR OLD

**LEDAIG**

SINGLE MALT
SCOTCH WHISKY

FROM

THE ISLE OF MULL

*aged*

*Aged 15 years*

This rare old single malt Scotch whisky
was distilled at the Ledaig Distillery
on the Isle of Mull by
Ledaig Distillers (Tobermory) Ltd.

PRODUCE OF SCOTLAND

TYPE: single malt
STRENGTH: 43% ABV
AGE IN CASK: 15 years
OWNERS: Burn Stewart
        Distillers plc
RATING: ✱✱✱

THE WHISKY SHOWS SMOKY TO A SURPRISING DEGREE. NOT A LOT of flavour otherwise, for a single malt. Better things are to be expected of this distillery in future since, after decades of haphazard operation, it is now under Burn Stewart stewardship.

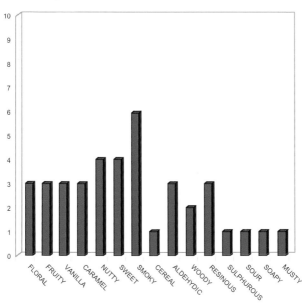

# LEDAIG
# 20 YEAR OLD

TYPE: single malt
STRENGTH: 43% ABV
AGE IN CASK: 20 years
OWNERS: Burn Stewart
        Distillers plc
RATING: *****

VERY DIFFERENT FROM ITS YOUNGER FELLOW. LOTS OF FLORAL
fruitiness and nutty caramel flavour, but not too sweet.
Cereals and aldehydics add substantially to the flavour base
to make for a perfectly delicious whisky.

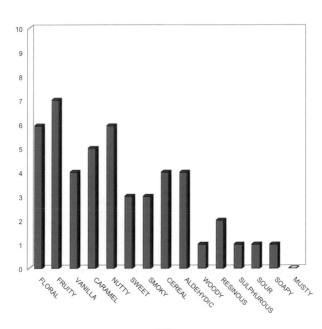

# LINKWOOD 1988: SIGNATORY BOTTLING

SIGNATORY
VINTAGE

Vintage 1988
Single Highland Malt Scotch Whisky

**Distilled at Linkwood Distillery**
on 31st May 1988

70CL    Matured in a sherry butt for 12 years    43% VOL
Bottled on 10th January 2001    Natural Colour
Butt No. 2791 · Bottle No.    of 992
This whisky has been selected, produced and bottled in Scotland for and under the sole responsibility of
Signatory Vintage Scotch Whisky Co. Ltd, Edinburgh EH6 5PY Scotland.

---

TYPE: single malt, private bottling
STRENGTH: 43% ABV
AGE IN CASK: 12 years
OWNERS: Signatory Vintage Scotch Whisky Co. Ltd
RATING: ***

---

A GOOD MALT IN AN INDEPENDENT BOTTLING: AT 12 YEARS OLD, IT is quite mature and shows a decent spectrum of flavours, though nothing out of the ordinary. It bears its year of distillation on the label, as though it mattered.

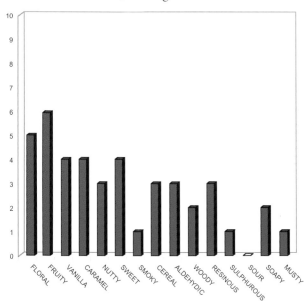

# LINKWOOD
# 17 YEAR OLD:
# ADELPHI BOTTLING

TYPE: single malt, private
bottling
STRENGTH: 64.2% ABV
AGE IN CASK: 17 years
OWNERS: Adelphi Distillery
Ltd
RATING: *****

the
**Directory**
regrets that
it was unable
to reproduce
this label

A TOTALLY SPECTACULAR SET OF FLAVOUR BARS IN THIS
Linkwood. Adelphi really can pick them. This shows just
how great is the influence of the individual cask in
producing the flavours of a mature whisky.

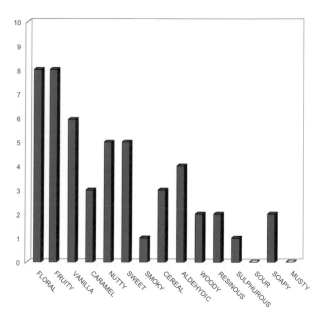

# LISMORE FINEST

LISMORE

*F I N E S T*

70cle BLENDED SCOTCH WHISKY 40%vol

---

TYPE: standard blend
STRENGTH: 40% ABV
AGE IN CASK: not stated
OWNERS: Wm Lundie & Co. Ltd
RATING: ****

---

A VERY GOOD STANDARD BLEND FROM WILLIAM LUNDIE.
Excellent flavours for the money and no faults at all.

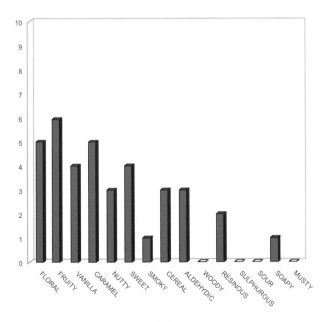

# LISMORE
# SPECIAL RESERVE
# 18 YEAR OLD

TYPE: de luxe blend
STRENGTH: 40% ABV
AGE IN CASK: 18 years
OWNERS: Wm Lundie & Co. Ltd
RATING: **

RATHER DISAPPOINTING, CONSIDERING IT IS MADE FROM OLDER whiskies and costs more than the standard blend from the same house.

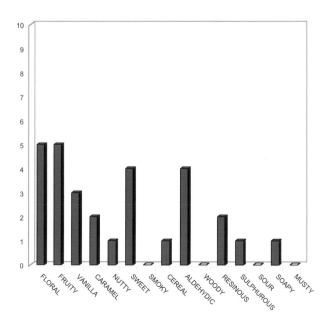

# LOCH FYNE

TYPE: premium blend
STRENGTH: 40% ABV
AGE IN CASK: not stated
OWNERS: Loch Fyne
        Whiskies Ltd
RATING: ***

A RESPECTABLE BLEND PRODUCED FOR THE WELL-KNOWN LOCH
Fyne retailer. Predominantly sweet: vanilla and caramel on
a fruity base. And not dear, either.

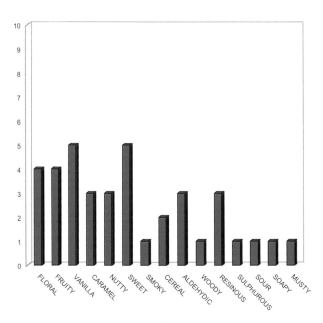

# LOCH LOMOND

TYPE: single malt
STRENGTH: 40% ABV
AGE IN CASK: not stated
OWNERS: Glen Catrine
            Bonded
            Warehouse Ltd
RATING: **

A NOT VERY INSPIRED SET OF FLAVOURS FOR A SINGLE MALT. ON this showing, it would be better used for blending than for drinking on its own.

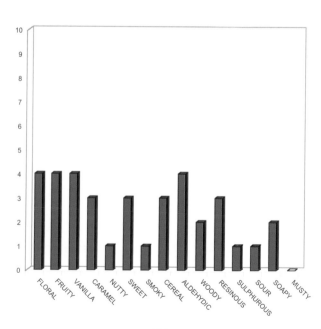

# LOCH RANZA

TYPE: premium blend
STRENGTH: 40% ABV
AGE IN CASK: not stated
OWNERS: Isle of Arran
          Distillers Ltd
RATING: ****

A VERY GOOD BLEND FROM THE FOLK WHO OPENED THE NEW distillery on Arran. Until their Arran malt reaches maturity, this is certainly good enough to be going on with.

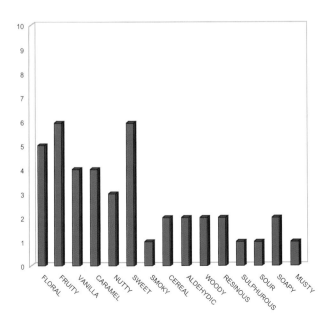

# LOCHSIDE
# 9 YEAR OLD:
# MURRAY McDAVID
# BOTTLING

TYPE: single malt, private
　　　bottling
STRENGTH: 46% ABV
AGE IN CASK: 9 years
OWNERS: Murray McDavid
　　　Ltd
RATING: ***

THE LOCHSIDE COMES OVER AS CONSISTENTLY FLORAL AND
fruity, even when bottled relatively young. The rest of the
flavours are a bit more patchy, though, when compared
with the older whisky from the same distillery.

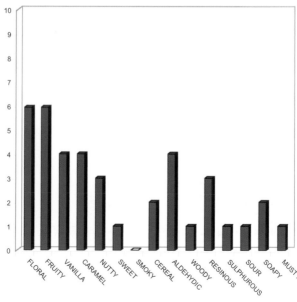

# LOCHSIDE 19 YEAR OLD: CADENHEAD BOTTLING

TYPE: single malt, single cask, private bottling
STRENGTH: 60.9% ABV
AGE IN CASK: 19 years
OWNERS: Cadenhead's
RATING: ****

FROM THE LONG-DEFUNCT MONTROSE DISTILLERY, THIS MALT HAS lots of flowery and fruity aromas. It shows itself to the palate sweetly toffee-like, against a solid background of the lesser aromas, with some evidence of age.

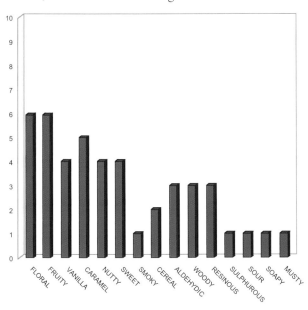

# LONG JOHN

TYPE: standard blend
STRENGTH: 40% ABV
AGE IN CASK: not stated
OWNERS: Allied Distillers
        Ltd
RATING: ****

AN ALLIED DISTILLERS STANDARD BLEND WITH NO AGE STATEMENT, this nevertheless exhibits a satisfactory slope of flavours. Good value for money.

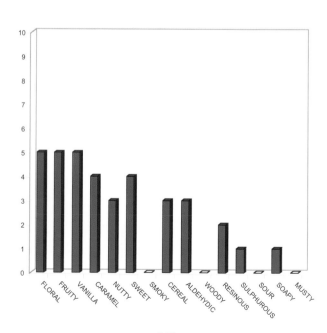

# LONGMORN
## 15 YEAR OLD

177

| | |
|---|---|
| TYPE: | single malt |
| STRENGTH: | 45% ABV |
| AGE IN CASK: | 15 years |
| OWNERS: | Chivas Brothers Ltd |
| RATING: | *** |

IT IS TO BE HOPED THAT CHIVAS BROTHERS, IN WHOSE PARISH THE Longmorn now lies, will take it in hand and produce a better bottled malt than this. Not that it's bad, simply that the Directory knows it could be a lot better.

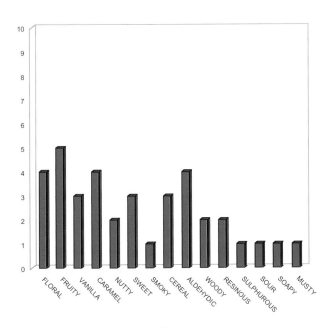

# LONGROW
# 10 YEAR OLD
# BOURBONWOOD

TYPE: single malt
STRENGTH: 46% ABV
AGE IN CASK: 10 years
OWNERS: Springbank
      Distillery Co. Ltd
RATING: ****

THE BOURBON CASK MATURATION PRODUCES A MORE CONSISTENT pattern of flavour than the sherry. More of everything except fruity flavours and altogether the more rounded of the two whiskies.

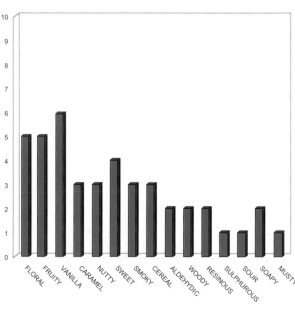

# LONGROW
# 10 YEAR OLD
# SHERRYWOOD

TYPE: single malt
STRENGTH: 46% ABV
AGE IN CASK: 10 years
OWNERS: Springbank
          Distillery Co. Ltd
RATING: ***

THE SHERRY-CASK WHISKY IS VERY STRONG ON FRUITY FLAVOURS, floral, moderately sweet and tasting of vanilla. Some aldehydic aromas, too. A good whisky but not overall as satisfactory as the bourbon-cask maturation.

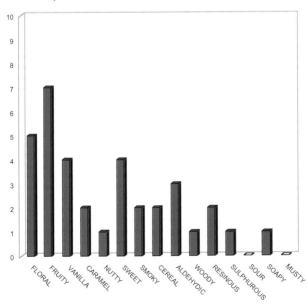

# MACALLAN
# 10 YEAR OLD

TYPE: single malt
STRENGTH: 40% ABV
AGE IN CASK: 10 years
OWNERS: Highland Distillers
Ltd
RATING: ***

THE CLASSIC MACALLAN AND A BENCHMARK FOR WELL-MADE whisky matured in sherry wood. The quality of the spirit derives more from the quality of its flavours than from their strength, hence the profile.

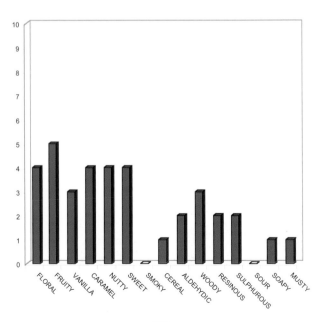

# MACALLAN
# 12 YEAR OLD

TYPE: single malt
STRENGTH: 40% ABV
AGE IN CASK: 12 years
OWNERS: Highland Distillers
              Ltd
RATING: ****

A CONSIDERABLE IMPROVEMENT ON THE 10 YEAR OLD AND, ALAS, not for sale in the UK. Macallan drinkers should petition the company for the repatriation of the 12 year old. All good flavours in the right sort of profile: high at the start, gradually declining.

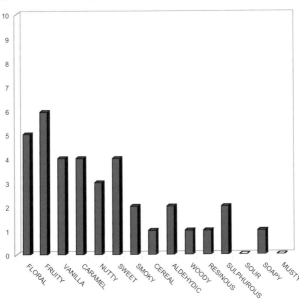

293

# MACALLAN
# 15 YEAR OLD

TYPE: single malt
STRENGTH: 43% ABV
AGE IN CASK: 15 years
OWNERS: Highland Distillers
      Ltd
RATING: ***

MACALLAN DOES WELL IN WOOD: THAT IS UNDENIABLE AND THIS flavour profile is evidence. Lots of fruits and nuts and sweetness, with a resinous, woody base and a touch of sulphur. The star rating does not do justice to its quality.

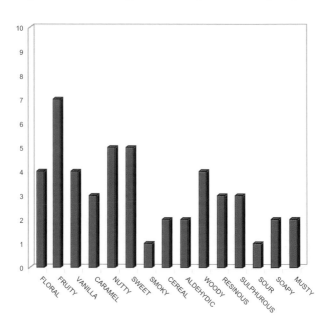

# MACALLAN
# 18 YEAR OLD 1982

TYPE: single malt
STRENGTH: 43% ABV
AGE IN CASK: 18 years
OWNERS: Highland Distillers
Ltd
RATING: ****

MORE AGE MEANS MORE OF THE SAME WITH THE EXCEPTION, curiously, of the sulphur-related aromas. An improvement on the 15 year old, though not necessarily on that account, for, with such levels of overall flavour, some sulphur is tolerable. Here only joys abound, and nuts.

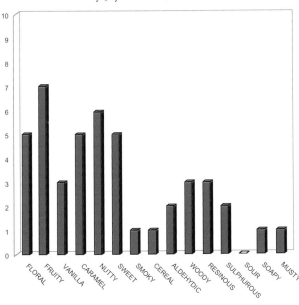

# MACALLAN
# 25 YEAR OLD

TYPE: single malt
STRENGTH: 43% ABV
AGE IN CASK: 25 years
OWNERS: Highland Distillers
Ltd
RATING: *****

SEVEN YEARS ON, WE SEE THE PATTERN MAINTAINED. THE WHISKY is just as fruity, if less floral, and with fewer nuts and more sweetness. Remarkably few woody flavours, given the great age of the whisky, and none of them offensive.

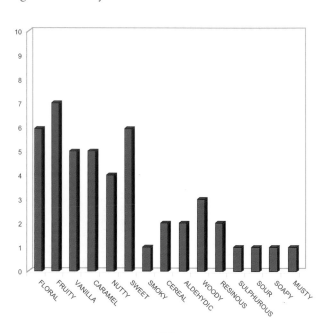

# MACALLAN
# 30 YEAR OLD

TYPE: single malt
STRENGTH: 40% ABV
AGE IN CASK: 30 years
OWNERS: Highland Distillers
           Ltd
RATING: ****

THE WHISKY IS NOW SERIOUSLY WOODY, RESINOUS AND sulphurous, but such flavours merely form a background for spectacularly high levels of fruitiness and nutty-caramel sweetness. One of the best old whiskies to be found.

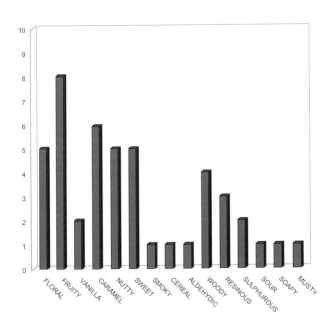

# 186
# MACALLAN
# 50 YEAR OLD 1949

TYPE: single malt
STRENGTH: 40% ABV
AGE IN CASK: 50 years
OWNERS: Highland Distillers
Ltd
RATING: ****

AT 50 YEARS OLD, MOST WHISKIES ARE WOODY AND BITTER. BY some strange alchemy, this is not true of the oldest Macallans. The flavour profile of the 50 year old shows quite low levels of woodiness, though most of the later flavours of the spectrum are substantially present.

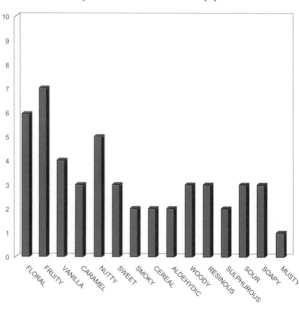

# MACALLAN
# GRAN RESERVA

| TYPE: single malt |
| STRENGTH: 40% ABV |
| AGE IN CASK: 18 years |
| OWNERS: Highland Distillers Ltd |
| RATING: ***** |

ANOTHER BOTTLING OF 18 YEAR OLD, WITH A SPANISH NAME TO distinguish it from the already distinguished 18 year old. Prodigiously fruity, it has a somewhat similar profile to the latter, but with more of a vanilla flavour.

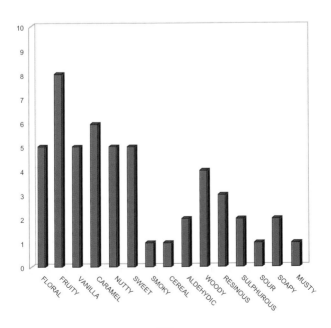

# 188

# MACARTHUR'S
# 12 YEAR OLD

TYPE: de luxe blend
STRENGTH: 40% ABV
AGE IN CASK: 12 years
OWNERS: Inver House
           Distillers Ltd
RATING: **

AN AGED VERSION OF THE BLEND OF THE SAME NAME. CLASSED AS
de luxe but not discernibly more luxurious than its cheaper,
younger brother.

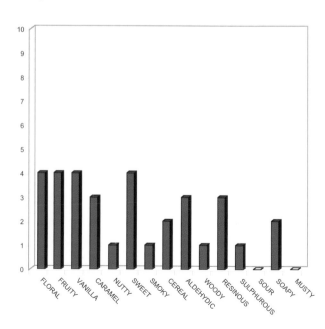

# MACARTHUR'S SELECT

TYPE: standard blend
STRENGTH: 40% ABV
AGE IN CASK: not stated
OWNERS: Inver House
          Distillers Ltd
RATING: ***

A STANDARD BLEND FROM INVER HOUSE. NOT AT ALL BAD, drinkable and inexpensive.

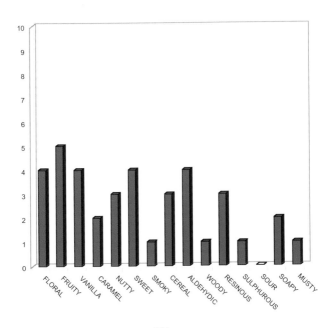

# MACDONALDS GLENCOE 8 YEAR OLD

TYPE: vatted malt
STRENGTH: 58% ABV
AGE IN CASK: 8 years
OWNERS: Ben Nevis
       Distillery (Fort
       William) Ltd
rating: ****

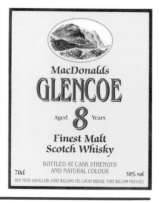

A VATTED MALT FROM BEN NEVIS DISTILLERY, SO PRESUMABLY
containing mostly Ben Nevis malt. Bottled at full strength.
A very tasty malt indeed and one which may help to
redeem the reputation of vatted malts.

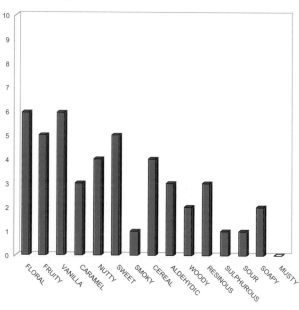

# MACLEOD'S SINGLE MALT HIGHLAND

TYPE: single malt, private
      bottling
STRENGTH: 40% ABV
AGE IN CASK: 8 years
OWNERS: P. J. Russell & Co.
      Ltd
RATING: **

THE FLAVOUR PROFILE OF THIS IS UNLIKELY TO HELP ANYONE
guess its distillery of origin. Low levels of flavour, as one
would expect of a youngish malt, but no serious defects
either.

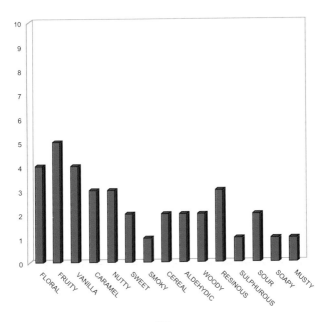

# MACLEOD'S SINGLE MALT ISLAND

TYPE: single malt, private
bottling
STRENGTH: 40% ABV
AGE IN CASK: 8 years
OWNERS: P. J. Russell & Co.
Ltd
RATING: ***

THE PRESENCE OF SMOKE-DERIVED FLAVOURS IN MODERATE
degree narrows the choice of distilleries down, given that
this is such a young malt and that smokiness declines with
age. The other flavours match the smoky ones to make this
a very pleasant dram.

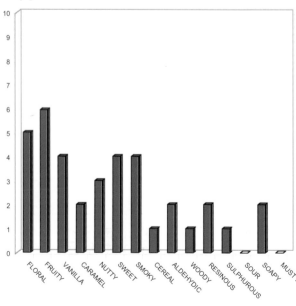

# MACLEOD'S SINGLE MALT LOWLAND

TYPE: single malt, private
     bottling
STRENGTH: 40% ABV
AGE IN CASK: 8 years
OWNERS: P. J. Russell & Co.
     Ltd
RATING: ****

A SINGLE MALT OF UNSTATED PROVENANCE. NO TRACE AT ALL OF peating, which may provide a clue as to where it came from: there aren't all that many lowland distilleries, and those which use unpeated malt number exactly one.

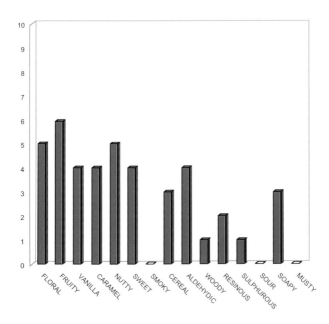

194

# MANNOCHMORE 1984 CONNOISSEURS CHOICE

TYPE: single malt, private
    bottling
STRENGTH: 40% ABV
AGE IN CASK: not stated
OWNERS: Gordon &
    MacPhail Ltd
RATING: ****

**CONNOISSEURS CHOICE**

*SPEYSIDE*
**Single Malt Scotch Whisky**

DISTILLED AT
**MANNOCHMORE**
DISTILLERY
Proprietors: John Haig & Co. Ltd.
DISTILLED
**1984**

Specially Selected, Produced and Bottled By
**Gordon & MacPhail**
Elgin . Scotland
Product of Scotland

70cl    40% vol

ANOTHER VINTAGE-DATED SINGLE MALT WITH NO AGE STATEMENT,
this time from the oldest of the private bottlers. The flavour
profile would suggest an oldish spirit, given the consistent
pattern of the flavour bars. Certainly a pleasant one to drink.

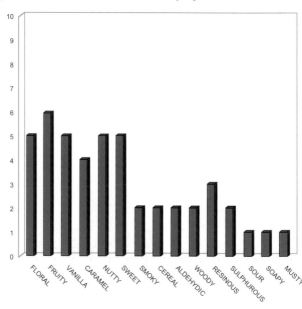

# McGIBBON'S
# SPECIAL RESERVE

TYPE: standard blend
STRENGTH: 40% ABV
AGE IN CASK: not stated
OWNERS: Douglas Laing &
          Co. Ltd
RATING: ***

A GOODISH STANDARD BLEND – AS WE HAVE COME TO EXPECT from Douglas Laing: the overall quality of the cheaper Scotch whiskies is probably better today than at any time in the last 500 years.

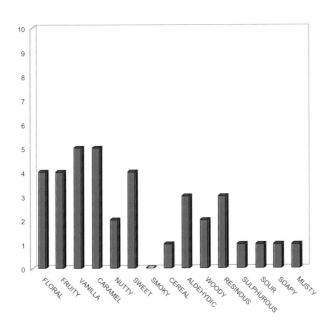

307

# MITCHELL'S
# 12 YEAR OLD

TYPE: de luxe blend
STRENGTH: 43% ABV
AGE IN CASK: 12 years
OWNERS: Springbank
           Distillery Co. Ltd
RATING: ****

A DE LUXE BLEND FROM THE OWNERS OF SPRINGBANK. A VERY FINE blend indeed, with lots of flavour and interest, reflecting the use of the Springbank malt in the blend. But well made, as well as having the advantage of a fine malt.

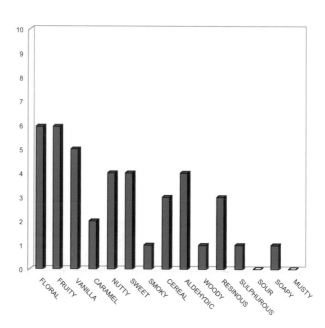

# MOSSTOWIE 29 YEAR OLD: CADENHEAD'S CHAIRMAN'S STOCK

197

| | |
|---|---|
| the **Directory** regrets that it was unable to reproduce this label | TYPE: single malt, single cask, private bottling<br>STRENGTH: 57.5% ABV<br>AGE IN CASK: 29 years<br>OWNERS: Springbank Distillery Co. Ltd<br>RATING: *** |

AN OLD WHISKY FROM THE GREAT CADENHEAD STOCKS. ENOUGH OF the right flavours to make it a good dram, but not at the levels one might expect – especially as regards woodiness – for a whisky of that age and strength.

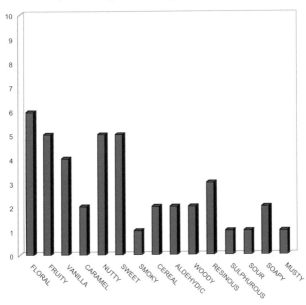

**198**

# NORTHERN ISLES SINGLE MALT 8 YEAR OLD

TYPE: single malt, private
bottling
STRENGTH: 40% ABV
AGE IN CASK: 8 years
OWNERS: London &
         Scottish
         International Ltd
RATING: ***

A GOOD-QUALITY, YOUNGISH MALT FROM AN ENGLISH BOTTLER. THE name would suggest an Orkney origin for the whisky, which narrows the field down to two distillers appearing in the Directory – the Scapa or the Highland Park. This whisky is sweeter than either of them.

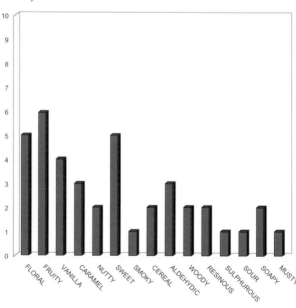

# OBAN 14 YEAR OLD

TYPE: single malt
STRENGTH: 43% ABV
AGE IN CASK: 14 years
OWNERS: United Distillers
        & Vintners Ltd
RATING: ****

FROM THE TOWN OF THE SAME NAME, A VERY GOOD MALT INDEED.
Lots of lovely flavours and an absence of faults fully justifies
its inclusion in the Classic Malts.

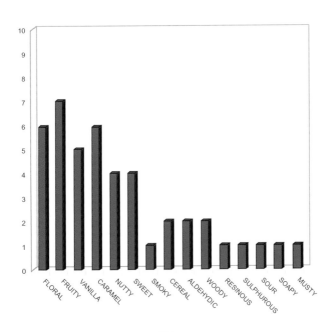

**200**

# ODDBINS OWN BRAND SINGLE ISLAND MALT 12 YEAR OLD

TYPE: single malt, private
    bottling
STRENGTH: 40% ABV
AGE IN CASK: 12 years
OWNERS: Oddbins Ltd
RATING: ***

single
island
malt
1987

scotch malt whisky
aged 12 years

70cl                    40%vol
Bottled for Oddbins by Scottish Independent
Distillers Company Ltd, Edinburgh, EH52 5BU

THE WELL-KNOWN HIGH STREET RETAILER HAS THE BUYING POWER TO secure supplies of good-quality malt for its in-house bottlings. That said, there isn't a lot of it about, which explains the lower than expected levels of flavour which are found here.

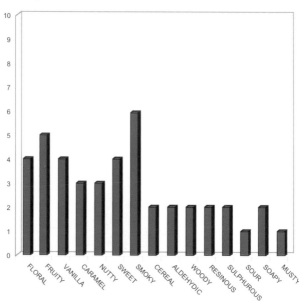

# ODDBINS OWN BRAND SINGLE SPEYSIDE MALT 25 YEAR OLD

single
speyside
malt
1974

scotch malt whisky
aged 25 years

70cl                    40%vol
Bottled for Oddbins by Scottish Independent
Distillers Company Ltd Edinburgh, EH52 5BU

TYPE: single malt, private
        bottling
STRENGTH: 40% ABV
AGE IN CASK: 25 years
OWNERS: Oddbins Ltd
RATING: ****

THE CHOICE OF SPEYSIDE MALTS IS MUCH WIDER THAN THE Islays and there are more whiskies to be had from good cask stock – hence the very high quality of this fruity, nutty Highland malt.

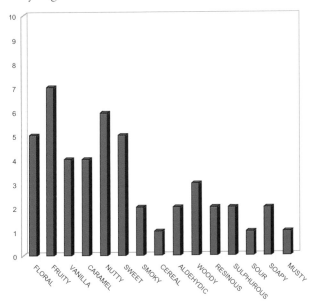

# OLD CROFTER

| | |
|---|---|
| TYPE: standard blend<br>STRENGTH: 40% ABV<br>AGE IN CASK: not stated<br>OWNERS: London &<br>        Scottish<br>        International Ltd<br>RATING: ** |  |

A STANDARD BLEND BY THE OWNER OF THE NORTHERN ISLES single malt. A bit below the average quality for standard blends, but cheap.

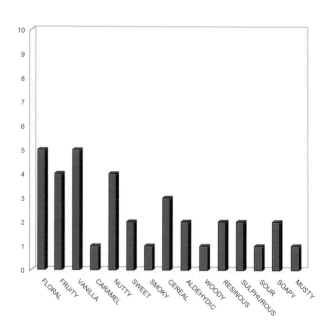

# OLD FETTERCAIRN
# 10 YEAR OLD

TYPE: single malt
STRENGTH: 40% ABV
AGE IN CASK: 10 years
OWNERS: Whyte & Mackay
Ltd
RATING: **

A DISAPPOINTING MALT FROM THE MEARNS DISTILLERY. MORE recent bottlings are now of a 12 year old, which is a great improvement, but alas they came too late for inclusion in the Directory.

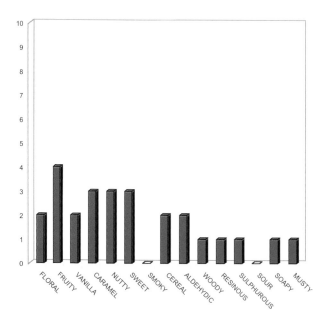

# OLD MULL

| | |
|---|---|
| TYPE: standard blend<br>STRENGTH: 40% ABV<br>AGE IN CASK: not stated<br>OWNERS: Whyte & Mackay<br>Ltd<br>RATING: *** |  |

A STANDARD BLEND WHICH IS VERY POPULAR ON THE ISLAND FROM which it takes its name, and rightly so, for it's not bad stuff at all, especially if consumed on Mull or – even better – on the adjacent island of Iona.

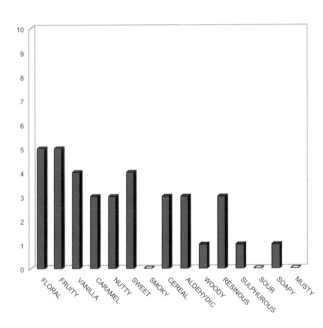

# OLD PULTENEY
# 12 YEAR OLD

> TYPE: single malt
> STRENGTH: 40% ABV
> AGE IN CASK: 12 years
> OWNERS: Inver House
>                Distillers Ltd
> RATING: ***

SOLID IF UNEXCEPTIONAL QUALITY FROM THE MOST NORTHERN OF the mainland distilleries. In rather an elegant bottle.

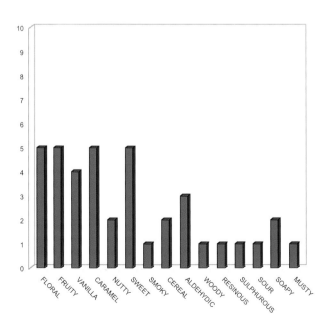

# OLD SMUGGLER

TYPE: standard blend
STRENGTH: 40% ABV
AGE IN CASK: not stated
OWNERS: Allied Distillers
Ltd
RATING: **

*Established* 1835
# Smuggler
## FINEST SCOTCH WHISKY
*100% Scotch Whiskies*
*Blended & Bottled by Jas. & Geo. Stodart Ltd.*
*Distillers ~ Forres, Dumbarton &*
70 cl e *Glasgow, Scotland.* 40% vol

A STANDARD BLEND BY ALLIED DISTILLERS, USING YOUNG whiskies and aimed at the cheaper end of the market, where it is likely to be drunk with mixers, for which purpose it is well suited.

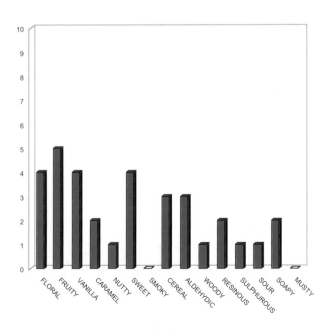

# THE ORIGINAL MACKINLAY 5 YEAR OLD

207

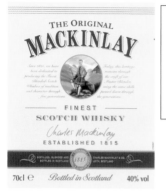

TYPE: standard blend
STRENGTH: 40% ABV
AGE IN CASK: 5 years
OWNERS: Whyte & Mackay
Ltd
RATING: ***

A LONG-ESTABLISHED AND RESPECTED NAME IN THE SCOTCH whisky industry, the Mackinlay brand is now owned by Whyte & Mackay. They do it justice with this blend, which is well made and flavoursome for a 5 year old.

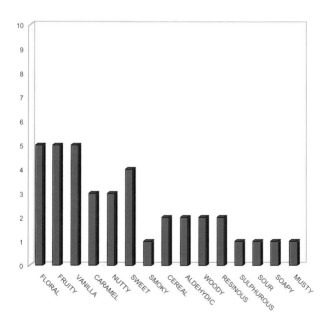

**208**

# THE ORIGINAL MACKINLAY 12 YEAR OLD

TYPE: de luxe blend
STRENGTH: 40% ABV
AGE IN CASK: 12 years
OWNERS: Whyte & Mackay
      Ltd
RATING: ****

A VERY GOOD BLEND INDEED, MAINTAINING THE MACKINLAY tradition of quality. Lots of flavour in the more desirable end of the spectrum and sufficient of the other flavours to ensure they are regarded as embellishments.

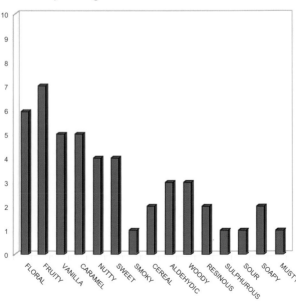

# PASSPORT

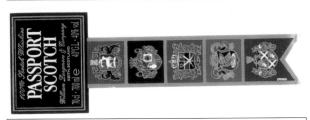

TYPE: standard blend
STRENGTH: 40% ABV
AGE IN CASK: not stated
OWNERS: Chivas Brothers Ltd
RATING: ****

A GOOD-QUALITY STANDARD BLEND BY CHIVAS BROTHERS. SOLD mostly overseas, this is a very respectable, traditional Scotch whisky.

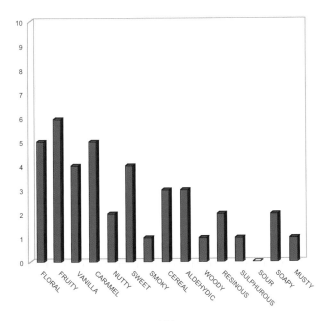

# PINWINNIE ROYALE

TYPE: de luxe blend
STRENGTH: 43% ABV
AGE IN CASK: not stated
OWNERS: Inver House
           Distillers Ltd
RATING: ****

THIS STRANGELY-NAMED (AND LABELLED) WHISKY IS DESCRIBED by its owners as a de luxe blend. Its flavour profile is as odd as its name, for cereal and aldehydic aromas are very powerful in relation to the other, more desirable flavours.

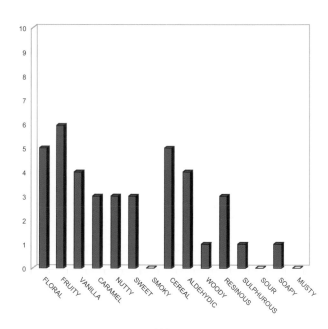

# POIT DHUBH
# 8 YEAR OLD

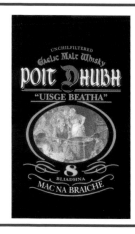

| | |
|---|---|
| TYPE: | vatted malt |
| STRENGTH: | 40% ABV |
| AGE IN CASK: | 8 years |
| OWNERS: | Praban na Linne Ltd |
| RATING: | **** |

THE WHISKY WHICH WAS BLENDED AS PART OF SIR IAIN NOBLE'S local renaissance on the Isle of Skye. It is well flavoured and there are no rough edges, despite its relative youth. Eight years is coming to be seen as a good age at which to bottle a blended whisky, provided active casks are used.

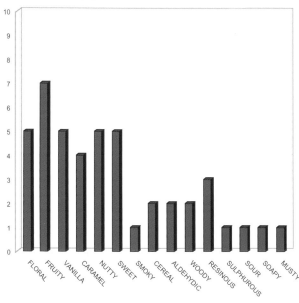

# POIT DHUBH
# 12 YEAR OLD

TYPE: vatted malt
STRENGTH: 40% ABV
AGE IN CASK: 12 years
OWNERS: Praban na Linne
Ltd
RATING: ****

A VERY GOOD WHISKY. MUCH LIKE THE 8 YEAR OLD, BUT fruitier.

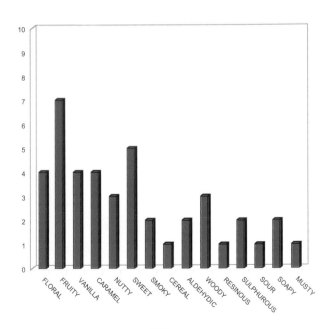

# PORT ELLEN
# 21 YEAR OLD:
# DOUGLAS LAING BOTTLING

213

A SINGLE Cask BOTTLING

DISTILLED AT
**PORT ELLEN DISTILLERY**

· SINGLE MALT Scotch WHISKY ·

DISTILLED 1982 FEBRUARY
BOTTLED 2003 DECEMBER

Aged 21 Years

NO CHILL FILTRATION. NO COLOURING
BOTTLED AT OUR PREFERRED STRENGTH OF 50% ALC/VOL
A BOTTLING FROM ONE CASK NUMBER 484

·Islay·  THIS BOTTLE IS ONE OF 348 BOTTLES FILLED FROM CASK  ·Islay·

700ml  DISTILLED, MATURED AND BOTTLED IN SCOTLAND
DOUGLAS LAING & CO LTD, GLASGOW  G3 8EQ  50% ALC/VOL
PRODUCE OF SCOTLAND

TYPE: single malt, private
bottling
STRENGTH: 43% ABV
AGE IN CASK: 21 years
OWNERS: Douglas Laing &
Co. Ltd
RATING: ****

THE DISTILLERY IS NOW A MALTINGS AND NO LONGER PRODUCES whisky. That it could produce very fine whisky is evident from this bottling. Very peaty, but, unlike so many peaty whiskies, it has some wonderful other aromas and tastes.

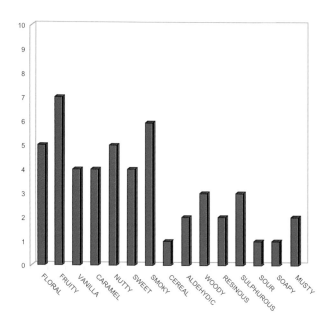

214

# THE REAL
# MACKENZIE

TYPE: standard blend
STRENGTH: 40% ABV
AGE IN CASK: not stated
OWNERS: Whyte & Mackay
        Ltd
RATING:***

A GOOD STANDARD BLEND. NO GREAT HEIGHTS, BUT THEN THAT IS not what standard blends are for. No low either, which is more important.

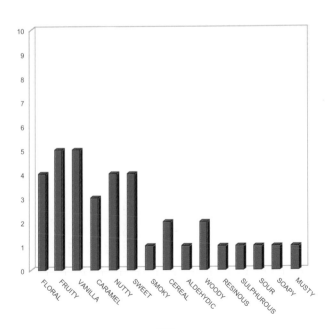

# ROBBIE DHU
# 12 YEAR OLD

TYPE: de luxe blend
STRENGTH: 43% ABV
AGE IN CASK: 12 years
OWNERS: William Grant &
    Sons
RATING: *****

A DE LUXE BLEND BY WILLIAM GRANT & SONS. THE RATHER OLD-fashioned label doesn't prepare one for the very fine whisky in the bottle. This is a flavour profile which many malt distillers would give their grannies to produce.

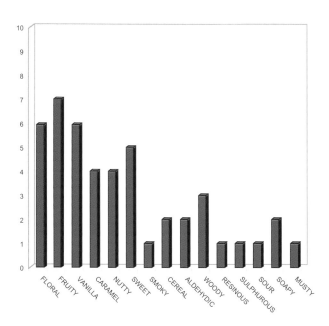

**216**

# ROSEBANK
# 11 YEAR OLD:
# DOUGLAS LAING BOTTLING

TYPE: single malt, private
bottling
STRENGTH: 43% ABV
AGE IN CASK: 11 years
OWNERS: Douglas Laing &
Co. Ltd
RATING: **

the
Directory
regrets that
it was unable
to reproduce
this label

ROSEBANK PRODUCED SOME GOOD MALT WHISKY, DESPITE ITS
industrial location. This example doesn't really do it justice,
for its lowish levels of flavour are oddly configured: floral
and fruity, cereal and aldehydic and not a lot else.

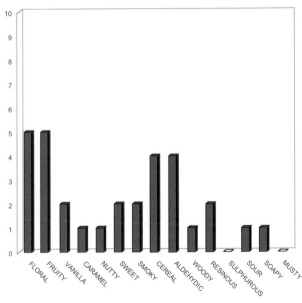

# THE ROYAL & ANCIENT

217

TYPE: standard blend
STRENGTH: 40% ABV
AGE IN CASK: not stated
OWNERS: Cockburn &
Campbell Ltd
RATING: ***

LOTS OF PEOPLE BUY THEIR WHISKY BECAUSE THE NAME ON THE label suggests something which they value, even though it is quite irrelevant to whisky: in this case, golf. With Royal and Ancient they get better than they deserve, for it's a decent enough blend.

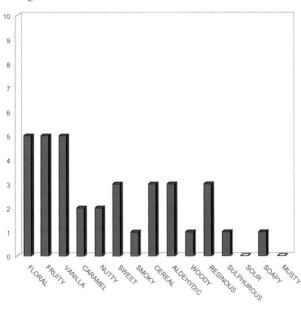

# THE
# ROYAL & ANCIENT
# 28 YEAR OLD

TYPE: de luxe blend
STRENGTH: 40% ABV
AGE IN CASK: 28 years
OWNERS: Cockburn &
          Campbell Ltd
RATING: \*\*\*

IF TO THE NAME OF THE GOLF CLUB A STATEMENT OF GREAT AGE IS added, no doubt the association is even more persuasive. Alas, the experience is likely to disappoint, for there is little in the flavour of the whisky to suggest such great age or justify the elevated price.

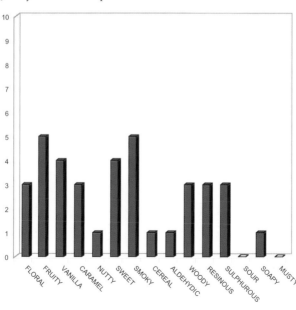

330

# ROYAL ISLAND
# 21 YEAR OLD

**219**

TYPE: de luxe blend
STRENGTH: 40% ABV
AGE IN CASK: 21 years
OWNERS: Isle of Arran
            Distillers Ltd
RATING: ***

ISLE OF ARRAN DISTILLERS HAVE ADDED TO THEIR PORTFOLIO OF blends two old whiskies, under the name of Royal Island. The whiskies will sell to people who buy on the naive assumption that there is a parallel between age and quality. In this case, they will be mistaken and would be better off with the younger Loch Ranza from the same firm.

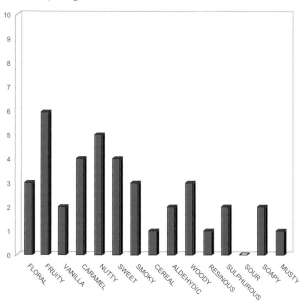

# ROYAL ISLAND
# 30 YEAR OLD

| TYPE: de luxe blend |
| STRENGTH: 40% ABV |
| AGE IN CASK: 30 years |
| OWNERS: Isle of Arran Distillers Ltd |
| RATING: *** |

THE ARGUMENT ABOUT THE 21 YEAR OLD APPLIES TO THIS WITH added force. It isn't a bad whisky, but not as good or as interesting as the premium blend – and a lot dearer. There is almost nothing in the flavour to indicate the age in cask and one must assume that old, worn-out casks were used.

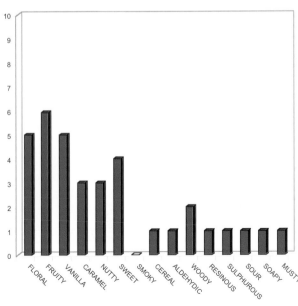

# ROYAL LOCHNAGAR
# 12 YEAR OLD

TYPE: single malt
STRENGTH: 40% ABV
AGE IN CASK: 12 years
OWNERS: United Distillers
        & Vintners Ltd
RATING: *****

A VERY FINE MALT INDEED FROM THE UDV STABLE. LOTS OF perfectly luscious flavours and no faults at all. The flavour profile is pretty close to the ideal malt whisky profile.

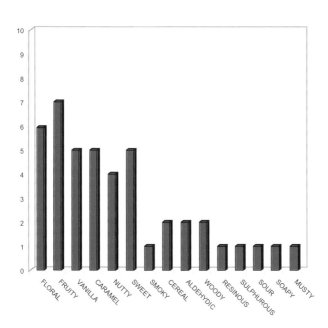

# ROYAL SALUTE
# 21 YEAR OLD

TYPE: de luxe blend
STRENGTH: 43% ABV
AGE IN CASK: 21 years
OWNERS: Chivas Brothers
        Ltd
RATING: *****

AN AGED BLEND FROM CHIVAS BROTHERS, IT IS A PARADIGM FOR old whiskies: lots of lovely fruity-flowery-sweet flavours, lots of aldehydes and wood, and low levels of everything else. Just great and, unusually among old whiskies, worth the money.

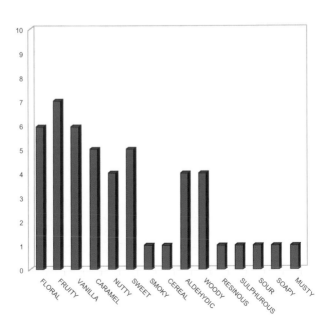

334

# SCAPA
# 12 YEAR OLD

TYPE: single malt
STRENGTH: 40% ABV
AGE IN CASK: 12 years
OWNERS: Allied Distillers
Ltd
RATING: ****

THIS IS THE OTHER ORKNEY WHISKY IN THIS GUIDE, FROM ALLIED
Distillers. It deserves to be better known than it is — it has
a better flavour profile than the Highland Park of that age.

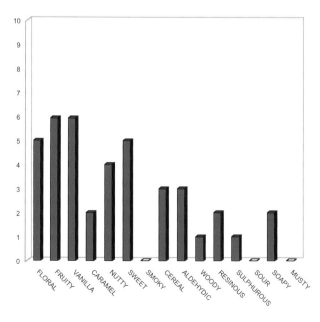

# THE SCOTCH MALT WHISKY SOCIETY CASK NO. 36.16

TYPE: single malt, single
cask, private bottling
STRENGTH: 57.8% ABV
AGE IN CASK: 19 years
OWNERS: The Scotch Malt
Whisky Society
Ltd
RATING: ****

| SINGLE CASK SCOTCH MALT WHISKY | |
|---|---|
| DATE DISTILLED | Jul 80 |
| DATE BOTTLED | Feb 00 |
| AGED IN OAK | 19 yrs |
| PROOF STRENGTH | 101.1° 57.8% vol e |
| CONTENTS BY VOL | 70 cl |

No. 36.16

THE SMWS BOTTLES INDIVIDUAL CASKS AT FULL STRENGTH. THIS
example of their wide range shows the practice to be justified
in terms of flavour, for it is a very good whisky – if not quite
up to the standard of some of the other private bottlers.

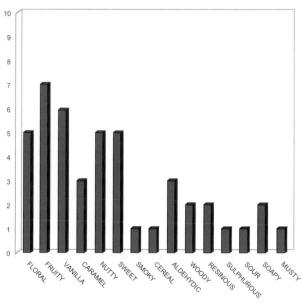

# SCOTTISH CASTLE

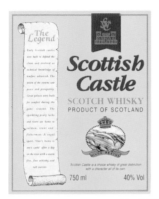

TYPE: standard blend
STRENGTH: 40% ABV
AGE IN CASK: not stated
BOTTLERS: Burn Stewart
               Distillers plc
RATING: **

THIS BURN STEWART ENTRY-LEVEL STANDARD BLEND IS QUITE sweet, and fine for the purpose to which it is most likely to be put – drinking with mixers – in which case the sulphurous and soapy flavours won't be noticed.

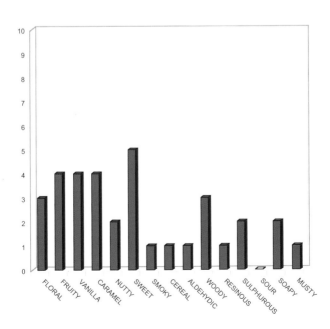

# SCOTTISH LEADER

TYPE: standard blend
STRENGTH: 40% ABV
AGE IN CASK: not stated
BOTTLERS: Burn Stewart
Distillers plc
RATING: ***

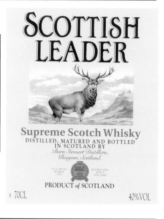

ALSO DESCRIBED AS A STANDARD BLEND, THIS IS A MUCH BETTER whisky than its predecessor: just as sweet, but the other pleasing flavours are at higher levels and the unpleasant ones at lower.

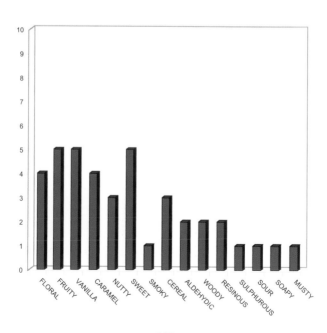

# SCOTTISH LEADER
# 15 YEAR OLD

TYPE: de luxe blend
STRENGTH: 40% ABV
AGE IN CASK: 15 years
BOTTLERS: Burn Stewart
          Distillers plc
RATING: ****

A VERY GOOD BLEND: VERY HIGH LEVELS OF FLAVOURS, especially fruity ones; some woodiness indicating age — and the touch of sulphur-related aromas augments such flavours, though they would diminish lesser ones.

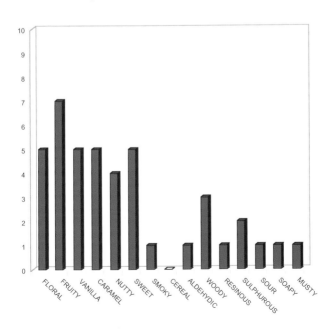

# SCOTTISH PRINCE
# 30 YEAR OLD

TYPE: de luxe blend
STRENGTH: 43% ABV
AGE IN CASK: 30 years
BOTTLERS Speyside
        Distillery Co.
        Ltd
RATING: ✳✳✳

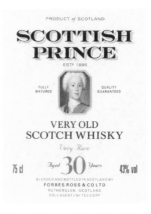

THE FLAVOUR PROFILE OF THIS DE LUXE BLEND IS A LITTLE disappointing, given the age: as floral and fruity as you could wish, but the sweetness is accompanied by rather low levels of the flavours one normally associates with such things and the rest of the spectrum is a bit flat.

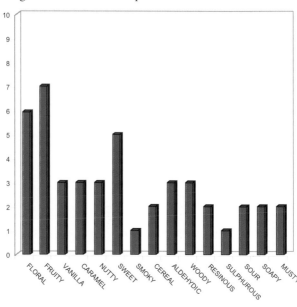

# SINGLETON
# 10 YEAR OLD

| | |
|---|---|
| the **Directory** regrets that it was unable to reproduce this label | TYPE: single malt<br>STRENGTH: 40% ABV<br>AGE IN CASK: 10 years<br>OWNERS: United Distillers<br>        & Vintners Ltd<br>RATING: *** |

WHISKY FROM A DISTILLERY WHICH WAS RENAMED QUITE RECENTLY because UDV thought folk wouldn't be able to say 'Auchroisk'. They were probably right, but on this showing this was no great loss, for it is a not an outstanding malt. That said, it's OK: just less than brilliant.

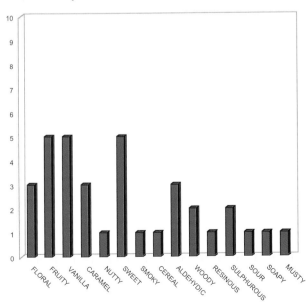

# SOMETHING SPECIAL

TYPE: de luxe blend
STRENGTH: 43% ABV
AGE IN CASK: not stated
OWNERS: Chivas Brothers
Ltd
RATING: *****

A FIRST-CLASS BLENDED WHISKY, WITH EVERYTHING YOU COULD ask for in a good dram: lots of fruit and toffee and enough of the lesser flavours to round it out to a complex and interesting potation. Its makers are to be congratulated on this. It really is special.

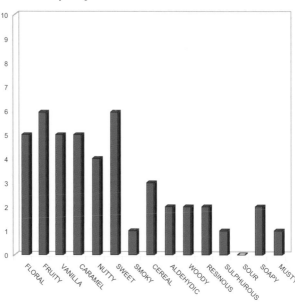

# SPEYBURN
# 10 YEAR OLD

TYPE: single malt
STRENGTH: 40% ABV
AGE IN CASK: 10 years
OWNERS: Inver House
          Distillers Ltd
RATING: ****

FROM A DISTILLERY OWNED BY THE INVER HOUSE GROUP, THIS whisky is a component in many of their good blends. From this profile, it is apparent why the blends are good, for it is a very good malt indeed. Again, the slope of the flavour profile indicates an interesting as well as a pleasing dram.

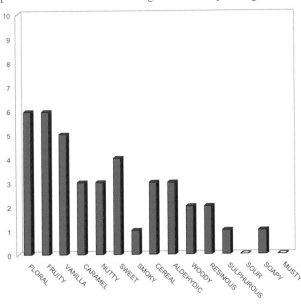

**232**

# SPEYSIDE
# 10 YEAR OLD

TYPE: single malt
STRENGTH: 40% ABV
AGE IN CASK: 10 years
OWNERS: Speyside
          Distillery Co. Ltd
RATING: ***

THE BEST WHISKY IN THE WORLD

AGE 10 YEARS

SINGLE HIGHLAND MALT

DISTILLED AND MATURED IN SCOTLAND

Estd 1895

SCOTCH WHISKY

PRODUCT OF SCOTLAND

LOWISH FLAVOUR BARS FOR HIGH QUALITY IN A MALT, BUT A sufficient spread of pleasing aromas makes it likely that the effort of inspecting it closely will be rewarded.

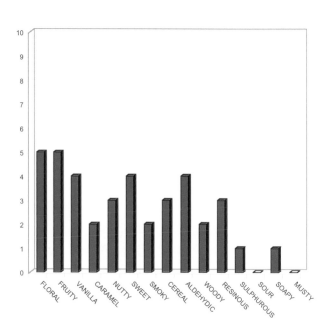

# SPRINGBANK
# 9 YEAR OLD:
# MURRAY McDAVID BOTTLING

TYPE: single malt, private
   bottling
STRENGTH: 46% ABV
AGE IN CASK: 9 years
OWNERS: Murray McDavid
   Ltd
RATING: ****

THIS IS A PERFECTLY GOOD WHISKY, BUT NOT PERHAPS AS GOOD AS one might have expected where a private bottler bottles something as wonderful as Springbank.

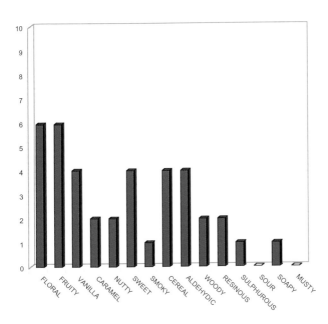

# SPRINGBANK
# 10 YEAR OLD

TYPE: single malt
STRENGTH: 46% ABV
AGE IN CASK: 10 years
OWNERS: Springbank
　　　　Distillery Co. Ltd
RATING: **

A DISAPPOINTING BOTTLING OF A MALT WHICH THOSE WHO KNOW IT of old know can be splendid. The low levels of flavour suggest that 10 years ago the distillers were using casks of rather poor quality. There is reason to think, though, that in time we shall see a 10-year-old Springbank which matches our expectations.

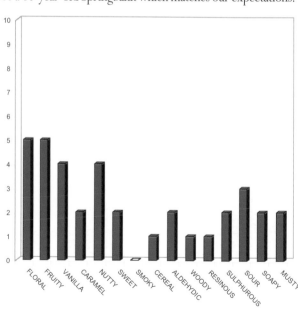

# SPRINGBANK
# 21 YEAR OLD

TYPE: single malt
STRENGTH: 46% ABV
AGE IN CASK: 21 years
OWNERS: Springbank
         Distillery Co. Ltd
RATING: ****

TWENTY-ONE YEARS AGO, SPRINGBANK WERE CERTAINLY USING very good wood indeed, as this bottling demonstrates. Lots and lots of lovely fruity, sweet flavours, and woody without being offensive. A perfectly lovely whisky.

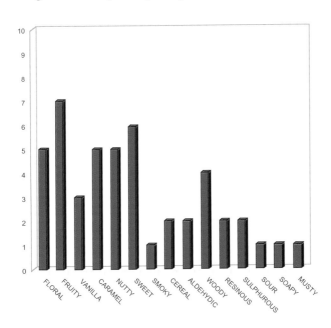

# 236 STEWART'S CREAM OF THE BARLEY

EST. 1831

RARE SELECTED

**STEWARTS CREAM OF THE BARLEY**

BLENDED SCOTCH WHISKY

DISTILLER BLENDED & BOTTLED IN SCOTLAND
STEWART & SON OF DUNDEE LIMITED
DUNDEE SCOTLAND
100% SCOTCH WHISKIES
40% vol          70 cl

TYPE: standard blend
STRENGTH: 40% ABV
AGE IN CASK: not stated
OWNERS: Allied Distillers
Ltd
RATING: ***

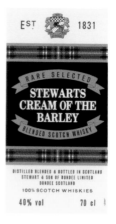

A POPULAR BLEND AMONG THE OPTICS IN SCOTTISH BARS. NOT A
bad lot of flavours for the cheaper end of the market and
fine for drinking mixed.

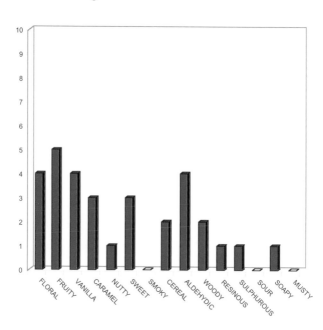

# STEWART'S FINEST OLD VATTED

**237**

TYPE: standard blend
STRENGTH: 40% ABV
AGE IN CASK: not stated
BOTTLERS: Whyte &
          Mackay Ltd
RATING: ***

NO RELATION TO THE PREVIOUS, THOUGH SIMILAR IN QUALITY: AN
unpretentious standard blend with some very nice flavours
and no nasty ones at all.

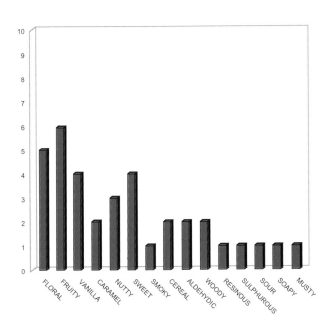

# ST MAGDALENE
# 24 YEAR OLD:
# CADENHEAD'S
# AUTHENTIC COLLECTION

TYPE: single malt, single-
    cask, private bottling
STRENGTH: 46% ABV
AGE IN CASK: 24 years
OWNERS: Springbank
        Distillery Co. Ltd
RATING: ***

WHISKY FROM A LONG-DEAD DISTILLERY, COURTESY OF CADENHEAD
bottlers, this is more of a curiosity than for serious drinking.
Not bad flavours, but nothing to suggest that the demise of
the distillery was a great loss to humankind.

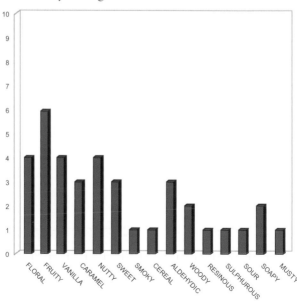

# STRATHISLA
# 12 YEAR OLD

the
Directory
regrets that
it was unable
to reproduce
this label

TYPE: single malt
STRENGTH: 43% ABV
AGE IN CASK: 12 years
OWNERS: Chivas Brothers
 Ltd
RATING: ***

A GOOD MALT WHICH IS RARELY ACCORDED CASKS OF QUALITY sufficient to allow it to distinguish itself. It can be a lot better than this decent, if unremarkable, bottling shows.

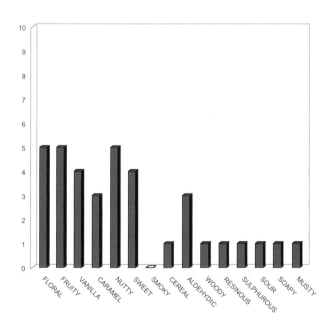

240

# TALISKER
# 10 YEAR OLD

TYPE: single malt
STRENGTH: 43% ABV
AGE IN CASK: 10 years
OWNERS: United Distillers
        & Vintners Ltd
RATING: ***

THE WHISKY DISTILLED ON SKYE, IT USED TO BE A BYWORD FOR peatiness and quality. It isn't now, and the flavour profile shows why. Smoky flavours predominate, but they do so only because of the flatness of the surrounding country.

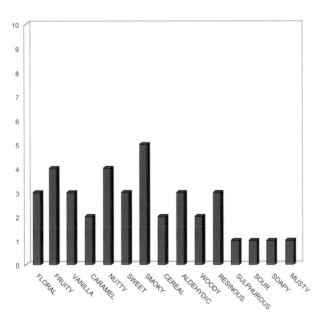

# THE TALISMAN

TYPE: standard blend
STRENGTH: 40% ABV
AGE IN CASK: not stated
BOTTLERS: The Tomatin
       Distillery Co.
       Ltd
RATING: ***

A BLEND FROM THE TOMATIN DISTILLERY CO., SO PRESUMABLY based on the Tomatin whisky. A well-made blend with all its flavours in due proportion.

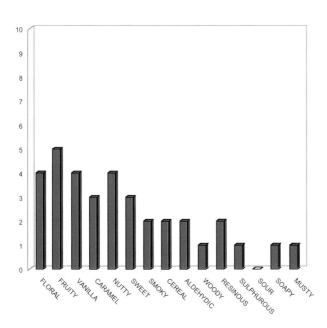

# TAMDHU

ESTABLISHED 1897
**TAMDHU**
SPEYSIDE SCOTLAND

TYPE: single malt
STRENGTH: 40% ABV
AGE IN CASK: not stated
OWNERS: Highland Distillers Ltd
RATING: ****

A VERY GOOD MALT INDEED AND ONE WHICH DESERVES TO BE better known. It is in the shadow of more famous relatives such as Macallan and Highland Park, though this bottling, which bears no age statement, is more flavoursome than the 10-year-old Macallan or the 12-year-old Highland Park.

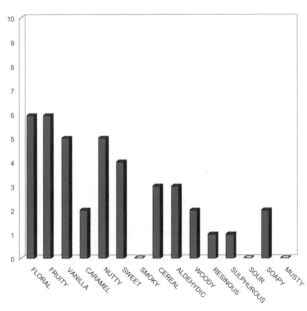

# TAMNAVULIN
# 12 YEAR OLD

TYPE: single malt
STRENGTH: 40% ABV
AGE IN CASK: 12 years
OWNERS: Whyte & Mackay
Ltd
RATING: ***

ONE OF THE WHYTE & MACKAY MALTS, IT HAS TO BE SAID THAT THIS does not exhibit any great range of flavour for a 12-year-old malt. Mostly used for blending.

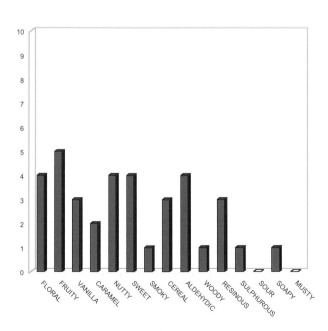

# TEACHER'S
# HIGHLAND CREAM

TYPE: standard blend
STRENGTH: 40% ABV
AGE IN CASK: not stated
OWNERS: Allied Distillers
      Ltd
RATING: ***

A MAJOR BLENDED WHISKY FROM ALLIED DISTILLERS. IT IS classed as only a standard blend, but has a flavour profile which warrants a much more eulogistic description. It fully deserves its popularity.

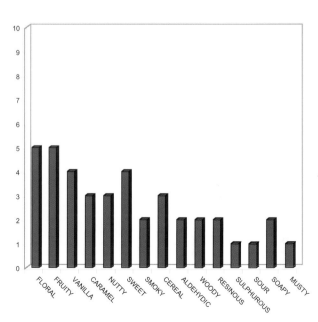

# TÉ BHEAG

TYPE: de luxe blend
STRENGTH: 40% ABV
AGE IN CASK: not stated
OWNERS: Praban na Linne
               Ltd
RATING: ****

ANOTHER DE LUXE BLEND FROM EILEAN IARMAINN IN SKYE. A VERY well-flavoured one: sweet, fruity, vanilla-tasting. Very good stuff.

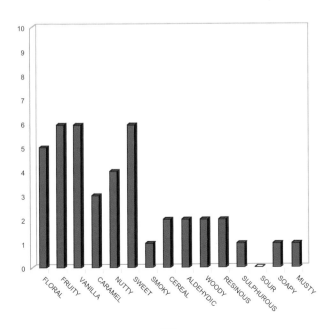

# TÉ BHEAG
# CONNOISSEURS
# BLEND – UNCHILLFILTERED

TYPE: de luxe blend
STRENGTH: 40% ABV
AGE IN CASK: not stated
OWNERS: Praban na Linne
         Ltd
RATING: ***

**CHILLFILTRATION OF WHISKY REMOVES FLAVOUR, SO ONE WOULD** expect this version of the Té Bheag to be more tasty than its filtered counterpart. Alas, that is not the case: it is more like a different whisky altogether.

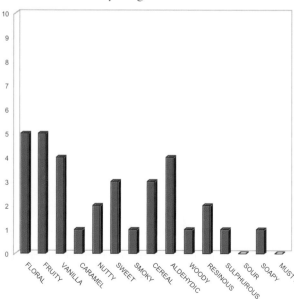

# TOBERMORY
# 10 YEAR OLD

TYPE: single malt
STRENGTH: 40% ABV
AGE IN CASK: 10 years
OWNERS: Burn Stewart
         Distillers plc
RATING: ***

THIS IS THE SAME WHISKY AS THAT BOTTLED UNDER THE NAME Ledaig. The whisky which bears the label 'Tobermory' shows little similarity to either of those from that distillery examined by the Directory, reflecting the vagaries of ownership of the distillery. Not a bad malt; powerfully aldehydic.

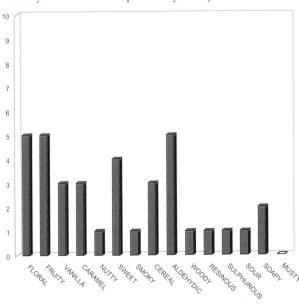

# TOMATIN
# 10 YEAR OLD

TYPE: single malt
STRENGTH: 40% ABV
AGE IN CASK: 10 years
OWNERS: The Tomatin
          Distillery Co. Ltd
RATING: ****

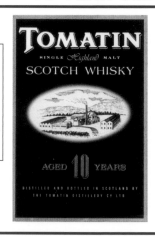

A FIRST-RATE MALT WHICH MUST HAVE BEEN KEPT IN GOOD WOOD
to produce those wildly floral aromas and all that fruit.
Plenty of other flavours besides and no defects.

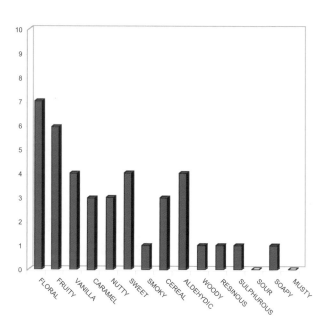

# TOMATIN
# 12 YEAR OLD

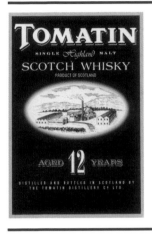

TYPE: single malt
STRENGTH: 43% ABV
AGE IN CASK: 12 years
OWNERS: The Tomatin
            Distillery Co. Ltd
RATING: *****

TWO MORE YEARS IN CASK HAVE MADE IT SWEETER AND HAVE concentrated the flavours in the floral-to-sweet segment of the spectrum. Very tasty stuff indeed and enough of the minor flavorants to let you know you are drinking Scotch whisky.

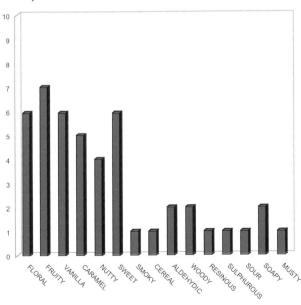

250

# TOMINTOUL
# 10 YEAR OLD

TYPE: single malt
STRENGTH: 40% ABV
AGE IN CASK: 10 years
OWNERS: Angus Dundee
Ltd
RATING: ****

the
Directory
regrets that
it was unable
to reproduce
this label

A VERY GOOD MALT, WITH LOTS OF NICE TASTES ON A MILDLY woody base. There is a slightly soapy off-note, but not enough to spoil it.

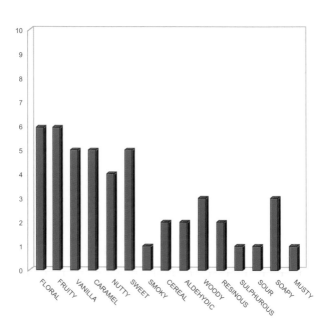

# TRIBUTE
# 5 YEAR OLD

PRODUCT OF SCOTLAND

TRIBUTE

AGED 5 YEARS

BLENDED
SCOTCH WHISKY

DISTILLED AND BOTTLED
IN SCOTLAND
WILLIAM LUNDIE AND CO LTD
GLASGOW
G3 7RW
MATURED IN OAK CASKS

70 cl                    40%vol

TYPE: standard blend
STRENGTH: 40% ABV
AGE IN CASK: 5 years
OWNERS: Wm Lundie &
              Co. Ltd
RATING: ***

AN ASTONISHINGLY SWEET WHISKY FROM WILLIAM LUNDIE, WHO
describe it as a standard blend, but give it an age statement,
which arguably implies some pretensions to higher status.
Its flavour profile could fairly be said to support these.

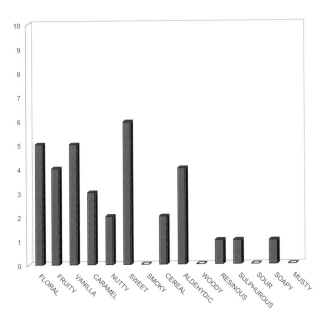

# TULLIBARDINE
# 10 YEAR OLD

TYPE: single malt
STRENGTH: 40% ABV
AGE IN CASK: 10 years
OWNERS: Tullibardine Ltd
RATING: ***

THIS LOWLAND MALT IS NOW UNDER NEW OWNERSHIP, WHICH IS just as well, for in its current state it bears a set of flavours which would not be particularly praiseworthy in a cheap standard blend. Perhaps the new owners will improve it.

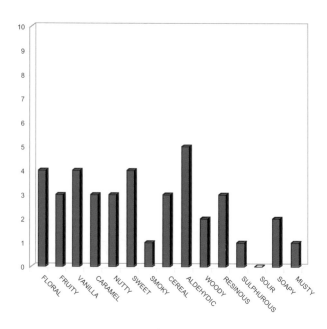

# VAT 69

TYPE: standard blend
STRENGTH: 43% ABV
AGE IN CASK: not stated
OWNERS: United Distillers
         & Vintners Ltd
RATING: ***

A VERY OLD BRANDED BLEND WHICH ONCE HAD A GREAT reputation. It is unlikely to regain one on this showing, though it's not a bad whisky.

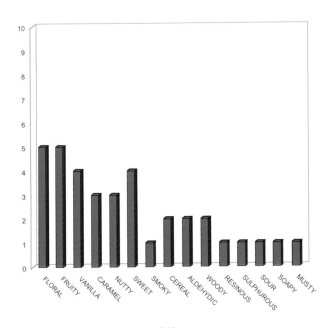

**254**

# WHITE HEATHER

TYPE: standard blend
STRENGTH: 40% ABV
AGE IN CASK: not stated
OWNERS: Chivas Brothers
          Ltd
RATING: **

A STANDARD BLEND FROM CHIVAS BROTHERS. UNPRETENTIOUS
and inexpensive – and commendable on both counts.

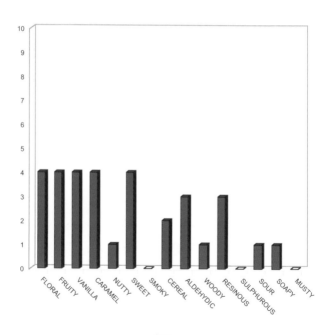

# WHITE HORSE

255

TYPE: standard blend
STRENGTH: 43% ABV
AGE IN CASK: not stated
OWNERS: United Distillers
       & Vintners Ltd
RATING: ***

THIS IS A ONCE-FAMOUS BRAND WHICH UDV INHERITED FROM ALL the whisky industry amalgamations and which it still produces, but does not promote much. No longer of note, but a perfectly decent whisky.

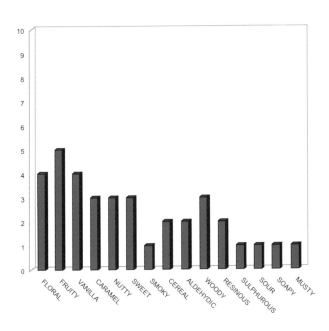

# WHYTE & MACKAY

TYPE: standard blend
STRENGTH: 40% ABV
AGE IN CASK: not stated
OWNERS: Whyte & Mackay
  Ltd
RATING: ✶✶✶✶

THE FLAGSHIP BRAND OF THE ONCE MORE EPONYMOUS COMPANY, the new owner having changed its trading name from Kyndal International Ltd back to Whyte & Mackay. Very high quality for a standard blend and a very good buy for the money.

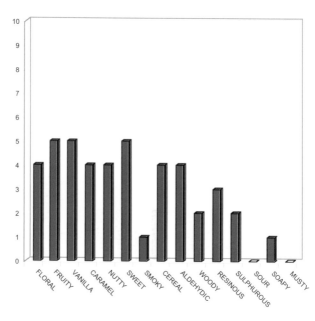

# WHYTE & MACKAY
# 12 YEAR OLD

**257**

TYPE: de luxe blend
STRENGTH: 43% ABV
AGE IN CASK: 12 years
OWNERS: Whyte & Mackay
      Ltd
RATING: ***

THE AGED VERSION IS BOTH BETTER AND WORSE THAN THE standard. It has more flavour both where it is desirable and where it is not. The soapy flavour rather spoils the show.

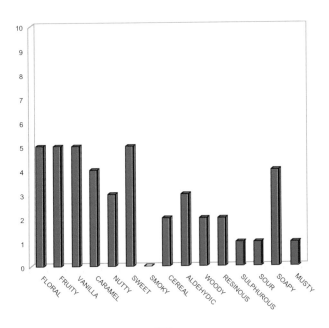

# WHYTE & MACKAY
# 15 YEAR OLD

TYPE: de luxe blend
STRENGTH: 43% ABV
AGE IN CASK: 15 years
OWNERS: Whyte & Mackay
         Ltd
RATING: ****

ANOTHER THREE YEARS AND WE HAVE A VERY FINE BLENDED whisky indeed. The combination of fruity flavours with vanilla is very distinctive and very pleasing, and the soapy taste has disappeared.

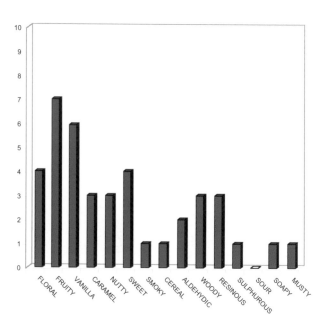

# WHYTE & MACKAY
# 18 YEAR OLD

FOUNDERS RESERVE
Of the finest Quality, this very special Scotch Whisky perfectly reflects the Partnership between the Founders. Mellow & refined, only the choicest malts are selected for this exceptional blend.

J. Whyte    C. Mackay

70 cl e    40% vol

BLENDERS OF FINE WHISKIES SINCE 1844

TYPE: de luxe blend
STRENGTH: 43% ABV
AGE IN CASK: 18 years
OWNERS: Whyte & Mackay Ltd
RATING: ***

THE WHISKY CHANGES AS IT AGES. WHILE THIS DOES NOT HIT THE peaks of the 15 year old, it is still a very good whisky, its flavours somewhat better integrated than those of the younger one.

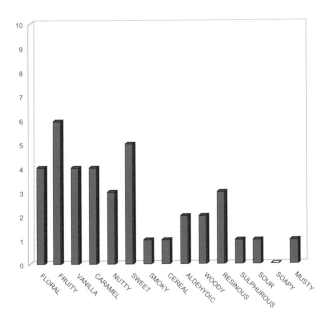

# WHYTE & MACKAY
# 21 YEAR OLD

**260**

TYPE: de luxe blend
STRENGTH: 43% ABV
AGE IN CASK: 21 years
OWNERS: Whyte & Mackay
   Ltd
RATING: ****

THERE IS GENERAL RAISING OF THE LEVELS OF FLAVOUR IN THE
earlier, more pleasing part of the profile, and it is difficult
to separate them, for they are closely bound together. The
minor flavorants form a discernible group against which the
others are set. Very good stuff.

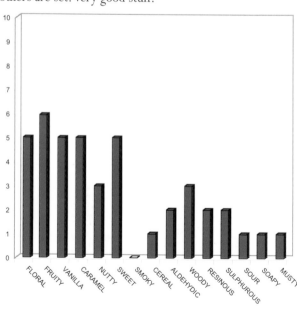

# WILLIAM GRANT'S FAMILY RESERVE

TYPE: standard blend
STRENGTH: 40% ABV
AGE IN CASK: not stated
OWNERS: William Grant &
Sons Ltd
RATING: ***

A STANDARD BLEND WHICH SELLS VERY CHEAPLY. IT IS TO BE commended for this: the more so in that it is also to be commended on account of its flavour profile, which is appropriate to a spirit of greater pretension and price.

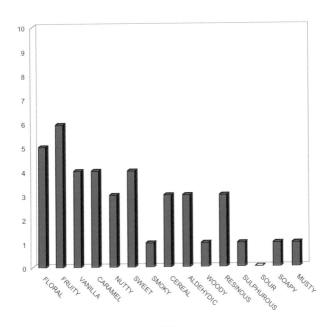

# WILLIAM GRANT'S HERITAGE RESERVE 15 YEAR OLD

**262**

TYPE: de luxe blend
STRENGTH: 40% ABV
AGE IN CASK: 15 years
OWNERS: William Grant &
        Sons Ltd
RATING: ****

THE FAMILY LIKENESS IS PRESERVED IN THIS OLDER VERSION. There are more of the delightful flavours and fewer of the lesser ones, so that the former stand out more. A very fine blend indeed.

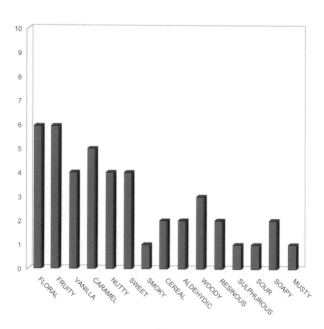

# WILLIAM GRANT'S CLASSIC RESERVE 18 YEAR OLD

TYPE: de luxe blend
STRENGTH: 40% ABV
AGE IN CASK: 18 years
OWNERS: William Grant &
        Sons Ltd
RATING: ****

THREE MORE YEARS HAVE PRODUCED ADDITIONAL FLAVOURS, BUT importantly, they have caused the balance to shift from floral to sweet and fruity, on a nutty caramel base. There are woody tastes as well, for the age is beginning to show.

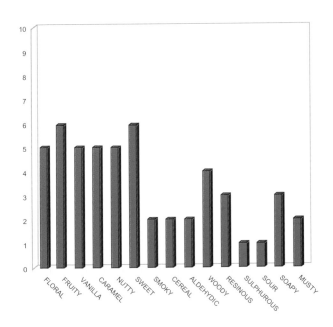

# WILLIAM GRANT'S
## 21 YEAR OLD

TYPE: de luxe blend
STRENGTH: 43% ABV
AGE IN CASK: 21 years
OWNERS: William Grant &
          Sons Ltd
RATING: *****

ON REACHING ITS MAJORITY, THE WHISKY EXCELS AND YIELDS quite spectacular quantities of fruit. There are lots of other fine flavours too, but inevitably they play second fiddle to the fruitiness. Brilliant whisky.

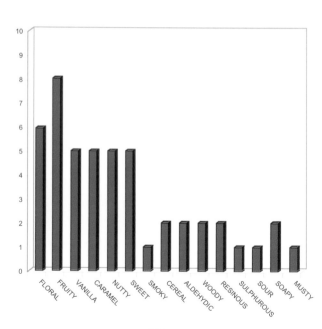

# WILLIAM LAWSON'S FINEST

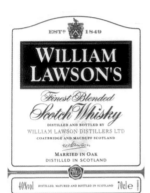

TYPE: standard blend
STRENGTH: 40% ABV
AGE IN CASK: not stated
OWNERS: John Dewar &
Sons Ltd
RATING: ✱✱✱

A STANDARD BLEND FROM JOHN DEWAR & SONS, IT DESERVES THE popularity it has among the discerning French. Lots of flavour for a standard blend, lots of sweet fruits and flowers, and enough of other tastes to make it a very useful, general-purpose whisky.

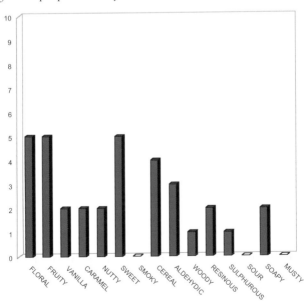

# INDEX

| 73. | Edradour 10 y/o | **** | 185 |
| 74. | The Famous Grouse | **** | 186 |
| 75. | The Famous Grouse Gold Reserve 12 y/o | *** | 187 |
| 76. | The Famous Grouse Prestige | **** | 188 |
| 77. | Findlater's Finest | **** | 189 |
| 78. | Glen Deveron 10 y/o | **** | 190 |
| 79. | Glendronach 15 y/o | ***** | 191 |
| 80. | Glenfarclas 10 y/o | *** | 192 |
| 81. | Glenfarclas 12 y/o | **** | 193 |
| 82. | Glenfarclas 21 y/o | **** | 194 |
| 83. | Glenfarclas 25 y/o | **** | 195 |
| 84. | Glenfarclas 105 | *** | 196 |
| 85. | Glenfiddich Ancient Reserve 18 y/o | **** | 197 |
| 86. | Glenfiddich Solera Reserve 15 y/o | *** | 198 |
| 87. | Glenfiddich Special Reserve 12 y/o | **** | 199 |
| 88. | Glen Garioch 8 y/o | ** | 200 |
| 89. | Glen Garioch 15 y/o | **** | 201 |
| 90. | Glen Garioch 21 y/o | ***** | 202 |
| 91. | Glengoyne 10 y/o | **** | 203 |
| 92. | Glengoyne 17 y/o | **** | 204 |
| 93. | Glengoyne 21 y/o | ***** | 205 |
| 94. | Glen Grant 5 y/o | * | 206 |
| 95. | Glen Grant 10 y/o | *** | 207 |
| 96. | Glen Keith 10 y/o | *** | 208 |
| 97. | Glenkinchie 10 y/o | **** | 209 |
| 98. | Glenlivet 12 y/o | *** | 210 |
| 99. | Glenlivet 12 y/o French Oak | ***** | 211 |
| 100. | Glenlivet 18 y/o | **** | 212 |
| 101. | Glenlivet 21 y/o Archive | **** | 213 |
| 102. | Glenlivet 1976: Signatory bottling | ***** | 214 |
| 103. | Glenlossie 17 y/o: Adelphi bottling | **** | 215 |
| 104. | Glenmorangie 10 y/o | **** | 216 |
| 105. | Glenmorangie 15 y/o | **** | 217 |
| 106. | Glenmorangie 18 y/o | *** | 218 |
| 107. | Glenmorangie Madeira Wood Finish | *** | 219 |
| 108. | Glenmorangie Port Wood Finish | **** | 220 |
| 109. | Glenmorangie Sherry Wood Finish | *** | 221 |
| 110. | Glen Moray Chardonnay | ** | 222 |
| 111. | Glen Moray Wine Cask 16 y/o | *** | 223 |
| 112. | Glen Ord | **** | 224 |
| 113. | Glenrothes 1987 | *** | 225 |
| 114. | Glen Scotia | *** | 226 |

| | | | |
|---|---|---|---|
| 157. | King of Scots 25 y/o | ***** | 269 |
| 158. | King Robert II | *** | 270 |
| 159. | Knockando 1986 | **** | 271 |
| 160. | Lagavulin 16 y/o | *** | 272 |
| 161. | Langs Supreme | ** | 273 |
| 162. | Laphroaig 10 y/o | *** | 274 |
| 163. | Laphroaig Cask Strength | **** | 275 |
| 164. | Leapfrog 12 y/o: Murray McDavid bottling | *** | 276 |
| 165. | Ledaig 15 y/o | *** | 277 |
| 166. | Ledaig 20 y/o | ***** | 278 |
| 167. | Linkwood 1988: Signatory bottling | *** | 279 |
| 168. | Linkwood 17 y/o: Adelphi bottling | ***** | 280 |
| 169. | Lismore Finest | **** | 281 |
| 170. | Lismore Special Reserve 18 y/o | ** | 282 |
| 171. | Loch Fyne | *** | 283 |
| 172. | Loch Lomond | ** | 284 |
| 173. | Loch Ranza | **** | 285 |
| 174. | Lochside 9 y/o: Murray McDavid bottling | *** | 286 |
| 175. | Lochside 19 y/o: Cadenhead bottling | **** | 287 |
| 176. | Long John | **** | 288 |
| 177. | Longmorn 15 y/o | *** | 289 |
| 178. | Longrow 10 y/o Bourbonwood | **** | 290 |
| 179. | Longrow 10 y/o Sherrywood | *** | 291 |
| 180. | Macallan 10 y/o | *** | 292 |
| 181. | Macallan 12 y/o | **** | 293 |
| 182. | Macallan 15 y/o | *** | 294 |
| 183. | Macallan 18 y/o 1982 | **** | 295 |
| 184. | Macallan 25 y/o | ***** | 296 |
| 185. | Macallan 30 y/o | **** | 297 |
| 186. | Macallan 50 y/o 1949 | **** | 298 |
| 187. | Macallan Gran Reserva | ***** | 299 |
| 188. | MacArthur's 12 y/o | ** | 300 |
| 189. | MacArthur's Select | *** | 301 |
| 190. | MacDonalds Glencoe 8 y/o | **** | 302 |
| 191. | Macleod's Single Malt Highland | ** | 303 |
| 192. | Macleod's Single Malt Island | *** | 304 |
| 193. | Macleod's Single Malt Lowland | **** | 305 |
| 194. | Mannochmore 1984 Connoisseurs Choice | **** | 306 |
| 195. | McGibbon's Special Reserve | *** | 307 |
| 196. | Mitchell's 12 y/o | **** | 308 |
| 197. | Mosstowie 29 y/o: Cadenhead's Chairman's stock | *** | 309 |